American Society for T

IN ACTION

Linking HRD Programs with Organizational Strategy

TWELVE

CASE STUDIES

FROM THE

REAL WORLD

OF TRAINING

ASTD

JACK J. PHILLIPS

SERIES EDITOR

WILLIAM J. ROTHWELL

EDITOR

Ordering information: Books published by the American Society for Training & Development can be ordered by calling 800.628.2783 or 703.683.8100.

Library of Congress Catalog Card Number: 98-71679
ISBN: 1-56286-087-9

Table of Contents

Introduction to the *In Action* Series v

Preface...vii

How to Use This Casebook xi

Linking HRD to Organizational Strategy: An Introduction....................1
William J. Rothwell

The Design of a Management Development Program........................27
University Medical Center
Maryjo Bartsch and Marilyn Repinski

Involving Employees in Making the Transition from
     Entrepreneurship to a Professionally Managed Company..............39
United Check Clearing Corporation
Paul O. Hardt

Strategic Planning and Customer Satisfaction: The Ultimate
     Drivers of Change Management...63
Financial Publishing Company
Beverly Hyman

Encouraging Human Potential: A Career Development
     Success Story..69
American Express Financial Advisors
Hilda C. Koontz, Laura L. Theis, Eugene J. Audette

Training for New Technology 85
Midwest Steel Company
Joseph T. Martelli

A Partnership for Integrating Work and Learning..............................97
Food-Processing Company
Gene L. Roth and Edward "Ted" Raspiller

Strategic Review of a Training and Development System.................109
BC TELECOM
Dale Rusnell

Workforce Education: A Model for Upgrading Skills
  of Foundry Workers 127
Southern Ductile Casting Company
Barbara E. Hinton

Evaluating Strategy Implementation in a Religious Organization:
  An Organizational Learning Approach 137
A Catholic Church
Jamie Callahan Fabian and Patrice Scanlon

Structured On-the-Job Training: Innovations in International
  Health Training...155
JHPIEGO Corporation
Rick Sullivan, Sue Brechin, and Maryjane Lacoste

Training Capacity Building for Poor Areas............................181
United Nations Develpment Programme Project in China
Jiping Zhang and Peter Sun

Moving to Manufacturing Professionals................................209
Michelin North America, Inc.
Barbara E. Hinton

About the Editor 219

About the Series Editor 221

Introduction to the *In Action* Series

As are most professionals, the people involved in human resource development (HRD) are eager to see practical applications of the models, techniques, theories, strategies, and issues the field comprises. In recent years, practitioners have developed an intense desire to learn about the success of other organizations when they implement HRD programs. The Publishing Review Committee of the American Society for Training & Development has established this series of casebooks to fill this need. Covering a variety of topics in HRD, the series should add significantly to the current literature in the field.

This series has the following objectives:

- *To provide real-world examples of HRD program application and implementation.* Each case will describe significant issues, events, actions, and activities. When possible, the actual names of the organizations and individuals involved will be used. In other cases, the names will be disguised, but the events are factual.

- *To focus on challenging and difficult issues confronting the HRD field.* These cases will explore areas where it is difficult to find information or where the processes or techniques are not standardized or fully developed. Also, emerging issues critical to success in the field will be covered in the series.

- *To recognize the work of professionals in the HRD field by presenting best practices.* Each book in the series will attempt to represent the most effective examples in the field. The most respected organizations, practitioners, authors, researchers, and consultants will be asked to provide cases.

- *To serve as a self-teaching tool for people learning about the HRD field.* As a stand-alone reference, each volume should be a very useful learning tool. Each case will contain many issues and fully explore several topics.

- *To present a medium for teaching groups about the practical aspects of HRD.* Each book should serve as a discussion guide to enhance learning in formal and informal settings. Each case will have questions for discussion. And each book will be useful as a supplement to general and specialized textbooks in HRD.

The topics for the volumes will be carefully selected to ensure that they represent important and timely issues in the HRD field. The editors for the individual volumes are experienced professionals in the field. The series will provide a high-quality product to fill a critical void in the literature. An ambitious schedule is planned.

If you have suggestions of ways to improve this series or an individual volume in the series, please respond directly to me. Your input is welcome.

Jack J. Phillips, Ph.D.
Series Editor
Performance Resources Organization
Box 380637
Birmingham, AL 35238-0637

Preface

The *In Action* casebook series focuses on important issues in human resource development (HRD), human performance improvement (HPI), and workplace learning and performance (WLP). To date, the American Society for Training & Development (ASTD) has published more than five volumes in the series. They have focused on such topics as measuring return-on-investment (two volumes), needs assessment, designing training programs, transfer of training, and learning organizations.

Target Audience

This book should be of value to anyone who is interested in linking HRD, HPI, WLP, or training initiatives to organizational strategy and needs. That should include just about everyone. After all, the key aim of most planned learning experiences in organizational settings is to realize improved performance that will help the organization remain in business, meet or exceed customers' needs, attain high quality, decrease costs, and increase productivity. When planned learning experiences do not meet that expectation, decision makers question whether they are valuable and are worth the time, money, and effort invested in them.

The primary audience for this book is the practitioner who manages, coordinates, or oversees a training department, training function, or training program. Those individuals are usually held accountable for achieving useful results—and are held responsible when they do not. Rather than providing specific how-to-do-it advice, this volume shows them how organizations of varied sizes and types have attempted to link HRD efforts to organizational strategy.

The second audience for this book is the HRD practitioner who does not bear management or programmatic responsibility. Although these individuals may not be personally involved in strategic planning discussions with top executives, they should be equipped to explain how their efforts contribute to meeting business needs and realizing strategic goals and objectives. This volume provides a frame of reference for that purpose, showing how that relationship can be made.

The third audience for this book is the researcher or academic who is looking for descriptions of how organizations are struggling to link HRD to organizational strategy amid daily crises. Researchers and academics alike will find such cases in this volume.

The fourth and final audience for this book is the line manager, the key stakeholder for many HRD efforts. For line managers, this book should illustrate when and how HRD has proved its value in realizing the organization's competitive strategy and strategic goals and objectives. The book raises—and addresses—many issues that they should consider when attempting to link HRD efforts to organizational strategy.

The Cases

The cases in this volume represent a broad cross section of real-world efforts in linking HRD with organizational strategy. Some cases are drawn from international settings and describe the macroeconomic implications of HRD in national economic development strategy. Most are drawn from U.S. domestic organizations, however, and show how HRD is linked with organizational strategy.

To find these cases, ASTD sought cases from its own members and from members of other organizations representing both practitioners and academics in the HR and HRD communities. Multiple mailings were undertaken to find authors. The volume editor also made numerous personal phone calls.

The cases represented here reveal a broad range of views and approaches. No effort has been made to make the cases conform to some contrived, or imposed, model of what linking HRD and organizational strategy should look like. Instead, the cases represent honest efforts to link HRD with strategic plans or strategic objectives.

Case Authors

The case authors were chosen for the quality of the cases they submitted. Collectively, they represent a broad range of experience—from government, business, education, and nonprofit sectors. Most have had significant experience in HRD.

Best Practices?

A funny thing happened on the way to preparing this volume. The editor ran into tremendous difficulty finding people willing to submit cases. Puzzled, he asked colleagues why that might be. Their answers were simple but thought provoking. In the words of one, a business professor specializing in corporate strategy: "Those organizations that have successfully linked HRD with corporate strategy have found it to be such a powerful weapon in their competitive arsenal that they do not want to talk about what they do or how they do it. This material is very sensitive and proprietary." Another colleague said, "The best-run companies have been doing this a long time but may not be willing to share the details of what they do. Other companies are not doing it, have nothing to describe, and their HRD managers are not willing to admit that."

As a result of the practical difficulties of finding case authors, the cases in this book do not represent best-practice cases. Although some cases embody best practices, most demonstrate the more typical, though realistic, struggles to link HRD with organizational strategy. But the latter experience is also worth hearing about because it matches many HRD practitioners' experiences.

Acknowledgments

Any edited work of this kind necessarily demands the help—and support—of many people. Allow me first to express my appreciation to the case authors for their time, patience, and effort in preparing their cases, all of which required dedication to the profession that is beyond the norm.

Second, I wish to thank Jack Phillips, editor of the *In Action* series, for the patience he demonstrated as we struggled to find good cases and prepare them for publication. His assistants Patti Pulliam and Tammy Bush were most helpful throughout this process and deserve praise for their patience with a volume editor as busy as I am. Special thanks also goes to Nancy Olson, vice president of publications at ASTD, for her extraordinary patience with this volume and its editor.

Third, I want to express my appreciation to my graduate research assistants Ning Li, Chris Howard, and Daryl Hunt for their willingness to help with details throughout the time this volume was in the making.

Fourth and finally, I wish to thank my wife, Marcelina, my daughter, Candice, and my son, Froilan Perucho, for their loving support during the time this book was assembled. This book was submitted on the day I left town to attend my son's wedding ceremony to our small family's most recent addition—my daughter-in-law, Kristen.

William J. Rothwell
State College, PA
June 1998

How to Use This Casebook

This book represents a broad cross section of efforts that aim to link human resource development (HRD) with organizational strategy.

Using the Cases

This book can be used in several ways. It provides real-world cases demonstrating the efforts of HRD practitioners and consultants to link HRD with organizational strategy. Following are descriptions of some of the ways in which the cases may be used:

- HRD managers will find that the cases that appear in this book are excellent and thought-provoking examples of practical efforts to link HRD to organizational strategy.
- Academics and researchers will find a source of useful information about actual practices in the field as a base of comparison with theoretical descriptions. This book describes how it is really done, providing a counterpoint to what should be done.
- HRD students will find this book to be a useful supplement to college textbooks that provide theory but often do not provide sufficient descriptions of how those theories may fare in application. Real cases demonstrating the difficulties inherent in application can enhance classroom discussion and provide a basis to discover, or test, theories.
- Line managers will find this book useful as they work with HRD practitioners to link HRD to organizational strategy. More specifically, understanding how other organizations have attempted the linkage of HRD and organizational strategy can provide a common language and basis for discussion and action.

Overview of the Case Studies

Table 1 provides an overview of the case studies appearing in this book. It lists the cases, indicating what industries, types of HRD efforts, targeted audiences, and types of linking efforts were attempted.

Table 1. Overview of the case studies.

Author's Name and Organization	Chapter Title	Industry	HRD Effort	Type of Linking Effort Attempted
Maryjo Bartsch and Marilyn Repinski *University Medical Center*	The Design of a Management Development Program	Academic medical institution	Management development	Building of management competencies to match organizational strategic needs
Paul O. Hardt *United Check Clearing Corporation*	Involving Employees in Making the Transition from Entrepreneurship to a Professionally Managed Company	Financial services	More than eight programs	Training to help an entrepreneurial business sustain growth
Beverly Hyman *Financial Publishing Company*	Strategic Planning and Customer Satisfaction: The Ultimate Drivers of Change Management	Publishing (within a financial-services organization)	Training based on customer desires	Training workers to perform in ways that match customers' requirements
Hilda C. Koontz, Laura L. Theis and Eugene J. Audette *American Express Financial Advisors*	Encouraging Human Potential: A Career Development Success Story	Financial services	Career development program	Linking career development to perceived employee and organizational needs

Joseph T. Martelli *Midwest Steel Company*	Training for New Technology	Manufacturing	Technical training	Linking training on new equipment to business needs
Gene L. Roth and Edward "Ted" Raspiller *Food-Processing Company*	A Partnership for Integrating Work and Learning	Food processing	Workplace literacy program	Creating partnerships among community college, manufacturing management, and manufacturing union
Dale Rusnell *BC TELECOM*	Strategic Review of a Training and Development System	Telecommunications (international)	Strategic training needs-assessment effort	Linking company strategic goals to company training needs
Barbara E. Hinton *Southern Ductile Casting Company*	Workforce Education: A Model for Upgrading Skills of Foundry Workers	Manufacturing	Basic skills training	Linking local education agencies and industries
Jamie Callahan Fabian and Patrice Scanlon *A Catholic Church*	Evaluating Strategy Implementation in a Religious Organization: An Organizational Learning Approach	Religious organization	Organization development intervention	Organizational learning

continued on page xiv

Table 1. Overview of the case studies (continued).

Author's Name and Organization	Chapter Title	Industry	HRD Effort	Type of Linking Effort Attempted
Rick Sullivan, Sue Brechin, and Maryjane Lacoste *JHPIEGO Corporation*	Structured On-the-Job Training: Innovations in International Health Training	Government/healthcare (international)	On-the-job training	Linking training to a national healthcare initiative
Jiping Zhang and Peter Sun *United Nations Development Programme Project in China*	Training Capacity Building Project for Poor Areas	Government (international)	Management training	Linking training to a national poverty reduction program
Barbara E. Hinton *Michelin North America, Inc.*	Moving to Manufacturing Professionals	Manufacturing	Workforce education	Linking workforce education to strategic planning

Follow-Up

Due to space limitations, some information about the cases had to be omitted. Readers who require additional information on any case may contact the authors directly at the addresses under "The Author" following the case.

Linking HRD to Organizational Strategy: An Introduction

William J. Rothwell

Human resource development (HRD) professionals have long discussed linking HRD with organizational strategy. Many people feel that if only HRD could be effectively linked to the organization's long-term strategy, then it would command top management's attention, galvanize management support, and attract additional resources. Strategy *is defined as the way an organization chooses to compete or meet customer or constituent needs.* HRD *means the "integrated use of training and development, organization development, and career development to improve individual, group, and organizational effectiveness"* (McLagan, 1989, p. 7). *This introductory chapter presents one model of how to link HRD with organizational strategy and summarizes in detail how that model can be applied. The author also reviews, briefly, some recent issues that have emerged on linking HRD with organizational strategy.*

Background

What is organizational strategic planning? What are the steps in the traditional strategic planning model? How can HRD efforts be linked with organizational strategy? What recent issues have emerged that relate to linking HRD with organizational strategy? This introductory chapter answers these key questions and, in doing so, lays the foundation for this casebook.

What Is Organizational Strategic Planning?

Strategic planning is the evolutionary step beyond its immediate predecessor, long-range planning. In the 1960s, it became increasingly apparent to senior executives, corporate planners, and others in the business world that existing models of corporate long-range planning were no longer appropriate. One reason was that external environmental change was happening too fast, and long-range planning tended to assume that the external environment would forever remain unchanged. A second reason was that long-range planning tended to extend assumptions of the past into the future, making the leap in logic that "the future will be an extension of past and present." The latter logic no longer holds true, of course (Rothwell & Kazanas, 1994b).

For both these reasons, decision makers began to look for a new approach to planning and invented strategic planning. More recently, various attempts have been made to reinvent strategic planning as it is carried out in many organizations (Bantel, 1994; Bechtel, 1996; Burton, Moran, & Burton, 1995; Camillus, 1996; Fogg, 1994; Gessner, McNeilly, & Leskee, 1994; Grant & Gnyawali, 1996; Heene, 1997; Kennedy, 1994; Mintzberg, 1993, 1994; Wall & Wall, 1995).

Strategic planning means the way an organization chooses to compete. Because a competitive focus is not appropriate in governmental or nonprofit sectors of the economy, strategy can also mean how an organization chooses to meet customers' or constituents' needs. Strategy is usually long term in its focus and is driven by dynamic and changing conditions in the world outside the organization (what is called the external environment).

Strategic planning is a process, whereas a strategic plan is the result or outcome of that process. This point deserves emphasis. Plans are easy to place on a shelf to gather dust, but the planning process unfolds on a daily basis as decision makers take action. Thus a distinction is sometimes made between *formal strategy* (what has been written) and *informal strategy* (what strategists carry around in their heads and use as the basis for their daily actions). Some people would say that formal strategy represents about 5 percent of all strategy, whereas *informal strategy* represents the remaining 95 percent.

What Are the Steps in the Traditional Strategic Planning Model?

A model is a simple depiction of an idea, object, or phenomenon that is otherwise more complex. Those who write about strategic planning often refer to the strategic planning model. Several variations of it exist, one version of which appears in figure 1. Each step in the model deserves a brief description.

- Step 1: Clarify a vision. A *vision* is an idealized way of thinking—a view of what the organization should be in the future and why

Figure 1. The strategic planning process.

Source: *Human Resource Development: A Strategic Approach, Revised Edition,* written by William J. Rothwell and H.C. Kazanas, copyright 1994, 1989. HRD Press, Inc. 22 Amherst Road, Amherst, MA 01002, 800.822.2801, 413.253.3488, fax 413.253.3490. Reprinted by permission of the publisher.

it should be that way. Most great leaders have been able to paint a picture of the future that people want to make a reality. That is the essence of visioning, the ability to create a compelling picture of what the world could and should be like in the future (George, 1997; Phillips, 1995).

- Step 2: Establish a mission or purpose. A mission answers the question, Why does the organization exist? Usually stated in one sentence, it captures the organization's essential reason for being. A mission statement, or purpose statement, is never as simple as, "We are here to make a profit," or "We want to please our customers." Such statements are obvious. A mission or purpose statement should at least describe the types of customers served, products or services offered, and a philosophy of doing business or carrying out operations (Jones & Kahaner, 1995).

- Step 3: Setting goals and objectives is the next step (Rothwell & Kazanas, 1994b). A goal is an idealized description of what results are sought in the future. Common goals might include increasing market share, improving performance, or improving customer satisfaction. Goals are timeless and measureless. Instead of providing specifics, they point the way in the general direction of transforming the mission or purpose into a reality on a continuing basis.

  Objectives take goals a step further. An objective answers, for each goal, such questions as How will that be measured? and Over what time span is that expected to be achieved? Objectives thus pinpoint what results are desired in a future period. They activate the mission or purpose as well as the goals, showing what must happen for the mission to be realized over time and how success can be determined.

- Step 4: Scan the external environment. Scanning the external environment means examining the world outside the organization for changes likely to pose future threats and opportunities to it. This fourth step of the model is key to successful strategic planning and is what distinguishes strategic planning from long-range planning. It is important because it is assumed that changes outside an organization will affect its ability to compete—or serve customers—in the future.

  During the scanning process, strategists typically analyze different segments of the external environment for possible future changes. These segments may include the following:
  — *Economic conditions:* What is the status of the economy expected to be? What changes are expected?

— *Market and competitive conditions:* What changes are happening in the industry of which the organization is a part? What new alliances are being struck? What mergers, acquisitions, and buyouts have occurred or are likely?

— *Social and human resource conditions:* How are lifestyle issues affecting the industry and the organization? What changes in customer lifestyles are expected? How widely available is the talent needed to succeed in the business?

— *Legal and regulatory conditions:* What changes in laws, rules, and regulations are occurring? How are they affecting the industry and the organization? Where are they occurring?

— *Technological conditions:* What changes are occurring in the technology needed to make the organization's products or deliver its services? How are technological changes likely to affect the work performed and the way the work is performed in the organization?

Scanning often requires two steps. In the first step, strategists ask, What is likely to happen in this area outside the organization? As a second step, strategists ask, What will those changes mean for the organization, and what threats and opportunities will they pose? Many trends have been identified that affect organizations generally and HRD activities specifically (see American Society for Training & Development, 1997; Aon Consulting, 1997; Schechter, Rothwell, & McLane, 1996).

- Step 5: Appraise the organization. Appraising the organization means assessing its present strengths and weaknesses. How well is the organization presently doing as it competes with others? What unique strengths set it apart from its competitors? What weaknesses are apparent? This step, which examines the internal environment (the world inside the organization), is often the most difficult because it requires strategists to be objective enough to critique what they have done and what they are doing. To help bring some objectivity to this process, some decision makers now favor using a balanced scorecard approach (Kaplan & Norton, 1996a, 1996b). Others prefer to rely on external, best-practices benchmarking (Day, 1995).

- Step 6: Consider the range of strategies available. How can the mission or purpose, goals, and objectives be realized, given the organization's present strengths and weaknesses and the future environmental threats and opportunities it will confront? Answering that question requires consideration of what strategies are available. Many strategies are possible, of course. They include:

— *Growth:* Doing more of the same.

— *Retrenchment:* Doing less of the same.

— *Diversification:* Branching out, entering new businesses and new industries.

— *Integration:* Moving up, down, or across the business chain by striking up closer ties with suppliers, distributors, competitors, or even key customers.

— *Turnabout:* Turning a losing business into a winner.

— *Combination:* Pursuing one strategy in one area while pursuing another strategy in a different area.

Although most people would like to see a growth strategy pursued, it is not always appropriate when the organization faces adverse external environmental conditions. In recent years, retrenchment has been a common strategy, as can be seen from the scope of downsizing, right sizing, and smart sizing efforts. New strategies are also emerging. One is strategic partnering by finding ways to link up with one or more other organizations to mutual advantage. (Strategic partnering includes outsourcing work and using contingent workers.)

- Step 7: Select a strategy. The seventh step in the strategic planning model, selecting a strategy, requires decision makers to select the best or the most realistic strategy. In this process, they should consider the organization's mission or purpose, goals and objectives, present strengths and weaknesses, and the future threats and opportunities to be confronted. Comparing present strengths and weaknesses to future threats and opportunities is called SWOT (for **S**trength, **W**eakness, **O**pportunity, and **T**hreat) analysis.

- Step 8: Implement the strategy. Implementation of the strategy involves orchestrating the best structure, people or leaders, policies and procedures, and rewards to facilitate strategy installation. *Structure* refers to reporting relationships (see Mintzberg, 1979). *People or leaders* refers to those who occupy positions of authority in the organization. *Policies and procedures* refer to the organization's statements about what should be done and how it should be done. *Rewards* refer to the match between what results are desired and what results are rewarded. These components should fit together harmoniously, consistently, and synergistically if a strategy is to be implemented successfully.

- Step 9: Evaluate the strategy. The ninth and final step of the model is evaluating the strategy. The goal of this step is to take stock periodically of the strategy and its results. Strategists can then make midcourse corrections as necessary or document the benefits that flowed from a strategy. The results of evaluation are (or should be) fed back into subsequent rounds of the strategic planning process in a continuous improvement loop.

How Can HRD Efforts Be Linked With Organizational Strategy?

According to Rothwell and Kazanas (1994a), there are 10 approaches by which to link HRD with organizational strategy.* They are not mutually exclusive and may be used individually or in any combination. Following is a summary of each.

- **The top-down approach:** In this approach, organizational strategy determines and dictates HRD offerings. For example, if the organizational strategic objectives involve increasing the market share by 5 percent over the next five years, then the question becomes, What HRD programs or initiatives would be most likely to contribute to meeting that organizational objective? The answer to that question becomes an acid test for setting HRD priorities. In other words, HRD efforts flow directly from organizational goals and objectives and are directly tied to them.

    An advantage of this approach is that few people, even the most hardened critics of HRD, can question the value of HRD activities that are directly linked with organizational objectives (and thus, presumably, to business or organizational needs). It follows logically that HRD activities must contribute to meeting the organization's goals and objectives.

    A disadvantage of this approach, of course, is that it may be very limiting to HRD. One reason is that organizational strategy is often focused on financial and marketing issues but not so focused on production, operations, or human resource issues. Consequently, such an approach casts HRD as a reactive rather than as a proactive function. Depending on the corporate culture in which the HRD program is carried out, that may (or may not) be appropriate. A second reason is that individuals may be employed by the same organization for their entire careers—a less common occurrence these days, but possible nevertheless—and their developmental span may encompass 30 or more years of employment, a time far exceeding the typical duration of most organizational strategic plans. Hence, HRD activities may actually have a longer impact time than strategic plans.

- **The market-driven approach:** In the market-driven approach, the HRD function or department identifies future learning needs on the basis of future market conditions confronting the organization. A variation of the top-down approach, it is more directly focused on meeting the needs of customers that the organization will serve in the future.

*This list is adapted from the strategic planning process outlined in figure 1.

A simple example may help to explain what this means. Suppose the organization markets vacuum cleaners to institutional customers. Decision makers want to diversify into selling to individual customers as well, but nobody in the organization has experience with serving the needs of individual customers. Consequently, the HRD program targets its efforts to building expertise and competence in that area.

The major advantage of this approach is that few critics can complain that the HRD effort is not meeting organizational needs because, after all, HRD efforts are directly related to organizational strategy. The major disadvantage of this approach is that it is reactive.

- **The career-planning approach.** In the career-planning approach, the HRD effort helps individuals prepare for the future against the backdrop of the organization's strategic plan. The people responsible—whether senior executives, HRD practitioners, the individuals themselves, or someone else—assess individual strengths and weaknesses against the organization's strategic objectives and give the individuals feedback on how well their competencies match up to those required for the future as portrayed in the strategic plan. Individuals are then encouraged to pursue training, education, and developmental activities that will help them contribute to the organization's strategy.

Consider a simple example: Suppose the organization is a regulated utility that is moving into a deregulated operating environment. Individuals who were hired, trained, and even promoted under one set of organizational assumptions must learn to function under new and different assumptions. Key questions include the following:
— What future competencies will be needed in the individual's work?
— What present competencies does the individual possess?
— What is the developmental gap between present and future competencies?
— By what training, education, and development experiences can the developmental gap be narrowed?
— How should those experiences be planned, monitored, carried out, and evaluated?
In this approach, individuals bear the most responsibility for preparing for the future.

The key advantage of this approach is that it cascades strategic planning requirements down to the individual level. Strategic objectives that might otherwise seem too general, too vague, or too distant to affect one person suddenly become individually focused. That helps implement the strategic plan throughout the organization.

The key disadvantage of this approach is that it can be very time-consuming. Someone has to monitor implementation and follow-up. Often those areas are weak and require oversight.

- **The futuring approach:** In this approach, the HRD function formally and directly assists top managers as they formulate organizational strategy. The idea is to link the HRD manager directly with the top manager strategists. One way to do that is to ask HRD managers to facilitate strategic planning retreats. In that way, HRD managers hear exactly what the organizational strategy means and what results the decision makers seek to accomplish. HRD efforts can then be targeted to support the strategy.

  This approach is advantageous in that it positions the HRD function in a powerful role, providing facilitation services to key decision makers as they ponder the future direction and competitive strategy of the organization. A key disadvantage of this approach is that such information is only as good as the persistency of the strategists. If rapid turnover affects the ranks of the strategists, then the HRD manager is left with information that may not be too useful.

- **The artificial experience approach:** In the artificial experience approach, the HRD function simulates the conditions the organization may face in the future. This information is then used to assess learning needs and set priorities for planned learning experiences. HRD practitioners thus take the lead to create a compelling simulation of what the future will be like. They then expose learners to it so that they may determine what their future learning needs will be and how well they are prepared to meet future work challenges. Two examples may show how this approach can be applied.

  First, a large retail company developed a working model of its store of the future. It built a store as it believed it would appear in the future, and that simulated store became the basis by which the organization could plan for the kind of people who would be required to work in the store and the competencies they would need to demonstrate successfully. That information, in turn, became the basis for identifying present HRD needs and establishing HRD priorities.

  In another example, a stockbrokerage company developed an in-basket activity in which performers were subjected to challenges expected in the future. That information was, in turn, used to establish HRD priorities and target areas in which training should be carried out in the future.

A key advantage of this approach is that it casts the HRD function as a leading-edge activity, pointing the way toward the future. Learners feel that the future has been made realistic to them. A key disadvantage of the approach is that it is risky because the future does not always unfold as expected. Consequently, HRD priorities that are identified in this way may not prove to be accurate—or even desirable.

- **The pulse-taking approach:** Perhaps more than any other function, HRD is at the forefront of communicating up, down, and across organizations. As HRD practitioners assess needs, design and develop instruction, deliver instruction, and evaluate results, they maintain a high profile. This unique position in the organization's communication chain is used to best advantage in the pulse-taking approach, where HRD professionals take the pulse of people and situations to find out how well existing organizational strategy is being implemented. They collect information about how well strategic plans are being implemented and feed that information back to strategists for use in making improvements to strategy.

A simple way to implement this approach is to add items to participant evaluation forms that are intended to show how instruction is perceived by participants to contribute to achieving the organization's strategic plan. At the same time, raising such questions draws attention to organizational strategy, thereby soliciting feedback about it from those who are most often serving customers and dealing with suppliers and distributors.

This approach is advantageous because it makes HRD activities a continuous feedback loop of qualitative information about how well managers and workers perceive that strategy as being successfully implemented. The approach is disadvantageous, however, because (like some other approaches) it tends to make HRD a reactive rather than proactive function.

- **The performance diagnosis approach:** While assessing training needs, HRD professionals often uncover performance problems or opportunities of strategic import. They relay that information, in turn, to top managers for their use in organizational strategic planning. In that way, feedback about organizational activities is continuous.

An advantage of this approach is that it positions the HRD function as a performance consulting effort that transcends mere "training" (an activity) and begins to focus on achieving improved performance (a result). That is the direction in which the field has been most recently headed. There is every likelihood that it will continue to move in that direction. A disadvantage of this approach is that the HRD function may tend to become misunderstood as managers and others attempt to determine exactly what it is responsible for doing and what results it is responsible for achieving.

- **The educational approach:** HRD practitioners attempt to link HRD with organizational strategy by teaching people how to think strategically as they do their work in the educational approach (see Schwenk, 1995). The applications of the traditional strategic planning model, as described in the first section of this introduction, transcend mere organizational strategy and may be applied to career issues, work issues, or even life-planning issues. By training people how to apply the strategic planning model to their work, HRD practitioners help people think beyond the immediate and anticipate problems or opportunities.

  A key advantage of this approach is that it can give people a powerful tool to apply to their work and to improve work processes. A key disadvantage of this approach is that it is less obviously linked directly with the organization's strategy and is focused instead on individual performers.

- **The interpersonal approach:** In this approach, HRD professionals interact with strategists to identify their beliefs and visions of the future, using that information when developing or prioritizing HRD efforts. Although similar to the futuring approach, the interpersonal approach does not require HRD managers to facilitate strategic planning retreats or to be directly involved in strategy formulation. Instead, the interpersonal approach is more informal and may involve socializing with strategists—talking strategy over lunch or even over a golf game. Because 95 percent of all organizational strategy is informal—and thus exists in the heads of the strategists—it makes sense to concentrate attention on getting to know the strategists and what results they are seeking. That is the rationale for this approach, which (admittedly) assumes that HRD practitioners can gain access to strategists.

  A key advantage of this approach is that it positions the HRD function as an important player, one in touch with the most important decision makers of the organization. A key disadvantage of this approach is that it may be difficult to engineer because HRD practitioners may not have easy access to the strategists.

- **The rifle approach:** The rifle approach takes its name from its laser-like focus on achieving pinpointed results. The term *rifle* is meant to distinguish this approach from a shotgun approach that attempts to do everything having anything to do with strategy but that may not be effective because scattergun efforts lack necessary focus.

In the rifle approach, HRD practitioners aim their efforts at areas of greatest need. For instance, on meeting the CEO, one HRD practitioner asked, "What is your most pressing business problem?" The CEO then related a story about the difficulty of selling to one large customer with which the organization did business. The HRD practitioner listened carefully to the story, summarized what he believed to be the problem (and received acknowledgment from the CEO that that was indeed the problem), and then returned to his department to devise a detailed strategy to use training to attack a part of the problem on which training could have an impact. The result was a focused effort on an area of perceived need to the key strategist. That approach worked well, giving the HRD practitioner sufficient credibility with the CEO to attack other targeted issues.

This approach has the advantage of building tremendous credibility for the HRD function with stakeholders and decision makers. Its key disadvantage, however, is that it tends to ignore what may be important, but otherwise mundane, operational problems in favor of issues of which top-level strategists are aware. That can make it highly political.

What Recent Issues Have Emerged on Linking HRD with Organizational Strategy?

Several issues have emerged in recent years that have a bearing on efforts to link HRD with organizational strategy. They include the following:
- planning strategically for the HRD function
- applying the principles of strategic planning to key steps in planning instruction
- linking HRD with key strategic issues
- linking HRD with the organization's core competencies
- linking human performance improvement with organizational strategy.

Each deserves brief mention.

Planning strategically for the HRD function. Planning strategically for the HRD function (or department) is often confused with linking HRD with organizational strategy. Planning strategically for the HRD function means establishing a strategic plan for the department (see Rothwell & Kazanas, 1994a; Sloman, 1994; Svenson, Rinderer, & Svenson, 1992). Although that is a laudable goal, it is (of course) possible to establish a strategic plan for the HRD function that has nothing whatever to do with the organization's strategy. At the same time, it is also possible to devise a strategic plan for HRD that dovetails with, or even leads, organizational strategy.

To plan strategically for the HRD function, HRD practitioners work by themselves or (more desirably) with such key stakeholders as top managers, line managers, and others to do the following (Rothwell & Sredl, 1992):

1. Clarify the vision for HRD.
2. Establish the mission or purpose of the HRD function or department.
3. Set HRD goals and objectives.
4. Scan the environment for future threats and opportunities affecting HRD.
5. Appraise the HRD function or department for present strengths and weaknesses.
6. Consider the range of HRD strategies available.
7. Select an HRD strategy.
8. Implement the HRD strategy.
9. Evaluate the results of the HRD strategy and improve continuously.

The worksheet in figure 2 can be helpful in carrying out this process.

Each step in strategic planning for the HRD function or department means essentially the same as it does for organizational strategic planning. The first step, clarifying the vision for HRD, means formulating a view of what the HRD function or department should be in the future and why it should be that way. The second step, establishing the mission or purpose of the HRD function or department, means determining why the HRD function or department exists. The third step, setting HRD goals and objectives, refers to developing general and specific results to be achieved. The fourth step, scanning the environment, is carried out to examine future threats and opportunities to HRD inside and outside the organization. The fifth step, appraising the HRD function or department for present strengths and weaknesses, pinpoints what the HRD function or department does especially well and what needs improvement. The sixth step, considering the range of strategies available, identifies directions in which the HRD function or department could head. These could include the following:

• growth (doing more of the same HRD activities)

Figure 2. A worksheet for an HRD function or department's strategic planning process.

Directions: Use this worksheet to guide the process of establishing a strategic plan for an HRD function or department. For each step and question appearing in columns 1 and 2, write your answers in column 3. There are no right or wrong answers in any absolute sense, although some answers may be better than others for one organization, HRD function, or department.

Column 1 Step Number	Column 2 Question	Column 3 Your Notes
1	• What do you believe the HRD function or department should be like in the future? • Why do you believe it should be like that?	
2	• What is the purpose or mission of the HRD function or department? (In one sentence, explain why it exists.)	
3	• What goals should be pursued by the HRD function or department? (How should the function or department activate its purpose or mission?) • What measurable and time-specific objectives should the HRD function or department achieve? (List them in measurable, time-specific terms that are directly linked to the mission or purpose as you have described it above.)	
4	• What threats and opportunities to the HRD function or department exist in the future inside and outside the organization it serves?	
5	• What are the present strengths and weaknesses of the HRD function or department?	

continued on page 15

- retrenchment (cutting back on what the HRD function is currently doing and outsourcing activities or partnering strategically with other organizations)
- diversification (moving into new and more profitable areas of business, such as selling HRD services to external groups)

Figure 2. A worksheet for an HRD function or department's strategic planning process (continued).

Column 1 Step Number	Column 2 Question	Column 3 Your Notes
6	• What range of strategies exist for the HRD function or department to realize its purpose, goals, and objectives, given the future threats and opportunities it faces from the external environment and the present strengths and weaknesses of the function or department? (Consider growth, retrenchment, diversification, integration, turnabout, or a combination.)	
7	• What strategy for the HRD function or department should be chosen that has the most realistic chance of providing successful guidance in realizing the HRD function or department's purpose, goals, and objectives—given its future environmental threats/opportunities and present strengths/weaknesses?	
8	• How should the strategy be implemented? • What changes in structure, policy, leadership, and rewards may be needed in the HRD function or department to provide the greatest chance of success in implementing the HRD strategy?	
9	• How should the HRD function or department's strategy be evaluated periodically?	

- integration (linking up to other providers of HRD products and services inside and outside the organization)
- turnabout (transforming failed programs into successful ones)
- a combination (that is, pursuing one HRD strategy in one part of the organization while pursuing other HRD strategies in other parts of the organization).

The seventh step, selecting an HRD strategy, means choosing one strategy to govern the long-term direction of the HRD function or department. The eighth step, implementing the strategy, means marshaling the structure, policy, leadership, and reward systems to match up to the HRD strategy. The ninth and final steps, evaluating the results of the HRD strategy and improving continuously, mean taking stock periodically of the HRD function or department's strategy and its results.

One variation on this approach is to use the development and implementation of an organization-specific HRD competency model to build the support to benchmark HRD best practices (Day, 1995), examine customers' views about the organization (Haines & McCoy, 1995), and secure flexible executive commitment (Chakravarthy, 1996). In fact, building an HRD competency model can have the side benefit of creating a solid foundation for an HRD strategy.

A second variation of this approach is to use the development and implementation of an organization-specific learning strategy as a way to create an HRD strategy. That may appeal to decision makers who want to make their companies learning organizations. As a side benefit, however, the process may produce an HRD strategy.

Applying the principles of strategic planning to key steps in planning instruction. Several writers in the HRD field have suggested that each step of the instructional design process can be carried out with a strategic and, thus, future-focused approach. It is possible to conduct training needs assessment, instructional design and development, instructional delivery, and evaluation with a future-focused rather than present- or past-focused approach in mind.

To understand how that works, think about training needs assessment (TNA). Writers on TNA typically describe it as a process of comparing what is happening (actual) to what should be happening (ideal). HRD practitioners usually focus their attention on present or past events. To determine what is happening, they may, for example, interview line managers and employees. But in doing that, they tend to focus on past events—what has been happening. To determine what should be happening, they may attempt to determine existing job standards—which were set in the past.

But if TNA is approached with a strategic orientation in mind, a paradigm shift occurs. HRD practitioners then seek to compare what is likely to happen (expected future actual) to what is desired to happen (expected future ideal) (Rothwell & Kazanas, 1994b). In the process they consider trends in the environment, both inside and outside the organization, affecting current and future performance. Many trends may exert influence, of course. Technological change alone can radically alter both expected future actual and expected future ideal. Other trends can also exert important influences.

The value of conducting TNA—or any other step in the instructional design process—by using a strategic approach is that, increasingly, the past is no indicator of what the future will be like. Radical events occur with greater frequency. There is need to think ahead, to try to avert performance problems, or to anticipate performance improvement opportunities.

Linking HRD with key strategic issues. An issue is a theme cutting across functions, divisions, departments, or programs. Examples of issues include diversity, quality, customer service, and many other important thematic areas that have attracted attention in recent years. Interest in issues has spawned an area called issues management, of which much has been written (Ewing, 1987; Heath, 1997; Renfrow, 1993).

When HRD is linked with a key strategic issue (see Cianni & Bussard, 1994), the HRD function or department sets its sights on applying the rifle approach by drawing a bead on the CEO's or strategic plan's top priority and unabashedly pursuing it. For instance, suppose that the number one organizational priority is improving customer service. As stated, of course, that is a goal because it is not timebound or measurable, as an objective is.

All or most HRD efforts are thus focused on that issue. The strategic planning model is refitted appropriately. For instance, HRD practitioners may ask such questions as these:

1. What is the desired vision of customer service to be realized by the organization? What is the role of the HRD function or department in realizing that vision?
2. What is the customer service mission or purpose of the organization, and how can the HRD function or department contribute to realizing that mission or purpose?
3. What are the customer service goals and objectives of the organization, and how can the HRD function or department contribute to achieving them?
4. What future external environmental trends will pose threats and opportunities to customer service for the organization, and how can the HRD function or department help avert the threats and seize opportunities?
5. What present internal strengths and weaknesses in customer service are apparent in the organization, and how can the HRD function or department contribute to building on the strengths or minimizing the weaknesses, or to doing both?
6. What range of strategies are available to improve customer service?
7. What organizational and HRD strategies should be selected to improve customer service?

8. How should the strategy to improve customer service be implemented? What should the HRD function or department do to help the organization realize its vision, achieve its mission or purpose, and meet its desired customer service goals and objectives?

9. How will the success of the customer service strategy be evaluated and improved continuously?

The same questions may, of course, be posed for any issue. These questions can thus become a way to organize an issue-oriented strategy.

Linking HRD with core competencies of the organization. A core competence (or competency) is, according to Hamel and Prahalad (1994), "a bundle of skills and technologies that enables a company to provide a particular benefit to customers" (p. 99). It means essentially the same thing as a capability. Both mean essentially the same thing as strategic strengths. They are what makes for success in a particular industry or line of work, and most competitive organizations have a few core competencies that set them apart from their competitors and constitute the essence of what makes them competitive.

Linking HRD with core competencies means building greater strength in the area that has already made the organization successful (Lado & Wilson, 1994; Long & Vickers-Koch, 1995). For instance, suppose the organization is known for the speed and reliability of its service, as Federal Express is. To link HRD with core competencies, the organization would focus its skill-building and competency-building initiatives in HRD around finding ways to enhance and strengthen the organization's existing core competencies. Every program, course, or effort of HRD would be aimed at enhancing the core capability or competency of the organization.

Linking HPI with organizational strategic plans. The HRD field has not stood still. Increasingly, HRD practitioners are expected to do more than offer courses (an activity) and are expected to achieve results (an outcome). Hence, interest has been growing in human performance improvement (HPI), defined as "the systematic process of discovering and analyzing important human performance gaps, planning for future improvements in human performance, designing and developing cost-effective and ethically-justifiable interventions to close performance gaps, implementing the interventions, and evaluating the financial and non-financial results" (Rothwell, 1996a, p. 79). HPI is a broader notion than HRD and transcends it (Rothwell, 1996b).

In a word, linking HPI with organizational strategy is more difficult than linking HRD with organizational strategy. First, it requires HRD-turned-HPI practitioners to involve line managers and employees in the process because HPI is not the responsibility of HRD practitioners alone. Second, it requires that all people involved in the process think more broadly about human performance improvement interventions and free their thinking of artificial limitations (such as thinking only about training, career development, or even organization development). They may begin by pondering such questions as these:

- What are the differences between the results people are achieving at present and what results they must achieve in the future if the organization is to realize its strategic vision, purpose, goals, and objectives?

- What are all the ways that the organization's environment can be made more supportive of individual performers so that they can best help realize the organization's strategic vision, purpose, goals, and objectives?

- What are all the ways that individual performance in the organization can be enhanced? How can these performance improvement interventions be implemented in a coordinated way? How can they be evaluated?

People who do HPI work think in broader terms than training, which is an isolated strategy. Instead, they try to view the total environment in which human performance occurs and ask how the environment—and the individuals in it—should be changed to help the organization realize the goals that have been established. Key areas for attention may thus include selection systems (how people are chosen, moved, and promoted), reward systems (how people are given incentive to perform and are rewarded for what they have done), tools and equipment (what people are given to carry out their work and achieve results), and supervision (what kind of people are overseeing performance and how they go about it).

Summary

This chapter has laid the foundation for this casebook by answering several fundamental questions.

First, strategic planning can be understood to mean the process by which an organization chooses to compete or meet customers' or constituents' needs. As a process, it is continuing. Hence, a difference exists between strategic planning and strategic plans.

Second, the steps in the traditional strategic planning model were listed:

1. Clarify a vision.
2. Establish the organization's mission or purpose.
3. Set goals and objectives.

4. Scan the external environment for future threats and opportunities.
5. Appraise the organization for its present strengths and weaknesses.
6. Consider the range of strategies available.
7. Select a strategy.
8. Implement the strategy.
9. Evaluate the results of the strategy and improve continuously.

Third, this chapter pointed out that there are at least 10 ways by which to link HRD with organizational strategy. They are as follows:

- The top-down approach: Organizational strategy determines and dictates HRD offerings.
- The market-driven approach: The HRD function or department identifies future learning needs based on future market conditions confronting the organization.
- The career-planning approach: The HRD effort helps individuals prepare for the future against the backdrop of the organization's strategic plan.
- The futuring approach: The HRD function helps top managers formulate strategy.
- The artificial experience approach: The HRD function simulates the future conditions the organization may face if the strategic plan is realized.
- The pulse-taking approach: HRD professionals take the pulse of people and situations to find out how well an existing organizational strategy is being implemented.
- The performance diagnosis approach: While assessing training needs, HRD professionals uncover performance problems or opportunities of strategic import. They provide that information, in turn, to top managers for use in organizational strategic planning.
- The educational approach: HRD practitioners link HRD with organizational strategy by teaching people how to think strategically as they do their work.
- The interpersonal approach: HRD professionals interact with strategists and attempt to identify their beliefs and visions of the future, using that information when developing or prioritizing HRD efforts.
- The rifle approach: HRD practitioners concentrate their efforts on areas of greatest need.

Fourth and finally, the chapter summarized several issues that have recently emerged on linking HRD with organizational strategic planning. These are as follows:

- Planning strategically for the HRD function: This means applying the organizational strategic planning model to HRD efforts.

- Applying the principles of strategic planning to key steps in planning instruction: This means using strategic thinking to guide instructional planning in one or all steps of the instructional design process.
- Linking HRD with key strategic issues: This means applying the strategic planning model to such issues as diversity, quality, or customer service.
- Linking HRD with core competencies of the organization: This means using HRD to enhance the organization's core competencies, capabilities, or strategic strengths.
- Linking HPI with organizational strategic plans: This means taking a broader view than linking HRD with organizational strategy to begin organizing all elements that affect human performance to be consistent with achieving desired organizational results.

As a final note, it should be emphasized that success in linking HRD with organizational strategic plans means that HRD function activities and results are perceived as useful in meeting business or organizational needs. That will often mean that decision makers regard HRD as providing a favorable return-on-investment.

References

American Society for Training & Development. *Trends That Affect Learning and Performance Improvement: A Report to the Members of the ASTD Benchmarking Forum* (3d edition). Alexandria, VA: Author, 1997.

Aon Consulting. *The 1997 Survey of Human Resource Trends Report.* Detroit: Human Resources Consulting Group, 1997.

Bantel, K. "Strategic Planning Openness: The Role of Top Team Demography." *Organization Management, 19*(4), 406–424, 1994.

Bechtel, M. "Navigating Organizational Waters With Hoshin Planning." *National Productivity Review, 15*(2), 23–42, 1996.

Burton, T., Moran, J., & Burton, T. *The Future-Focused Organization: Complete Organizational Alignment for Breakthrough Success.* Englewood Cliffs, NJ: Prentice-Hall, 1995.

Camillus, J. "Reinventing Strategic Planning." *Strategy & Leadership, 20*(3), 6–12, 1996.

Chakravarthy, B. "Flexible Commitment: A Key to Strategic Success." *Strategy & Leadership, 24*(3), 14–20, 1996.

Cianni, M., & Bussard, D. "CEO Beliefs, Management Development, and Corporate Strategy: An Exploratory Study." *Group & Organization Management, 19*(1), 51–66, 1994.

Day, L. "Benchmarking Training?" *Training & Development, 49*(11), 26–30, 1995.

Ewing, R. *Managing the New Bottom Line: Issues Management for Senior Executives.* Homewood, IL: Irwin, 1987.

Fogg, D. *Team-Based Strategic Planning: A Complete Guide to Structuring, Facilitating, and Implementing the Process.* New York: AMACOM, 1994.

George, S. "Focus Through Shared Vision." *National Productivity Review, 16*(3), 65–74, 1997.

Gessner, S., McNeilly, M., & Leskee, B. "Using Electronic Meeting Systems for Collaborative Planning at IBM Rochester." *Planning Review, 22*(1), 34–39, 1994.

Grant, J., & Gnyawali, D. "Strategic Process Improvement Through Organizational Learning." *Strategy & Leadership, 24*(3), 28–33, 1996.

Haines, S., & McCoy, K. *Sustaining High Performance: The Strategic Transformation to a Customer-Focused Learning Organization.* Delray Beach, FL: St. Lucie Press, 1995.

Heath, R. *Strategic Issues Management: Organizations and Public Policy Challenges.* Thousand Oaks, CA: Sage, 1997.

Heene, A. (Ed.). *Competence-Based Strategic Management.* New York: John Wiley, 1997.

Jones, P., & Kahaner, L. *Say It & Live It: 50 Corporate Mission Statements That Hit the Mark.* New York: Doubleday, 1995.

Kaplan, R., & Norton, D. *The Balanced Scorecard: Translating Strategy Into Action.* Boston: Harvard Business School Press, 1996a.

Kaplan, R., & Norton, D. "Strategic Learning and the Balanced Scorecard." *Strategy & Leadership, 24*(5), 18–24, 1996b.

Kennedy, J. "Strategic Employee Surveys Can Support Change Efforts." *Journal for Quality and Participation, 17*(6), 18–20, 1994.

Lado, A., & Wilson, M. "Human Resource Systems and Sustained Competitive Advantage: A Competency-Based Perspective." *Academy of Management Review, 19*(4), 699–727, 1994.

Long, C., & Vickers-Koch, M. "Using Core Capabilities to Create Competitive Advantage." *Organizational Dynamics, 24*(1), 7–22, 1995.

McLagan, P. *Models for HRD Practice.* Alexandria, VA: ASTD, 1989.

Mintzberg, H. *Structuring of Organizations: A Synthesis of the Research.* Englewood Cliffs, NJ: Prentice-Hall, 1979.

Mintzberg, H. *The Rise and Fall of Strategic Planning: Reconceiving Roles for Planning, Plans, Planners.* New York: The Free Press, 1993.

Mintzberg, H. "The Fall and Rise of Strategic Planning." *Harvard Business Review, 72*(1), 107–114, 1994.

Phillips, N. *From Vision to Beyond Teamwork: 10 Ways to Wake Up and Shake Up Your Company.* Chicago: Irwin Professional, 1995.

Renfrow, W. *Issues Management in Strategic Planning.* Westport, CT: Quorum Books, 1993.

Rothwell, W. *The Strategic Planning Workshop.* Amherst, MA: Human Resource Development Press, 1989.

Rothwell, W. *The ASTD Models for Human Performance Improvement: Roles, Competencies, and Outputs.* Alexandria, VA: ASTD, 1996a.

Rothwell, W. *Beyond Training and Development: State-of-the-Art Strategies for Enhancing Human Performance.* New York: Amacom, 1996b.

Rothwell, W., & Kazanas, H. *Human Resource Development: A Strategic Approach* (rev. ed.). Amherst, MA: Human Resource Development Press, 1994a.

Rothwell, W., & Kazanas, H. *Planning and Managing Human Resources: Strategic Planning for Personnel Management* (rev. edition). Amherst, MA: Human Resource Development Press, 1994b.

Rothwell, W., & Sredl, H. *The ASTD Resource Guide to Professional Human Resource Development: Roles and Competencies* (2d edition, volumes I and II). Amherst, MA: HRD Press, 1992.

Schechter, S., Rothwell, W., & McLane, S. "Think Tank Uses Reverse Delphi Process to Reach Consensus on Top Trends/Competencies." *Issues & Trends in Personnel,* 8–9, 1996, June 19.

Sloman, M. *A Handbook for Training Strategy.* Brookfield, VT: Gower, 1994.

Svenson, R., Rinderer, M., & Svenson, R. *The Training and Development Strategic Plan Workbook.* Englewood Cliffs, NJ: Prentice-Hall, 1992.

Schwenk, C. "Strategic Decision Making." *Journal of Management, 21*(3), 471–493, 1995.

Wall, S., & Wall, S. "The Evolution (Not the Death) of Strategy." *Organizational Dynamics, 24*(2), 6–19, 1995.

Additional Resources on Linking HRD with Organizational Strategy

Aloian, D., & Fowler, W. "How to Create a High-Performance Training Plan." *Training & Development, 48*(11), 43–44, 1994.

Atkinson, A., Waterhouse, J., & Wells, R. "A Stakeholder Approach to Strategic Performance Measurement." *Sloan Management Review, 38*(3), 25–37, 1997.

Bantel, K. "Strategic Planning Openness: The Role of Top Team Demography." *Organization Management, 19*(4), 406–424, 1994.

Bassi, L., Gallagher, A., & Schroer, E. *The ASTD Training Data Book.* Alexandria, VA: ASTD, 1996.

Blakely, G., Martinee, C., & Lane, M. "Management Development Programs: The Effects of Management Level and Corporate Strategy." *Human Resource Development Quarterly, 5*(1), 5–19, 1994.

Burrows, D. "Increase HR's Contributions to Profits." *HRMagazine, 41*(9), 103–110, 1996.

Cosgrove, G., & Speed, R. "What's Wrong With Corporate Training?" *Training, 32*(1), 53–58, 1995.

Cyr, D. *The Human Resource Challenge on International Joint Ventures.* Westport, CT: Quorum Books, 1995.

Darling, P. *Training for Profit: A Guide to the Integration of Training in an Organization's Success.* New York: McGraw-Hill, 1993.

"Four Ways You Can Make Training a Strategic Business Imperative." *Training Directors' Forum Newsletter, 11*(11), 7, 1995.

Galpin, T., & Murray, P. "Connect Human Resource Strategy to the Business Plan." *HRMagazine, 42* (3), 99–104, 1997.

Hale, J., & Westgaard, O. *Achieving a Leadership Role for Training.* New York: Quality Resources, 1995.

Hall, D. "Executive Careers and Learning: Aligning Selection, Strategy, and Development." *Human Resource Planning, 18*(2), 14–23, 1995.

Hamel, G., & Prahalad, C. *Competing for the Future: Breakthrough Strategies for Seizing Control of Your Industry and Creating the Markets of Tomorrow.* Boston: Harvard Business School Press, 1994.

Harp, C. "Link Training to Corporate Mission." *HRMagazine, 40*(8), 65–68, 1995.

Lorange, P. "Strategic Planning for Rapid & Profitable Growth." *Strategy & Leadership, 24*(3), 42–48, 1996.

Martell, K., & Carroll, S. "How Strategic Is HRM?" *Human Resource Management, 34*(2), 253–267, 1995.

Matejka, K., & Dunsing, R. *A Manager's Guide to the Millenium: Today's Strategies for Tomorrow's Success.* New York: AMACOM, 1995.

Mayo, A. "Balancing Organizational Intervention in Career Management With Personal Career Ownership." *Career Planning and Adult Development Journal, 11*(1), 4–8, 1995.

Pickens, J., & Dess, G. "Out of (Strategic) Control." *Organizational Dynamics, 26*(1), 35–48, 1997.

Raelin, J., & Colledge, A. "From Generic to Organic Competencies." *Human Resource Planning, 18*(3), 24–33, 1995.

Raghuram, S. "Linking Staffing and Training Practices With Business Strategy: A Theoretical Perspective." *Human Resource Development Quarterly, 5*(3), 237–251, 1994.

Raimy, E. "Before You Tinker With T & D." *Human Resource Executive, 8*(2), 38–41, 1994.

Raimy, E. "Start Planning in the Trenches." *Human Resource Executive, 9*(6), 20–25, 1995.

Robinson, A., & Stern, S. "Strategic National HRD Initiatives: Lessons From the Management Training Program of Japan." *Human Resource Development Quarterly, 6*(2), 123–147, 1995.

Saggers, R. "Training Climbs the Corporate Agenda." *Personnel Management, 26*(7), 40–45, 1994.

Torraco, R., & Swanson, R. "The Strategic Roles of Human Resource Development." *Human Resource Planning, 18*(4), 10–21, 1995.

Williams, L. *Human Resources in a Changing Society: Balancing Compliance and Development.* Westport, CT: Quorum Books, 1995.

Wills, J. *The ASTD Trainer's Sourcebook: Strategic Planning.* New York: McGraw-Hill, 1997.

Yeung, A., Woolcock, P., & Sullivan, J. "Identifying and Developing HR Competencies for the Future: Keys to Sustaining the Transformation of HR Functions." *Human Resource Planning, 19*(4), 48–58, 1996.

Zuckerman, A. "Are You Really Ready for Knowledge Management?" *Journal for Quality and Participation, 20*(3), 58–61, 1997.

The Design of a Management Development Program

University Medical Center

Maryjo Bartsch and Marilyn Repinski

This case provides the rationale and strategy for linking human resource development to organizational strategy as well as an application of that strategy in the design and implementation of a management development curriculum.

The Case for Human Resource Development Integration

Organizations today recognize a stronger need than ever before to identify and successfully implement business processes that will most effectively enable them to meet or exceed their goals. Increasing demands on time have not brought about an increase in available resources. The tale of restricted financial resources and limitations in staffing is a familiar one to most businesses. These limitations combined with stronger competition increase the need for solutions and decrease the time to find them.

Finding the one right process for any given situation to enable an organization to reach a particular goal seems to be the solution, or so it would appear. Many sound theories and practices are available for consideration. There are offerings of total quality management, continuous quality improvement, right sizing, multirater 360 feedback, project teams, and the like.

There is, no doubt, an increased awareness that there is no one-size-fits-all solution to organizational needs. Often, an organization

This case was prepared to serve as a basis for discussion rather than to illustrate either effective or ineffective administrative and management practices. All names, dates, places, and organizations have been disguised at the request of the author or organization.

tries a process on for size only to find that it does not seem to fit. A search for which processes to select should consider what makes a process work effectively within an organization.

For example, one process most organizations have in common is performance management of some form. Simply stated, it involves the establishment of performance goals and the measurement or assessment of performance, and it should include a plan for continued employee development. There are many options that vary from multirater 360 feedback to self-assessment to no formal assessment.

Historically, companies have tried on various forms of performance management processes in search of the right fit. Organizations may change the type of process implemented to coincide with their business operations or because they believe the current process doesn't work. In examining why a process needs to be changed or "doesn't work," an organizational fit is often overlooked. Whether the goals set for individuals and the performance factors that are assessed are in sync with the organization's values and goals has as much to do with the success of a process as the process itself.

The way in which a process is integrated and supports the goals of the organization is a primary determinant in whether a sustained success will be realized. The human resources function needs more than ever to link the development of training and education to organizational strategy.

When Strategy and Process Are Not Integrated

The best planning and the best selection of a process in and of themselves will not bring about overall success. Without the integration of the process into the overall framework of the organization, success, if obtained at all, will be short-lived.

There are many implications from a human resource development (HRD) perspective. For example, the organization may decide that teams are the most effective basis from which to run its operations. However, if the employment function in HR has not been established to hire individuals who possess the technical and academic credentials and can and want to work within the team framework, the organization will be left with a concept that cannot be successfully implemented. Further, if managers and supervisors are not equipped to function in this new structure and ongoing staff are not given the proper foundation within which to work, teams, as a process, become no more than a group of individuals who happen to work together.

Another example is evident in the design of a training and development curriculum. As a primary step, doing a needs analysis may be one of the processes selected. If the resulting curriculum design takes only the results of the analysis into consideration, it will not be enough to have a lasting impact. Included in an integrated approach to HRD would be an examination of organizational values expressed through a variety of sources. This examination could include an evaluation of its performance review process; workplace issues in general and disciplinary and legal issues in specific and how the organization addresses them; and plans for growth, right sizing, or downsizing that might emphasize needs for the development of skills that are transferable and support growth and change. Training could then be designed to go beyond serving an immediate need to supporting not only the development of skills needed, but also the values and direction of the organization.

From Concept to Implementation
Organization Profile

The work described in this case study was conducted in a private academic medical institution affiliated with a regional medical center. The population consisted of approximately 2,200 staff and 950 faculty. Although most of the population was located on the grounds of the medical center, staff worked in any one of 42 locations throughout the city and state. Some of the unique challenges included the following:

- Approximately 70 percent of the workforce did not work in the employer's workplace but in departments that the organization ran that were located in other health-care institutions or clinics.
- No prior programming existed in the desired areas. The curriculum and methodology had to be developed from the ground up.
- Although a strategic organizational plan existed, planning and development within departments had been segmented and was not divided along organizational lines. Strategic thinking needed to be developed using the programming as a primary source.
- People were hired into the positions of the targeted population at a relatively high level of education and experience. Therefore, the organization did not readily perceive the need for human resource development and the specific areas to be developed in these roles.

A number of key issues were taken into consideration in the development of the management development program curriculum. The first was that the organization had in place a strategic plan but lacked a detailed plan for implementation. In the area of human resources, and separate from the plan document, there was an objective to develop the management program. This objective came as the result of a variety of analyses described later in this case study. Therefore, another key issue was how HR could link itself to the organization's goals and objectives throughout the curriculum goals and content. It was not sufficient for HR alone to have determined that such a program would add value to HRD. It was necessary that a need be created or shown through the linkages that were developed.

The HRD function could be linked to several objectives in the organizational strategic plan. The Human Resources Department created a strategic development plan, using these objectives and strategies as key components. The following excerpt from the HRD plan states how the linkage of HRD within the strategic organizational plan was developed:

> Employees are strategic resources in accomplishing organizational objectives. Human Resource Development is instrumental in translating the goals of the organization and the departments to the job the employee is doing. By linking the strategic HRD plan to the goals, objectives, and strategies of the organization, the (organization) can work to ensure maximum utilization of its human resources and the development of its staff to their fullest potential.

Following are some of the objectives and strategies to which HRD was linked:

Objective: *Staff*—recruit, train, and foster the professional development of an outstanding staff, skilled in a broad range of disciplines and dedicated to the mission of the organization.

Objective: *The workplace*—create and sustain an environment that respects the dignity of each individual, promotes teamwork and the sharing of skills and ideas, and embodies the principles of fairness, honesty, and integrity.

Strategy: Create supportive opportunities for the employment and professional development of the organization's staff.

Strategy: Encourage the recruitment and development of underrepresented minorities.

Strategy: Enhance the administrative skills of both faculty and staff to extend their supervisory and leadership capability.

The authors, as part of the Human Resources Department, implemented a skills inventory by reviewing the functions listed in the position descriptions for the roles in the management and supervisory classifications. From this inventory, a strategic needs assessment was conducted to determine the frequency and the extent to which the targeted staff performed all or a portion of the functions.

Included in the consideration was that there had been a relatively low rate of turnover, requiring that existing mental models be taken into consideration. Incumbents in the targeted positions were assumed to be functioning at a relatively higher skill level given the degree and experience level required at the time of hire. Therefore, they were not readily perceived by the organization as being in positions needing further development. Again, it was critical to demonstrate the need for the specific skills included in the curriculum.

Further, although the organization had not experienced a perceived turnover problem, there had been relatively little organizational change in the years preceding the development of the management program. It was known that the organization would experience many changes due to the nature of its business in the health-care industry, requiring a curriculum responsive to present and ongoing needs.

The authors also did an analysis of factors including progress interviews taken six weeks following a new hire; feedback on how new hires were incorporated into their roles; issues expressed through grievances and charges filed through external agencies; and HRD needs as expressed through performance reviews and feedback from exit interviews. Information gathered from all of the analyses was used in both the development of the program curriculum and in designing the strategy of linking HRD to organizational development.

HRD Function Profile

The human resource development function was positioned within the human resources department of the organization. The primary focus of the HRD function was management and staff development that supported the mission of HRD: to provide programming and services essential to the development of the skills, knowledge, and ability of staff in their role with the organization and to their contribution to the overall missions of the organization.

Description of the Effort

As a result of the strategic needs assessment, 12 management competencies were identified. Seven were core competencies: interviewing and hiring, orienting and teaching adults, performance management, handling discipline and dismissal issues, oral and written communication, leadership in diversity, and knowledge of current legislation with respect to sexual harassment and the Americans with Disabilities Act (ADA). The five additional competencies identified were time management, team building, managing conflict and confrontation, championing change, and goal setting.

A training module was then established for each competency, and objectives were set. For example, course objectives for the interviewing and hiring module were that participants would be able to do the following:
- prepare a preemployment job analysis on any positions for which they were interviewing candidates
- follow organizational policies and legal guidelines and use company resources when recruiting for all positions
- demonstrate an ability to assess résumés and applications received against the essential functions of the job
- conduct an interview, which follows legal guidelines (including ADA) and asks behavioral interviewing questions
- conduct effective reference checks.

The next step was to establish behavioral indicators or criteria, which would be used to assess whether the training objectives were being achieved. To do this, a link was made with the educational services department of the organization and a doctorate-level senior evaluation specialist who helped define those indicators. Again, using the interviewing and hiring module as an example, behavioral indicators for the ability to assess résumés and applications were as follows:
- conducts job analyses to determine required skills and abilities
- detects strengths and weaknesses in résumés and applications
- determines top candidates based on qualifications and skills relative to job duties
- documents decision-making processes and is able to support one or more selections.

The following were behavioral indicators for the ability to conduct an interview:
- demonstrates knowledge of ADA and Equal Employment Opportunity Commission by adhering to questioning guidelines
- asks behavioral interviewing questions
- applies legal guidelines uniformly
- conducts applicant interviews consistently (that is, the same for each candidate)
- documents all activities.

Target Population

Given that this was a two-person training and development department with finite resources, it was necessary to identify and then prioritize the target population. To do that, the authors distributed a questionnaire to all employees whose job titles indicated they would be performing job duties or essential functions involving the established competencies. The questionnaire listed functions such as interviewing job candidates, making final hiring decisions, and writing performance appraisals. From that feedback, those employees within each department that indicated they were performing most or all of the functions were the first to be targeted for participation in the management development program. Administrators, administrative coordinators, supervisors, and senior administrative assistants were some of the most likely employees to be performing the targeted management functions. Out of 2,200 employees (not including faculty), the authors selected 180 to have top priority to register for the program.

Although involvement in the management development program was voluntary, a variety of steps were taken to encourage participation. The director of human resources sent a letter to all department heads indicating that once the program was under way participation in or completion of the program would be an expectation for internal transfer and promotion for managers and that it should be included in future job descriptions for management positions. Briefings were held for administrators where the senior vice president for administration spoke of his support for the program. They were also used to introduce the philosophy and mechanics of the program to the people who would be key in supporting and encouraging participation in the program at the department level. These briefings were very helpful in overcoming resistance, clarifying expectations, and garnering support organization wide.

Program Description and Delivery

The program consisted of a series of four-hour workshops (with the exception of communication skills workshops, which lasted a full day). To complete the program, it was necessary to attend the seven workshops based on the seven core competencies, and three of the five workshops based on the other competencies. This equates to five and a half days or 45 hours of managerial training. External consultants were contracted to assist with facilitation. The frequency of the workshops allowed participants to finish the program in one year, although there was no time limit for completion placed on the participants—once enrolled, they could go at their own pace.

Every workshop in the development program had curriculum designed specifically for its audience. The assumption was that these workshops were oriented toward skills enhancement and were not remedial in nature. All of the participants were practicing managers, many with advanced education and years of work experience. Curriculum design incorporated basics of adult education theory. All workshops were interactive and incorporated delivery methods such as small group activities, large and small group discussions, videos, self-assessments, and case studies. Case studies were based on actual situations from within the organization.

Evaluation

Once the coursework was completed, participants could earn their management skills certification by completing a written review. Again the senior evaluation specialist ensured that the test accurately reflected the objectives and behavioral indicators established in the beginning. Questions were essay, and they presented workplace scenarios and asked the managers to indicate how they would respond to them based on the knowledge and skills they acquired in the workshops. For example, the following is a question regarding interviewing and hiring skills:

> You have been interviewing applicants for a frontline position in your department. This person will be very visible, and will be the first point-of-contact with your internal and external customers. One applicant in particular is very qualified, experienced, and seems to have all the skills needed to do the job. As you are interviewing her, however, you have some concerns:
>
> (a) At the University Medical Center, your current staff is primarily 40–60 years old, very conservative and professional. This applicant is in her 20s.
>
> (b) The applicant's appearance also concerns you. She is wearing extremely trendy clothes, has purple hair, and wears an earring in her nose.
>
> (c) She has described her previous work environments as very loose and unstructured, and you wonder how she'll fit in with your more structured organizational culture.
>
> Address how you would handle these three concerns:
> 1. Are any (or all) of the concerns relevant to your hiring decision?
> 2. How would you phrase questions to address your concerns to the applicant: Give examples.
> 3. What statements would you make to the applicant to address your expectations in these areas? Give examples.

Managers who did not successfully complete the review the first time were tutored and coached by the training and development specialist and could retake the review at their convenience. The intent of the review was to ensure that certification signified that the manager had indeed acquired the knowledge and skills necessary to perform essential managerial functions, rather than that the manager had simply "attended" the workshops.

After sufficient time had passed for the first group of 180 managers to earn certification, a self-assessment was distributed to determine whether or not the knowledge and skills acquired in the program were actually being applied in the workplace. For example, the assessment asked the managers to grade the following on a scale from 1 to 4, where 1 equaled not at all, and 4 meant to a great extent: "To what extent do you used behavioral interviewing questions when conducting an interview?" and "To what extend do you define the skills and abilities necessary to do the job in addition to the technical expertise and education?" Responses indicated that on average (2.5 to 3.25), managers were applying their skills in the workplace.

Consequences

The main consequences of the establishment of this management development program were that it laid a foundation within the organization for developing managers within their roles, provided a foundation for the competencies needed when hiring new managers, and led to other processes that aided the development of managers.

One such process was the development of a performance management system within the organization. This involved establishing a performance management resource group of managers who were trained to act as liaisons between the human resources office and the departments in the area of performance management. This group met regularly for training as well as to tackle performance-related issues such as the redesign of the organization's performance appraisal form.

Conclusions and Recommendations

The early linkages made between HRD and organizational strategy along with the strategic approach taken to determine management development needs was integral to the success of this program. Also, the willingness to build momentum and acceptance for the program from the ground up was very important. Ironically, although this program operated in an academic environment, there was some resistance to the idea of continuous learning. It was assumed on the part of some that if their managers had advanced or terminal degrees, that this translated into "terminal learning." The fact is that although this was a voluntary program, it was well received, and demand for the program continues.

To establish return-on-investment and for HRD to have lasting value, HRD must be linked to organizational strategy. It is necessary to take a macro view of the organization before determining needs. It is also helpful to ask who the key stakeholders are and how a program such as this can enhance their ability to function strategically within the organization. In other words, what's in it for them to participate in such a program? It is essential to create the need and obtain their buy-in.

The skills developed and the method by which they were developed became an integral part of the overall organizational strategy. It became recognized that HRD is the strategic link, which provides the continuous incremental learning essential to successful business development.

Questions for Discussion

1. What are the implications of linking HRD to organizational strategy?
2. In the planning of HRD, what considerations should be given to the strategy as stated in the organization's development plan?
3. How can HRD planning be linked to the organization when no organizational strategic plan exists?
4. In what ways could HRD be successfully implemented in an organization without clear support from senior management?
5. Consider what analysis should be done to ensure the long-term success of HRD.
6. Discuss current organizational processes, such as project teams, and why they might not succeed in a given organization.
7. Examine the role of HRD in today's workplace and any changes that might be developing.
8. In what ways has competition shaped the need for employers to invest in HRD?

The Authors

Maryjo Bartsch, the corporate training specialist for Fiserv, Inc., a leading provider of financial data-processing systems and related services to the financial industry, has 20 years of experience in management and organizational training and consulting. Prior to joining Fiserv, she was an independent consultant in organization and employee development, providing consulting, curriculum design, and training for clients in management development, performance management, communication, and team effectiveness.

She also has experience as a training and development specialist for a university medical center where she designed, wrote curriculum, and facilitated management development and staff development programming. She developed an organization-wide performance management system and was the college's liaison to the medical center's campuswide valuing-diversity initiatives. She was also a member of several campuswide committees charged with improving patient relations and customer service. Bartsch gives presentations nationwide as a conference seminar speaker, teaches continuing education courses, and has written articles for publication on management development topics. She has a bachelor's degree in business administration and a master's degree in adult education and is past president of the Southeastern Wisconsin Chapter of the American Society for Training & Development. Bartsch can be reached at Fiserv, Inc., 255 Fiserv Drive, Brookfield, WI 53045; phone: 414.879.5721.

Marilyn Repinski is manager of human resources for the Blood Center of Southeastern Wisconsin. She has more than 20 years of experience in human resources, including experience as administrator of employee relations and training and development at a university medical center. Repinski has established training departments, including performance management and management development certification programs. She is a graduate of the University of Wisconsin—Milwaukee and holds certification as senior practitioner human resources (SPHR).

Involving Employees in Making the Transition from Entrepreneurship to a Professionally Managed Company

United Check Clearing Corporation

Paul O. Hardt

Chaos seems to reign supreme in young, fast-growing companies. The order-entry system that was just right for a $1 million company is suddenly woefully inadequate for sales of $5 million. The sales department that once comprised the owner and one or two trusted confederates now has 10 salespeople, and more need to be recruited. The computer system that was just fine for 10 employees now can't possibly keep up with 100 employees. This case shows how one company handled the growth.

Background

Human resource management and development are certainly not exempt from this swirl of activities. When the company had a handful of employees, it was acceptable to have an informal hiring process, for the owner to do the orientation, and for performance appraisals to be done as needed. With a rapidly growing employee group, the entrepreneurial organization finds itself writing employee handbooks, compensation policies, and disciplinary procedures. All of these are examples of the paradox of growth in entrepreneurial organizations. An entrepreneur may begin the business as an escape from a large, inflexible, bureaucratic market-dominating corporation. The aspiring entrepreneur wants nothing of the chains of red tape, policy, and procedure that shackled his or her own adventurous, free spirit. Yet, as the entrepreneur realizes the dream of growing an exciting, vibrant business, he or she finds some of the same constraining forces encroaching

This case was prepared to serve as a basis for discussion rather than to illustrate either effective or ineffective administrative and management practices.

on the fledgling company's original maverick spirit. The entrepreneur fears the re-creation of the very behemoth he or she fled and seems trapped in a fatalistic mindset that it is inevitable.

Is it possible to make the transition from entrepreneurship to a professionally managed company while maintaining the company's original break-free-from-the-herd spirit? One successful company in the Midwest, United Check Clearing Corporation, implemented an organizational development process aimed at planned growth and increased competitive advantage while retaining the original entrepreneurial spirit of the founder. It is achieving this purpose by involving all of its 65-plus employees in structuring itself for maximum "customer intimacy." This is the company's story.

Organizational and Industry Profile

Elloyd Hauser, a Minnesota entrepreneur, founded United Check Clearing Corporation (UCCC) in 1984. The mission of the organization was to offer check-processing and depository services to organizations that received high volumes of low-dollar checks. UCCC chose to focus on four major industry groups that have these large volumes of low-dollar checks: magazine publishers, fund-raisers, consumer product manufacturers, and direct marketers. Over the years, services that were originally contracted to outside vendors were consolidated within the company, and new services were added. A significant shift in company operations took place in 1990, when the company vertically integrated its check-processing services. In other words, UCCC could now handle internally virtually every step in processing a check. Today, UCCC processes over 100 million checks in a year, using proprietary software. In addition to check processing, UCCC offers outsourced services including forms management and management of accounts payable. As the company grew, Hauser brought family members into the business, including his three daughters, his son, and a son-in-law. UCCC remains a family-owned business.

UCCC does business in a market dominated by large banks. There are other third-party check processors like UCCC, but banks do most of the check processing. Although some people have predicted the advent of the checkless society, there has been an annual growth of 1 percent to 2 percent in check volume for the past 10 years. It is anticipated that annual national check volume will grow from 64 billion checks in 1996 to somewhere between 68.4 billion and 75.6 billion checks by the year 2005. Such growth means two things. First, there is still a tremendous opportunity for growth in the check-processing business, and UCCC aims to capitalize on this growth opportunity. Second, with such a tremendous flow of paper, the use of information-systems technology is crucial to this industry. Truncation, the process of converting the information on checks from paper information to digitized bits, has become an increasingly important process. Those organizations that can master this process have a decided advantage in containing costs. Considering the tremendous volume of checks being processed, savings of even a fraction of a penny can mean millions in reduced costs to processors and customers. UCCC has found a niche for itself in this highly cost-competitive market by leveraging its expertise in information-systems technology.

Besides gaining competitive advantage through information-systems technology, UCCC has searched for other ways of establishing itself as a distinctly different third-party check processor. UCCC's primary competitors, huge national banks, try to establish their competitive advantage through what Treacy and Wiersema (1995) call operational excellence (see table 1). These huge banks try to cut price through volume processing. However, check processing is a money-losing business for many banks. Banks make their real money by making loans. Check processing is an added service that can tie a customer more tightly to the bank. In many cases, there is little incentive to spend resources on the check-processing part of a bank's business and even less incentive to spend lots of time getting to know the customer. For most banks, the only people who really get to know the customer are loan officers or investment bankers. UCCC has chosen a very different route to establishing competitive advantage. UCCC has chosen the customer-intimate value discipline as the driving force behind its campaign to find chinks in the armor of its huge competitors. Because of its size and technical expertise, UCCC can be more flexible in creating the total solution for its customers' check-processing needs.

At the same time, UCCC experiences the same challenges that many young companies face. As the company has prospered, employee numbers have increased. The company faces the inevitable tensions around keeping internal and external communication lines short and customer focused. Employees in this kind of fast-growing company can become progressively distanced from customers as layers are added to the organization. UCCC adopted a banklike organization chart, with vice presidents of functional areas reporting to a president and CEO. This arrangement was not satisfactory. The organization design seemed to result in inadequate communications, duplication of effort, and banklike red tape. Under these circumstances, management was

Table 1. Operating models.

Operating Model	Focus	Business Structure	Management System	Culture	Examples
Operational excellence	Optimized, streamlined product supply and basic service to minimize cost and hassle.	Standardized, simplified, tightly controlled, centrally planned; few decisions left to discretion of rank-and-file workers.	Integrated, reliable systems that focus on high-speed transactions and compliance to norms.	Abhors waste and rewards efficiency.	• General Electric Appliances • Price-Costco • Dell Computer
Product leadership	Invention, product development, market exploitation.	Loosely knit, ad hoc, ever changing to adjust to entrepreneurial initiatives and redirections.	Management that is results oriented; measures and rewards new product success; and doesn't punish experimentation.	Encourages individual imagination, accomplishment, out-of-the-box thinking. Driven by desire to create the future.	• Johnson & Johnson's "Vistakon" • Nike • MTV • Disney
Customer intimacy	Solution development (i.e., helping the customer understand exactly what's needed), results management (i.e., ensuring solutions get implemented), and relationship management.	Decision making delegated to employees who are closest to customer.	Systems geared to creating solutions for carefully selected and nurtured clients.	Embraces specific rather than general solutions and thrives on deep and lasting client relationships.	• IBM • Cable & Wireless Communications

torn between wanting the benefits of growth and fearing the costs of greater bureaucracy. On the one hand, growth means more revenue, more satisfied customers, and greater capacity for being a bigger player in the market. On the other hand, more employees mean more people to coordinate more rules and regulations and more bureaucracy. UCCC's efforts to reinvent itself into an organization in which employee involvement was "hard wired" into its structure and culture were direct responses to this dilemma.

UCCC used the process depicted in figure 1 as a guide in dealing with this situation. UCCC's experience will be used to explain what happens in each phase of the process.

The Project

This section describes the project's phases.

Phase One: Building the New Foundation

In an effort to upgrade the competence of its employees and in a search for a better way of doing business, UCCC started to send employees to a variety of training programs in the fall of 1995. UCCC people went to sales training courses as well as to courses in team building and team leadership. Through these courses, UCCC personnel started to conceive a foundation for the business that would be built on a set of commonly held principles. In addition to this training, members of the UCCC organization read James A. Belasco and Ralph C. Stayer's (1993) *Flight of the Buffalo,* a book that presents principles that seemed to capture a hint of what UCCC wanted to happen in the organization. It emphasizes that employees should acquire a greater sense of ownership of their jobs and the company and that employers should be clear about what good performance looks like, align operations with company goals, engage the whole employee in the business, develop employees' capabilities, and never rest on their laurels.

At about the same time, UCCC decided to take the temperature of the organization through an employee opinion survey. The opinion survey and interviews with employees showed problems that were similar to those Eric Flamholtz (1990) cited in his book *Growing Pains.* Flamholtz described the following problems in organizations making the transition from an entrepreneurship to a professionally managed company:

- People feel that there are not enough hours in the day.
- People spend too much time putting out fires.

Figure 1. Organization design and implementation process.

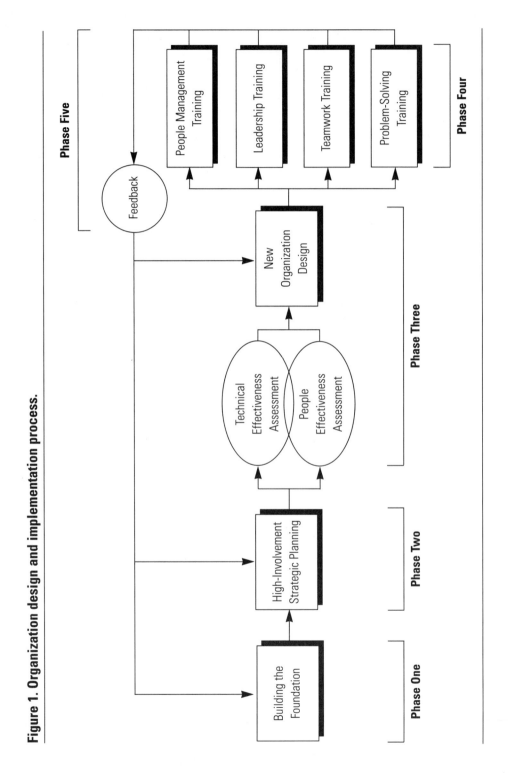

- People are not aware of what other people are doing.
- People lack understanding about where the firm is headed.
- There are too few good managers.
- People feel that they have to do it themselves if they want to get it done correctly.
- Most people feel that meetings are a waste of time.
- When plans are made, there is little follow-up, so things don't get done.
- Some people feel insecure about their place in the firm. (pp. 53–54)

To compound UCCC's situation, there were few best-practice human resource systems. Besides these symptoms, UCCC leaders noticed some of the same ones Ralph Stayer (1990) saw when he became concerned about the lack of employee involvement at Johnsonville Foods: the lack of a sense of ownership in the company or in individual jobs, a sense of trying to maintain instead of improve, and a sense that people were just going through the motions and not taking a real interest in their work or the company. All of these symptoms led the management of UCCC to ask these questions:

- What is our vision of UCCC for the next five to 10 years?
- How can we organize ourselves so we can make this vision come alive?
- What systems must we improve or create to implement our new organization design (NOD)?

To answer these questions, UCCC decided to embark on a series of high-involvement strategic planning sessions in August 1996.

Phase Two: High-Involvement Strategic Planning—August 1996 to November 1996

The company conducted three strategic planning sessions in August, September, and October 1996. In contrast to a conventional series of strategic planning retreats in which a select group of company managers go off to a retreat center to mix golf and mission writing, UCCC decided to take a risk and involve as many employees as possible in this activity. Twenty employees, almost one-third of all company employees, representing nearly every function and all levels in the organization, met in late August to start the process. Using an outside facilitator, the Strategic Planning Group (SPG) began by reviewing the history of the company, why it was founded, and some of the turning points in its history. This activity was helpful because several of the retreat participants were relatively new to the company.

The review set the stage for a review of the company's internal and external environments, beginning with its internal operating values. Through small group brainstorming sessions, the following values emerged:

- Employees are our number one asset. Employee satisfaction is important.
- We want to promote decision making throughout our company.
- We want to seek solutions and partnerships that add value.
- We want to be customer focused, internally and externally.
- We want to develop a profitable business that promotes growth and stability.
- We want to operate in an ethical, socially responsible manner.
- While sticking to boundaries that will define our marketing strategies, we also want to challenge paradigms, such as "the way we've always done things."

Following this affirmation of key operating values, the SPG used what it called a SWOT (for strengths, weaknesses, opportunities, and threats) analysis. On balance, the group found that, although the company had many strengths and opportunities, internal weaknesses were preventing the company from growing in the direction the group desired.

The SPG next summarized what it thought UCCC's core competencies were:

- flexible employees and systems
- customer-focused orientation
- innovative approach
- ability to manage diverse relationships
- dedication to their niche
- a positive working environment.

The SPG affirmed these core competencies, but recognized that the company would have to develop a common mission and vision that built on past success at the same time as it aligned with future efforts. At this point, the SPG considered the concept of an organization design based on a strategic business unit (SBU). An SBU is a self-managed, cross-functional team of employees that focuses its efforts on a customer group. In an organization that uses SBUs, functional silos are broken down to facilitate customer-focused activities. Some staff functions—information systems, accounting, human resource management—may be "seeded" into these SBUs, or they may become Resource Centers that provide support services to the SBUs. This design concept challenged the SPG's thinking about the existing, conventional organization design (a pyramid) by offering an alternative that other organizations have found promoted the kind of customer-intimate organization UCCC wanted to see itself as, regardless of how large it became.

As a tentative move in the direction of an SBU-based organization, the original SPG broke into three groups, each with responsibility for developing mission and vision statements that captured the essence of what UCCC was and wanted to be in the future. The three groups worked independently and then presented the results of their discussions to the whole SPG. After considerable discussion, the following statements were adopted:

- United Check Clearing Corporation's mission is to manage the flow of financial transactions for clients who issue or receive high volumes of low-dollar payments.
- Our services are valued because they are innovative, reliable, and responsive to our clients' needs.
- We operate in a highly ethical manner in all that we do. We respect all stakeholders and their unquestionable right to expect superior performance from our organization.
- We challenge ourselves to improve and remain flexible, exceeding the expectations of our stakeholders.
- We evaluate our success in achieving our mission through growth in
  — client satisfaction,
  — employees' skills and career fulfillment,
  — suppliers' abilities to offer us improved products, services, and return on stockholders' investment.
- Growth in all of these areas sustains our success.
- Our vision is to be an extension of our clients in facilitating financial transactions between our clients and their customers.

UCCC had thus answered the first question it faced in the strategic planning process, "What is our mission and vision for this company?" UCCC now faced the question of how to structure itself to carry out this mission. This question was the focus of the next phase in the strategic planning process.

Phase Three: Assessment of People Systems and Technical Systems— November 1996 to February 1997

At this point, the SPG formed three proto-SBUs (SBUs in name, but not in operation), each based on one of the industry foci, to delve deeper into how the company could be divided into the three industry groups (see figure 2). Besides gathering more technical and financial information, these groups turned their attention to the specific question of how to organize the people systems of UCCC to support the new organization design. A nucleus of two people formed the core of each group. A cross-functional representation from every department in the company augmented this. Areas that have traditionally been staff functions—information systems, finance, human resources— were designated as Resource Centers that would provide resources to the SBUs. The SPG designated the operations area as a super-Resource Center because it was not known at this time how its functions could be divided by industry. A management team made up of the president, vice president of sales and marketing, the vice president of operations, the chief financial officer, the director of information systems, and an outside consultant would advise the proto-SBUs. A Steering Committee made up of the management team and one representative from each proto-SBU would coordinate the proto-SBUs. These representatives would serve a six-month term, and then they would rotate out of this role, allowing another SBU member to be a representative to the Steering Committee.

The management team worked with each SBU to allocate the accounts that each SBU would be responsible for as well as the sales, cost of sales, and volumes of checks that each account generated. The management team would also help SBUs create a plan to communicate the reorganization to clients.

The management team charged the SBUs with setting preliminary sales and gross profit goals for the coming year. In addition, the SPG charged each proto-SBU with making a recommendation to the Steering Committee that each employee would be assigned to an SBU or Resource Center. The goal was to make the SBUs self-sustaining mini-businesses, so Resource Center membership would be kept to a minimum and as many employees as possible would be assigned to an SBU. Finally, the SPG charged each proto-SBU with developing a responsibility chart, which was a team job description for its SBU that would clearly identify the responsibilities their SBU would carry out and the level of authority the SBUs would have in fulfilling these responsibilities. The target date for presentations of their results by the proto-SBUs was set for mid-January 1997. After these presentations, the Steering Committee would meet and give final approval of the SBU mission and vision statements, sales and gross profit goals, SBU membership, and responsibility charts. After these preliminary de-

Figure 2. Preliminary SBU design.

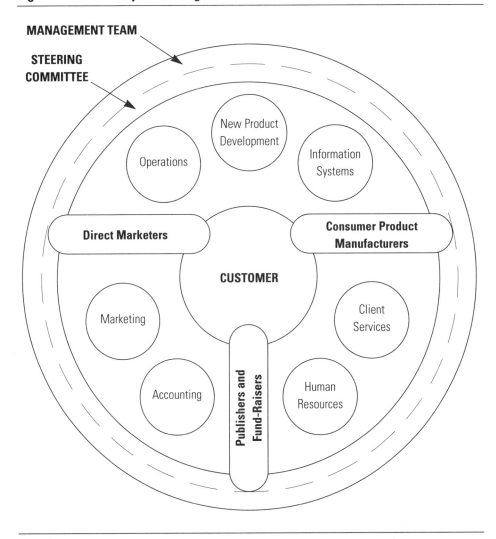

cisions were made, SBUs were charged with presenting final sales and gross profit goals as well as marketing plans and with being up and running by March 31, 1997.

To assist the proto-SBUs in their task, each group attended a training program titled "Working Together as a Team." The topics of the program included:

- **How to manage a team with diverse styles:** Each participant completed a self-scoring version of the Myers-Briggs Type Indicator (Myers & Myers, 1993), compared results with their team members, and discussed the stresses and strains posed by a diverse team membership.

- **Team-based motivation:** Members learned how teams could be structured to enhance motivation.
- **Meeting management methods:** The emphasis was put on effective time management so teams would get the most out of their meetings.
- **Navigation skills:** Organization design concepts—chain of command, levels of authority, span of control—were presented to help team members effectively design their SBUs. Preliminary mission and vision statements for SBUs were developed in this session.

The proto-SBUs met intensively during late December 1996 and early January 1997. On January 17, 1997, the groups presented their recommended goals, responsibilities charts, preliminary resource needs, and proposed rosters. The Resource Centers next met with a similar agenda between January 17 and early February to develop their own boundary markers. At this time, the vice-president of operations left the company. This departure caused a delay while a replacement was found (the chief financial officer was given additional responsibilities for managing the operations area). The Steering Committee struggled with the SBUs' proposals. Although there was considerable interest in putting everyone on an SBU, there was confusion about what membership meant. Did it mean people would spend 100 percent of their time on their SBU's business and be unavailable to work on business relating to other SBUs? Some people felt the company did not have the resources to have a pure SBU design. The Steering Committee seemed at a loss to make a final determination on SBU membership.

To help it out of this fix, the Steering Committee returned to some of the original principles that drove the company to consider an SBU design in the first place (see figure 3). By reviewing these principles, the Steering Committee could use them as the basis for deciding how to proceed. The consultant summarized the principles in the figure, and this review seemed to break the deadlock. The Steering Committee reached a final agreement on SBU membership and responsibilities on February 13, 1997. Figure 4 shows the final organization design. The Steering Committee decided that although each employee would be a member of an SBU, only a small number of employees, mostly salespeople, would spend 100 percent of their time on business in their customer area. The rest of the employees would spend less time on SBU-focused business and more time on activities based in the Resource Centers that the SBUs shared. Although the Steering Committee reached an agreement, its members knew that the organization design they adopted would create tension between the SBUs and the Resource Centers. In essence, two centers of gravity were set up. On the one hand, employees would feel the pull of their SBU. On the other hand, employees who were also members of a Resource Center would feel its pull. Recognizing that no organization design was going to be perfect, UCCC decided to proceed with the design.

The Steering Committee concluded this phase by charging the SBUs with refining their sales and marketing plans, developing plans to help all SBU members feel an allegiance and ownership of their SBUs, and participating in planning a number of initiatives to improve the human resource management system.

Phase Four: Implementing the New Organization Design—March 1997 to August 1997

Implementation of the new organization design (NOD) was carried out in three areas of activity: SBU activities, human resource management system improvements, and training and development for all employees.

Figure 3. A new paradigm for employee involvement.

OWNERSHIP

People are motivated by owning—psychologically or materially—a task, job, or team. Ownership means responsibility to self and others.

Set the goal, then get out of the way.	Design work so people get the information, training, power, and resources they need to get the work done.	Plan change so that peoples' values are respected.	Making the transition to greater employee involvement requires superior leadership and management skills.	The value of any person, group, or activity is judged by how it delivers value to the customer.	No person, group, or activity is an "island." Everything is related to everything else.

CONTINUOUS AND CONSTANT IMPROVEMENT

Stay open to change. The necessity of change is not a sign of failure.

Figure 4. Final organizational chart.

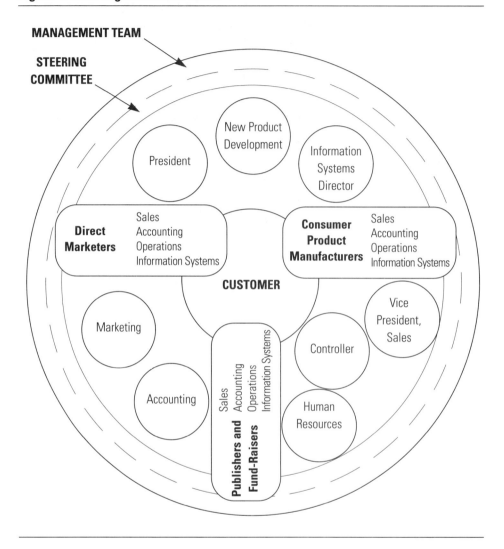

SBU ACTIVITIES. The SBUs began meeting almost immediately after approval of the final design in February. Although none of the SBUs had a formal leader, each one's Steering Committee representative tended to take the lead in calling these meetings. At the meetings, all SBU members were introduced to one another, the planning process was reviewed, and the charges that the SBUs had to complete were presented to the members. SBUs met at least weekly to undertake the planning tasks that faced them. The operations area continued to fine-tune the way in which their employees were assigned to SBUs. The Finance Department began to gear up for providing financial information on an SBU-by-SBU basis.

HUMAN RESOURCE MANAGEMENT SYSTEM IMPROVEMENTS. One of the messages that came through clearly in UCCC's employee opinion survey in the spring of 1996 was that the company needed to improve all its human resource management systems. The NOD process was an ideal opportunity to start out fresh with new ideas to construct a comprehensive human resource management system that would support the NOD. Throughout 1997, UCCC developed the following new systems:

- **Interviewing and selection:** The Steering Committee worked with the author, in his capacity as an outside consultant, to develop methods for assessing the knowledge, skills, and abilities needed to fill positions. The author taught best practices for interviewing and selection methods to everyone involved in hiring decisions. This training was delivered at nearly all levels of the company, so that SBUs could start selecting their own employees.

- **Compensation:** UCCC had only an informal compensation system at the beginning of the process. After doing a market survey to determine where the company's compensation levels were in relation to those of the marketplace, the author developed a comprehensive compensation system for all positions. The operations area started to explore a skill-based pay system. Skill blocks would be identified, workers would be assessed against these skill blocks, and compensation would be assigned on the basis of the skill blocks a worker could perform. The company hoped that such a system would allow flexible use of all employees and would encourage employees to learn and grow.

- **Performance feedback and coaching:** The Steering Committee formed a task force of employees and charged them with developing an objective, standards-based performance appraisal system that would support the NOD. After two months' work, the task force produced a form and process, which the Steering Committee endorsed. For formal job performance feedback and compensation assignment, the system relies on manager-to-employee feedback, but allows for peer-to-peer feedback in more informal development reviews.

- **Employee handbook:** An employee handbook was part of the effort to build a greater sense of ownership in the company. Company management wanted to open the books on company policies and procedures, just as it had done with its financial information. The management team developed this handbook for introduction to employees in the fall of 1997.

- **Supervisor handbook:** Contrary to what some people may think happens in a self-directed work team, supervisory responsibilities still need to be carried out, but a wide variety of people may carry them out. Training and guidance in carrying out policies and procedures are essential if a wider spectrum of employees is to do these supervisory tasks. To aid this effort, a supervisory handbook that contains processes, forms, and other tools was written for distribution at about the same time as the employee handbook.

- **Gain sharing:** UCCC's owners instituted a formal gain-sharing program in the spring of 1997. Under this plan, quarterly profit goals were set for the company. If these goals are met, all employees share a percentage of the profits. This program is designed to encourage employees to develop cost-saving and revenue-generating ideas that can result in benefits for all employees. Such a program also encourages employees to learn more about all aspects of the business—finance, sales, marketing, and operations.

The vision that unifies all these efforts is that of a best-practice HR management system. The company deliberately did not develop these systems with the primary focus of compliance in mind. Instead, the focus of all these systems is on building a greater sense of ownership in the company and a greater sense of personal empowerment within the employee.

TRAINING AND DEVELOPMENT FOR ALL EMPLOYEES. The foundation of the training programs delivered to nearly every employee at United Check Clearing is the "Leadership for Quality and Involvement Model" (Hardt, 1997) (see figure 5). This model has its basis in a study of the leadership practices of 11 companies in Minnesota that have striven to establish world-class quality and employee involvement programs.

In this model, there are eight competencies grouped into two clusters with one of those competencies—personal power—shared by the clusters. The two clusters and eight competencies are the following:

- creation skills needed primarily in the creation of the NOD:
  - navigation skills needed to establish and maintain the landmarks (mission statements, job descriptions, team charters, ground rules) that will help people find ways to work productively in the new organization
  - change management skills needed to encourage, solicit, and implement employee-generated ideas for system improvement; the ability to support people as they go through change events

Figure 5. Leadership for Quality and Involvement Model.

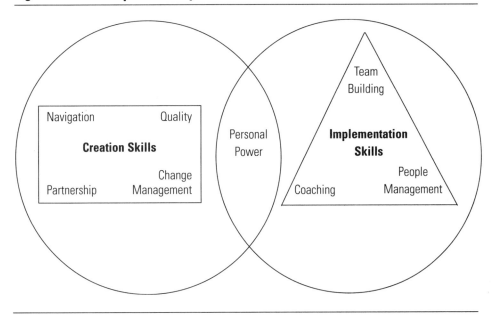

— partnership skills to help employees feel like partners in the business of the company

— quality skills, which are knowledge of quality improvement processes and fact-based problem-solving methods

• implementation skills needed to implement and "live in" the NOD:

— people management skills to establish systems that select, orient, train, and give feedback and rewards to people as they carry out organization goals; the ability to train others to lead through employee involvement

— coaching skills to give feedback to others and support them as they act to improve their performance

— team-building skills to form and support teams in the workplace; the ability to participate as a productive, positive team member

• the linking skill needed in creating and implementing the NOD:

— personal power to set personal goals, reward oneself, seek feedback and challenge one's own thinking as one develops as well as such characteristics as flexibility, trustworthiness, endurance, willingness to admit when one may be wrong, patience, sense of fairness, resiliency, realism, up-beat attitude, and organization skills.

Training was also planned in the concept of open book management (OBM). UCCC's finance department developed an in-depth training program in the basics of finance. This training supported the gain-sharing program and helped employees understand key financial measures used to judge the success of their SBUs.

The management team received training first, then the SBUs and individual employees were trained. The management team began its training with a multirater 360 feedback assessment on the basis of the "Leadership for Quality and Involvement Model."

SBUs began their training with an enhanced version of the training program "Working Together as a Team" that was delivered to the proto-SBUs in late 1997. Everyone received the same training, although the SBU membership had expanded and the training was slightly redundant for some members. The training consisted of 11 hours of training spread over a month's time. The sessions began with an ice breaker problem-solving session to get everyone acquainted. Then each group assessed its development according to Carew, Parisi-Carew, Stoner, Finch, and Blanchard's (1991) stages—"orientation," "dissatisfaction," "resolution," or "production". All SBUs were introduced to the concepts embodied in the navigation skills competency—the necessity of building clear chains of command, lines of sight, and levels of authority to help their teams function. Meeting management was covered in a one-hour session. Diversity was handled as before, with a workshop using the *Myers-Briggs Type Indicator* (Myers & Myers, 1993). Partnership skills were dealt with as a separate topic to help the SBUs start thinking about how they could build a greater sense of ownership in the business of their SBU. Finally, all groups learned an eight-step problem-solving process for use on improving processes that affected their businesses.

Because the management team encouraged the SBUs to play an active role in carrying out the traditional human resource management functions of a supervisor for their own members, they provided training in interviewing and selection and orientation and training. Both skills are part of the people management skills competency category. Many SBU members also took a two-hour workshop in coaching skills in an effort to learn more about how to communicate with other team members about performance problems. Team leadership was dealt with in a workshop titled "Situational Leadership" (Blanchard, Carew, Parisi-Carew, 1990). Using Blanchard's approach to situational leadership, attendees learned how to assess the maturity level of their team and how to assess their own preferred leadership style.

A four-hour workshop covered the personal power competency. For self-improvement, participants learned how to set personal improvement goals, monitor their behavior, and keep a journal about self-defeating beliefs and how to apply these self-improvement methods in the areas of building trust, optimism and endurance, and organization and time management skills. Under the leader's guidance, participants analyzed each of these elements of personal power and encouraged one another to identify ways in which they were already personally powerful and ways in which they could increase their personal power. Personal power is an essential part of building employees and teams that can be self-directing. Training in giving performance feedback was introduced early in 1998.

Phase Five: What Next?

After a year of unprecedented change, the employees and management of UCCC wanted to stop, take stock, and set their direction for the coming year and beyond. In mid-August 1997, 23 UCCC employees met for two half-day retreat sessions to talk about what had gone well, what hadn't gone well, and what they had learned. The group listed these lessons:

- Although people are learning to work together, there is still confusion about the role of SBUs and Resource Centers, and there is confusion about the responsibilities of individuals in the NOD. Questions remain about the SBUs' and Resource Center's levels of authority and their interrelationships. The pulling and hauling that existed between the functional departments are echoed in the interactions between SBUs and Resource Centers. At the same time, there is unprecedented sharing of information, goals, and improvement ideas. Individual differences are being recognized and valued. The entire organization will have to continue to work on clarifying roles and goals.

- Old paradigms die hard. Although there is interest and some enthusiasm for the new paradigm (see figure 3), it is still very easy to fall back into old modes of thinking.

- Change creates a wide variety of reactions. In the course of the most recent planning retreat, a whole spectrum of reactions to change was revealed. Some felt there was a lack of commitment to the change process and that there was a lack of a sense of ownership in SBUs. Low morale and resistance were cited. At the same time, many participants voiced great support for the change process. There were frequent affirmations of the company's ability to make the NOD work.

- Training is essential. The NOD required that employees at all levels of the organization practice a vast array of new skills. Training in the elements of the Leadership for Quality and Involvement Model was cited as a crucial success factor.

- Resources must be made available while the change is happening. Although the organization is going through change, resources of all kinds—information, people, time, money—must be allocated. Without these resources, people cannot attend meetings, understand the change process, or bring about the personal change that is necessary for the NOD to work.

- Communication has been one of the successful outcomes. Although some people complain about the time spent in meetings, these meetings—regular SBU and company meetings, open book management meetings, forums that the president of the company presents, and task force meetings—have all contributed to a greater sense of buy-in to the change process.

These lessons were the basis for the planning group's top priority goals for 1998:

- **Training:** Although training was one of the strengths of the initial phase of the process, even more must be done to train people in job-specific, SBU-specific, and companywide topics. Specific goals must be established for this training. Eventually, the goal is to get all SBUs to a high level of group maturity and productivity.

- **Objective standards and an objective performance appraisal system:** The planning group wanted to see more work done in these areas and to see the performance appraisal system in full operation by the end of 1998.

- **Communicate the vision:** The planning group discussed the challenges of communicating a clear, coherent vision to the whole organization. Although UCCC has taken unprecedented steps to try to align all employees with its vision, more needs to be done. Plans are under way for the planning group to participate in retreat sessions, which will focus specifically on developing a fuller, richer vision of the company and methods of communicating this vision.

- **Strategic growth:** Just as at the beginning of this process, UCCC continues to deal with the stresses and strains of trying to grow, and at the same time, trying to keep all employees involved and feeling ownership in the process. The planning group wants to see the gain-sharing program continue to succeed. It also wants to see each SBU develop a strong sense of individual identity, which it can take to the marketplace. The SBUs will also need to establish pricing strategies to support the company's strategic growth.

- **NOD role clarification:** All agreed that if SBUs are to move to their optimum levels of maturity and productivity, their roles, responsibilities, and levels of authority and those of each individual in the organization must be clarified.
- **Upbeat, motivational, employee-focused culture:** The planning group wants to see more done to develop a positive, high-energy culture that attracts the right kind of new employee to UCCC and fosters a sense of ownership among all employees.

Conclusion

Can employees from all levels and functions in an organization come together to plan the future of that organization? The answer seems to be yes, based on the experience of this case. UCCC's experience shows that the organization that wants to foster in all its employees a sense of ownership can find new ways to structure the organization and then live and work in that new organization. These new ways will be a combination of theory, the experiences of other organizations, and most important, the experiences of the people going through the process. The experience of UCCC shows that by taking the plunge into experiencing this change process and by reflecting upon this experience, an organization like UCCC can learn to make the transition from entrepreneurship to becoming an empowering, professional organization where competitive advantage is realized through employee involvement.

Questions for Discussion

1. What were the forces pressuring UCCC to move to a customer-intimate value discipline? Besides the actions described in the case, what are some other steps UCCC could have taken to create a more customer-intimate organization?

2. Treacy and Wiersema advocate an organization that chooses one value discipline and sticks closely to that discipline. Were there other value disciplines contending for the attention of UCCC's management and employees? What were these disciplines? How could UCCC reconcile the competition between these disciplines?

3. Could larger organizations use the high-involvement strategic planning methods described in this case? What would be some limitations of using these methods in larger organizations? How might these methods help a larger organization?

4. Was it appropriate for all employees to receive the training described in the "Implementing the New Organization Design" section

of this article? What training seemed most appropriate? What was least appropriate?

5. What kinds of barriers would you see to using some of the methods described in this case in the organization in which you work? What forces within and outside the organization in which you work might promote the use of some of these methods?

6. How was the overall effort evaluated? Do you think this evaluation effort was appropriate and effective? How could it have been improved?

The Author

Paul O. Hardt, Ed.D., has over 25 years of experience in the human development field. He has been a teacher, training manager, consultant, and developer of volunteers. He specializes in working with small to medium-size organizations, helping them overcome the growing pains that seem inevitable when an entrepreneur wants to grow his or her company. He has published articles in the *Human Resource Development Quarterly* and *Performance Improvement*. He conducted a study of 11 companies that the Minnesota Council for Quality recognized for their world-class quality efforts. The study resulted in Hardt's doctoral dissertation on the leadership practices of first-line leaders (team leaders, facilitators, boundary managers) in these organizations. Hardt has been a frequent speaker at local, regional, and national training events. Most recently, he has presented papers at two of the annual conferences of the Academy of Human Resource Development. Hardt can be reached at Creative Work Systems, 3905 Highland Drive, Shoreview, MN 55126-7015; phone: 612.483.9619; e-mail: hardt007@tc.umn.edu.

Notes

I am deeply indebted to the entire staff of United Check Clearing Corporation, Plymouth, Minnesota, for their cooperation in carrying out the process described in this case study. I am especially indebted to Joe Keller, UCCC's president, for his constant support in all aspects of this project, including the documentation of all the planning meetings throughout the NOD process and the editing of this case study.

References

Belasco, J., & Stayer, R. *Flight of the Buffalo: Soaring to Excellence, Learning to Let Employees Lead*. New York: Warner Books, 1993.

Blanchard, K., Carew, D., & Parisi-Carew, E. *The One Minute Manager Builds High Performing Teams.* New York: William Morrow, 1990.

Carew, D., Parisi-Carew, E., Stoner, J., Finch, F., & Blanchard, K. *Group Development Stage Analysis: Team Profile.* Escondido, CA: Blanchard Training and Development, 1991.

Flamholtz, E. *Growing Pains: How to Make the Transition From an Entrepreneurship to a Professionally Managed Firm.* San Francisco: Jossey-Bass, 1990.

Hardt, P. *Creating Effective Organizations.* Shoreview, MN: Creative Work Systems, 1997.

Myers, P., & Myers, K. *Myers-Briggs Type Indicator: Form G Self-Scorable* (rev. edition). Palo Alto, CA: Consulting Psychologists Press, 1993.

Stayer, R. "How I Learned to Let My Workers Lead." *Harvard Business Review,* November–December 1990, 66–83.

Treacy, M., & Wiersema, F. *The Discipline of Market Leaders.* Reading, MA: Addison-Wesley, 1995.

Strategic Planning and Customer Satisfaction: The Ultimate Drivers of Change Management

Financial Publishing Company

Beverly Hyman

This case illustrates how bringing the stakeholders into the process from the outset drives change management. This financial services publishing company implemented vast changes by reflecting the strategic plan and going out to customers to get their buy-in.

Background

On a spring day, the publisher of six well-known monthly technical financial service publications called his director of publishing services into his office. The publisher charged his subordinate with making the publications user friendly. The CEO had announced that customer service was one cornerstone of the new strategic plan. A second cornerstone was professionalizing the skills of the organization by making an investment in the professionals in the firm. In the publishing arm of this 3,000-person, multiservice, highly visible financial services corporation, succeeding in the second endeavor was an awesome feat.

The Players

The following six levels of key players lay between the CEO and the subscribers who ultimately read and used the financial information XYZ published:

- Eight executive directors, one for each business unit: The publishing end of the business was minor for them compared with product sales

This case was prepared to serve as a basis for discussion rather than to illustrate either effective or ineffective administrative and management practices. All names, dates, places, and organizations have been disguised at the request of the author or organization.

of tangible financial services. It was not that they thought the publications were trivial, but their bottom line was not directly dependent on them.

- The publisher: He had a high stake in this plan. He wanted tangible evidence of change to demonstrate his ability for the CEO.
- The director of publishing services: He was a true professional in publishing and saw this plan as an opportunity to significantly upgrade the publishing products for which he was responsible.
- The editor in chief of the flagship publication: He hoped that this effort would solve some of the day-to-day business problems he had receiving articles and other written material from as many as 800 in-house business analysts, economists, and financial services specialists each year, none of whom were professional writers.
- The editorial staff: They hoped this effort would empower them and make them less at the mercy of the nonprofessional contributing writers whom they served on a daily basis.
- The writers: They initially thought this plan would be nothing much—just business as usual.

The Problems

The director of publishing services fleshed out the problems:
1. How would the customers, or subscribers, like to see the publications change? The director of publishing services had undertaken a large readership survey about content only a year ago. Content was in line with subscribers' tastes; format and style got lower grades.
2. Assuming publishing services management could determine the needed format and style, how could those managers get all the people involved to agree on the changes and, much harder, get those format and style changes implemented? The changes had to take place at the level of each individual contributor. Editors had neither the time nor expertise to rewrite the huge numbers of long, technical articles submitted to them.

The Steps

There were 11 steps to implementing the change:
1. The director of publishing services shopped for a consultant. He wanted someone who met the following criteria:
- was local and could be easily available
- had a track record with companies in the industry
- was seasoned and credible to the highly educated, well-paid professionals at the firm

- had experience in writing for publication
- was an outstanding course developer and trainer
- was with a firm that was large enough to handle this size job.

2. Before making his final choice, the director of publishing services invited four executive directors (EDs) and the publisher to a joint interview with the consultant. He asked the consultant to meet one-on-one with the other four EDs. The information she derived from these meetings, the familiarity she established with each ED, and the goodwill she established set the tone for the whole project.

3. After the director of publishing services hired the consultant, he quickly brought other team members into the process. The manager of marketing, the senior editors, and the most prominent writer-contributors all oriented the consultant to the task at hand.

4. With the manager of marketing, the consultant set about designing and conducting focus groups to reach consumers and determine what style and format changes were desirable. Before conducting the outside focus groups, the consultant ran trial focus groups with internal people, mostly contributing writers. Focus groups were designed to represent each of the types of subscribers to the publications. The focus groups were videotaped, and the CEO watched an edited version.

5. Many concrete recommendations came out of the focus groups. These were discussed with the EDs, the publisher, the director of publishing services, the editor in chief and the editors. They were codified into a simple-to-use manual for the whole company with lots of examples of right and wrong style and format usage.

6. The consultant designed a highly interactive hands-on two-day workshop to train all writer-contributors in the new style and format.

7. Editors were the first people to go through the workshop so the consultant could address their practical problems in dealing with writer-contributors.

8. The EDs went through the workshops next. From then on, letters of invitation to the workshops came from the EDs to their direct reports and below.

9. The workshops were rolled out quickly, with as many as four two-day workshops conducted, off site, with 10 writer-contributors in each, per week. The workshops opened with videotape excerpts from the focus groups with client-subscribers talking about what they did not like or did not find useful in the present style and format of the publications. Everyone attending a workshop had to submit writing samples in advance from work he or she had published previously in the publications. The consultant critiqued them and used them as examples

in each workshop so the material in each workshop was unique to the people present. The consultant solicited samples from each participant after the workshops as well.

10. The feedback about the workshops really helped to market the program. The (somewhat arrogant) professionals who attended were surprised by the tangible results they saw in their own writing because they now had formats and concrete style principles to follow. They liked the tremendous individual feedback as well as the give and take in the workshops, and they very much liked hearing and seeing their readers on tape.

11. Word-of-mouth made the workshop very popular. Within six months, several tangible results materialized:

- The publications looked and read much differently, incorporating the new changes. This was a permanent change.
- People coming into the workshops were coming in with a head start. A new ethic had been established—the right way to do it. New people coming into the company were using the style manual and starting out writing the right way.
- Administrative assistants, secretaries, systems people, and a whole host of other players in the company wanted courses for themselves. Writing had become an ethic in the company.
- Contributing writers requested an advanced course. Supervisors requested a remedial course.
- Customer feedback was enthusiastic.
- The CEO pronounced the effort the "single most successful training and development effort I have seen in my career."
- The publisher was promoted.
- Another major print product was singled out for overhaul, and the consultant got that job, too.

Questions for Discussion

1. Describe how you would conduct the focus groups. How many people would you invite to attend? Who would conduct them and how? What types of questions would you ask? How would the facilitator or facilitators get people to contribute? How would the data be captured and used?

2. If you had been responsible, describe what the format of the two-day workshop would have been. How would so much individual feedback be provided to each participant? Would groups be homogeneous or heterogeneous—that is, grouped by business unit (retail analysis, insurance, manufacturing, and so forth) or mixed? Why?

3. One of the outcomes of the effort that was not as successful as the rest of the project was the empowerment of editors. Editors continued to feel at the mercy of writer-contributors. They could not get writers on the telephone to request permission to make changes and could not make substantive manuscript changes because of the technical financial meanings involved. What else could be done for editors to help them facilitate their work with contributors? What electronic communications might help them? What support? What added training?

4. Although the changes became permanent and the new style was uniformly adopted, the consultant has never been able to get many people to send her a new writing sample within three months of completion of a writing workshop. What would encourage people to get that final feedback? Is this necessary or important?

5. The firm was so thrilled with the outcome of this initiative that it set about doing the same thing with its public speaking efforts. Its professionals are constantly asked to speak, and the company puts on many technical seminars for its clientele. Although the same consultant used the same systematic approach, why were the public speaking efforts less successful? What might be different about public speaking skills?

The Author

Beverly Hyman is internationally known as the Trainer's Trainer. Her organizational development and training firm, Beverly Hyman, Ph.D. & Associates, solves internal and external communications problems and trains in curriculum design, presentation skills, facilitation, sales, negotiation, interpersonal skills, influence, strategic planning, team building, and technical and business writing. To date, the company has trained more than 20,000 trainers. Hyman is the author of *Training for Productivity* and *How Successful Women Manage* as well as articles and interviews in such periodicals as *Fortune* and *Ms.* She has been a featured speaker at national and international conferences including the United Nations Conference to End the Decade for Women, the National Human Resources Conference of the American Management Association, and the AFL-CIO Professional Employees Conference. Hyman holds a Ph.D. from New York University in communication and an M.S. in education. She can be reached at Beverly Hyman, Ph.D. & Associates, 369 Lexington Avenue, New York, NY 10017; phone: 212.983. 6250; fax: 212.983.6342.

Encouraging Human Potential: A Career Development Success Story

American Express Financial Advisors

Hilda C. Koontz, Laura L. Theis, and Eugene J. Audette

This case illustrates how a major financial services company developed an internationally recognized career development program serving 5,400 corporate office employees. The company began the program in response to negative employee feedback but now uses it as a successful recruitment and retention tool.

Background

American Express Financial Advisors' vision includes their aim to become the "Best Company for Our People." The vision statement says in part, "We have become, for all involved, a place of realized potential."

The company conducts an employee survey each September that helps to determine how well the organization is achieving its vision. Called the LEAPS/American Express employee survey (the former means Leadership Effectiveness and People Satisfaction), it also provides a mechanism by which corporate employees and people in the field can evaluate their leaders and the organization as a whole. The results of the 1993 survey indicated that corporate employees and the people in the field did not feel that American Express Financial Advisors was a best company in the area of career development and perceived that leaders didn't have the skills to provide that kind of assistance. The scores employees gave for this function were consistently low both in the corporate office and the field. The LEAPS index for career

This case was prepared to serve as a basis for discussion rather than to illustrate either effective or ineffective administrative and management practices.

development items in 1993 was only 49 percent favorable in the corporate office. To be considered a strength, the index needs to be at least 70 percent favorable.

At the same time, American Express Financial Advisors was undergoing a top-to-bottom restructuring that resulted in a much flatter organization. Opportunities to move in many directions across a career lattice were replacing career moves up the traditional ladder. The LEAPS results, combined with organizational restructuring, coalesced and created an opportunity to improve organizational performance by addressing the need for career development. A better match between employees' strengths and job demands would result in improve-ments in performance, employees' being more comfortable with organizational change, improved staff satisfaction, reduced turnover, and increased ability to attract top talent. The initial focus of the career development initiative at American Express Financial Advisors was on employees in the corporate office, although much information would subsequently be communicated to people in the field.

Organizational and Industry Profile

American Express Financial Advisors, formerly known as IDS Financial Services, is a major financial services company that owns or manages nearly $130 billion in assets and serves more than 2 million clients throughout the United States. IDS Financial Services was founded in Minneapolis in 1894 and acquired by the American Express Company in 1984. The organization was rebranded as American Express Financial Advisors in January 1995. The company has over 5,400 employees in its corporate headquarters in Minneapolis.

The financial planning industry is immense and highly competitive. Competition is increasing as banks and brokerage houses attempt to enter the field. One of American Express Financial Advisors' goals has always been to build, support, and maintain long-lasting relationships with its clients. To accomplish that, the organization needs to attract, develop, and retain the best possible human capital at all levels of the company.

Key Players

The senior leadership team gave its support and commitment to a career development initiative as soon as it saw the results of the 1993 LEAPS. This team was responsible for the redeployment of financial and human resources to facilitate the effort and were visible advocates throughout the initiative. The leaders included the chief executive officer and the senior vice president for human resources (SVP-HR).

Within the Human Resources (HR) division, the key players were the vice president for leadership assurance, the director of leadership assurance, the leadership assurance consultant, and the career specialist. The leadership assurance consultant was an extant human resources employee who was reassigned to the full-time task of implementing the career development program. The career specialist was external talent hired specifically to develop and staff the on-site career center.

Seven volunteers from different areas of the corporate office served on a career advisory board. The members had an expressed interest in career development and provided suggestions and feedback as the initiative progressed. This group was instrumental in developing support for the initiative from all parts of the organization.

A career development psychologist, who is also a professor at a nearby regional university, provided the initial external consulting services for the initiative.

A national career management firm was the external vendor that consulted on the initial program design, delivered short-term services to employees, conducted pilots of career development training, facilitated train-the-trainer sessions, and provided ongoing career development training for leaders.

The Career Development Initiative

Once career development had been identified as a corporate priority, American Express Financial Advisors initiated a rapid response. Figure 1 shows the timeline of this phase of development.

In early 1994, senior leadership approved a variance in the HR budget to fund the career development effort. By March an HR staff employee had been redeployed on a full-time basis to guide the program through its initial phase.

The research and communication phase began in earnest in April 1994 and involved seven concurrent activities. These activities were
1. obtaining assistance from an outside consultant
2. developing a career development philosophy
3. benchmarking external organizations
4. doing an internal scan to determine what career development resources already existed
5. conducting a needs analysis to determine employee expectations

Figure 1. Timeline for research and communication phase of the career development initiative.

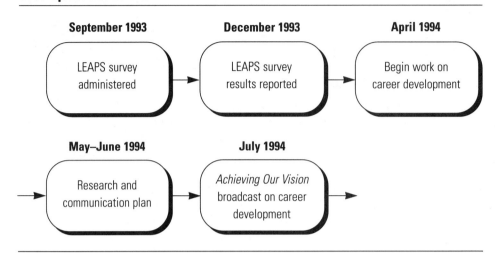

6. engaging an outside vendor to provide short-term career development services
7. creating an integrated communications plan.

The outside consultant was engaged in April 1994. His role as a consultant included brainstorming approaches and setting priorities and timelines with the leadership assurance consultant. He also researched models of career development delivery systems that could be suitable in a corporate environment and suggested tangible processes that would help the company achieve its goals. His search of the literature focused on adaptations of models that would fit the company's identified needs and could be linked to performance management, individual development planning, and reward systems.

Early in the process, the consultant suggested that a career development philosophy be developed. The statement needed to define what career development meant within the organization, and it needed to be congruent with the company's overall mission and philosophy. The leadership assurance consultant, in consultation with the director of leadership assurance, the advisory board, and the consultant, developed the following philosophy statement:

> Career Development is a partnership between the organization, leaders and American Express Financial Advisors people.
> • Individuals are primarily responsible for their own Career Development, and leaders support and encourage this development.

- American Express Financial Advisors provides resources people may need during the Career Development process.
- Career enrichment involves creating a plan for individuals to grow and develop skills to enhance performance in their current position or prepare them for other opportunities.

The consultant also advised the company of the need for an ongoing, high-profile communications effort that would keep employees apprised of the organization's commitment to career development and the tangible results of that commitment.

Finally, the consultant recommended that an outside vendor be engaged to provide two types of service that the company could not then provide internally. The outside vendor would provide short-term services to employees, such as career-related brown bag sessions as well as in-depth career development training for both leaders and individual contributors. From a field of 15 possible outside vendors, five local and national career development management firms were chosen to submit proposals. From this group, a national company was selected to deliver the career services.

By July 1994, the work of the outside consultant was formally concluded. However, he has maintained an ongoing personal and professional interest in the career initiative at American Express Financial Advisors.

Concurrent with the work of the consultant, the HR staff member did an external scan to learn what career development services other major local and national corporations were providing. This research revealed that there was no consistent model for delivering such a service. Some companies had few resources, some were just beginning such programs, and others had highly developed programs that had been in place for many years.

Similarly, an outside survey firm looked at what other career development activities had taken place in the organization during the previous few years. In 1993, there had been five such initiatives, including an informational memo, relevant training packets, workshops, and an education fair. More such initiatives had begun after the 1993 LEAPS results were published, but these departmental efforts lacked an across-the-company linkage.

From inception to operation, the hallmark of the career development effort at American Express Financial Advisors is that it has been shaped in large part to reflect what the employees said they wanted in such a program. The company's internal needs assessment in the spring of 1994 exemplifies this approach. A local human resource development consulting group conducted 18 one-on-one interviews and five focus groups in May and early June 1994 and received random written commentaries from employees. The group asked participants questions about career development, leadership, and performance management issues.

The results of this needs assessment indicated that employees wanted the following resources to support career development:

1 an on-site resource person with specialized training in the area of career development
2. computer-based career assessment tools
3. information about the organization and career opportunities that might be available in other parts of the company
4. in-depth career training for both leaders and individual contributors
5. an on-site, accessible resource center filled with career-related books, videos, audiotapes, and various company-specific materials.

The final activity that was key to the first phase of this career development initiative was an intense, integrated communication effort. Regular communications to the organization kept career development issues visible and provided employees with updates on the progress of the initiative.

In addition to the CEO's and the SVP-HR's ongoing communications in the company's publication of record and in the e-mail system, they participated in a live video broadcast to the entire company in July 1994. Titled *Achieving Our Vision,* the broadcast again communicated the importance that senior leadership attached to the issue of career development. In the broadcast, Beverly Kaye, a nationally known career development consultant, explained what the career development process looks like, what people can do to take charge of their careers, and what a leader's role is in career development.

During the second half of 1994, HR staff focused on obtaining resources, continuing to publicize and build support for the career initiative, and implementing programs. (See figure 2.) In September and October, the external vendor facilitated the pilots of the in-depth career training programs titled "Career Focus," which is for employees, and "Partners in Career Management," for leaders. Both levels of training provided 16 hours of instruction around the career development model to employees representing many different areas of the company.

In November, the external vendor provided lunchtime brown bag sessions called "Work in the '90s" and "Career Development Process."

Figure 2. Program implementation timeline.

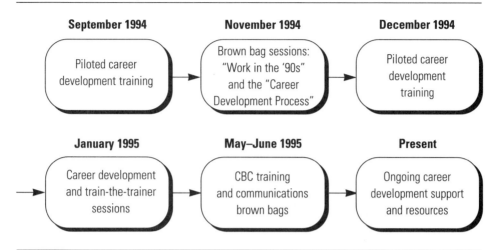

These sessions provided employees with some useful career information until a formal resource center and its services became available.

In November, external talent with expertise in career development came on board to physically set up and staff the resource center. The following concurrent activities were carried out during November and December:

1. selection of print, video, and audio resources
2. selection of a computer-based career development software program
3. selection of assessment tools
4. obtainment of and organization of company-specific information
5. obtainment of catalogs for all postsecondary institutions in the area
6. marketing of the career center to employees.

As part of the ongoing communications effort, a contest was held to choose a name for the new career resource center. The HR staff chose the name Career Enrichment Center (CEC), and the contest winners received career counseling services from the external vendor. The inclusion of the word *enrichment* in the name is significant because this career effort emphasizes growth of the individual within the company and has no connection with any outplacement function.

At the end of December 1994, the CEC began operating. On January 6, 1995, a formal grand opening took place at which both the CEO and the SVP-HR gave presentations on the importance of career development. The CEC occupies 954 square feet of highly visible space in the IDS Tower in downtown Minneapolis. Many of the resources are accessible to employees 24 hours a day, seven days a week.

At the time of its opening, the CEC library contained about 500 resources in the areas of career development, personal growth, workplace trends, life balance, communications, leadership effectiveness, customer service, management, and retirement options. Career development software titled *DISCOVER for Organizations,* was available on two computers. Also available was detailed information about company organization, department descriptions, current and historical job postings, and company-sponsored training opportunities.

First-Year Activities

In its first year of operation, American Express Financial Advisors delivered the career development program by providing:
1. ongoing communications about career issues
2. resources in the CEC
3. training through the "Career Focus" and "Partners in Career Management" programs
4. lunch-hour brown bag sessions on various career issues
5. an internal consultant function, which supported individualized career development projects in other parts of the organization.

The ongoing suggestions and requests of the employees have shaped all the components of this effort. The circulating CEC resources, for example, have increased in number and diversity due to employee feedback. The collection has grown to about 1,000 resources, including those from the company's Work and Family unit, the Toastmasters chapter, and the Finance Leadership Resource Center. The CEC display area, containing handouts on career, stress management, work and family balance, performance management, and training and educational opportunities, has doubled in size. A career bulletin board on the e-mail system has been established and provides current information on CEC resources, events, training, and other career-related information. Twenty-three internal trainers were certified to deliver "Career Focus" training.

Costs

The funding for the career initiative at American Express Financial Advisors came from the budget of Leadership, Organization Effectiveness and Staffing, which is an area of HR. Senior leadership approved a generous variance in the HR budget, which was more than adequate to fund the start-up costs through 1995.

Precise cost figures are not being provided in this case study because expenditures can vary widely depending on the costs of space, whether an organization engages the services of outside consultants and trainers, whether licensed products are being utilized, and if any of the services being provided are charged back to units or to individuals. American Express Financial Advisors does not charge individuals or units for the services provided in the CEC or through special presentations. There is a unit charge-back for materials used as part of the in-depth career training.

Results

The CEC provided nearly 4,000 services in 1995. By 1997, annual usage had risen to 5,000. The services provided include one-on-one career coaching, Myers-Briggs Type Indicator and Strong Interest Inventory assessments, mock interviews, computer-based training for career and personal development, seminars, library services, and learning tours of the facility.

The CEC has been benchmarked nationally and internationally, and the authors of this case study have made presentations about this career initiative at the conventions of both the Minnesota Career Development Association (MCDA) and the National Career Development Association in 1995. A tour of the CEC was also a scheduled event for the Academy of Human Resource Development international convention in March 1996. The CEC received the MCDA Merit Award in 1996.

American Express Financial Advisors does not see career development as a one-time program, but as the way the company operates. As a result, career development was integrated into other HR systems as follows:

- The compensation system rewards lateral moves.
- Leaders designate 25 percent of their goal weighting for leadership effectiveness.
- Career development is seen as fitting into each step of performance management and individual development planning.
- Career training is included in all new manager training.
- The Employee Assistance Resource program is familiar with career resources for referral purposes.
- A tour of the CEC is part of the new employee orientation program.

The annual LEAPS survey is the main measure of the success of this career initiative. The satisfaction rating of career development was 49 percent in 1993. As the effort was beginning in 1994, the rating increased to 57 percent favorable. The LEAPS data of 1995 show that, after the CEC and other career components became operational, the career development index increased to 72 percent favorable and it then rose to 73 percent in 1996. The CEO communicated the results of this survey (see figure 3) to the company in a memorandum and in the company's publication of record.

For all major components of this career development initiative, clients' overall satisfaction ratings on a scale from 1 to 5 were as follows for 1995:

- CEC: 4.8
- "Career Focus" training: 4.7
- "Partners in Career Management" training: 4.5
- brown bag sessions: 4.4.

The CEC is used proactively as a recruitment and retention tool in the very competitive Minneapolis job market.

Conclusions and Recommendations

On the basis of the quantitative LEAPS data, the qualitative personal comments that accompanied them, and the overall satisfaction ratings received for the various services, it appears that the career development initiative at American Express Financial Advisors has been extremely successful. Two key factors have contributed to these results. First, senior leadership made career development a company priority and visibly supported the effort throughout its development. Second, the employees themselves have continually shaped the resources and programs in this effort. As a result of the company's responding positively to employee feedback, the employees have a sense of ownership in the effort and know that their needs are being respected.

Figure 3. Career development results.

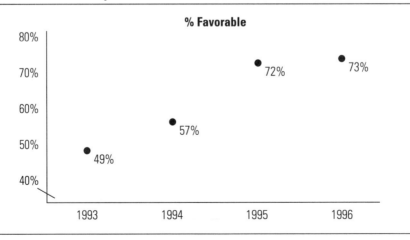

Although the needs of every organization are unique, a tangible career center, such as the CEC, would most easily lend itself to replication in other organizations. The scope and physical size could range anywhere from a large center with round-the-clock accessibility to a simple display rack with career-related handouts.

On the basis of the knowledge the case authors gained in beginning this career initiative, they have the following recommendations for companies embarking on a similar initiative:

1. Generate a clear and explicit career development philosophy statement that is in harmony with the vision, mission, and publicly stated annual goals of the organization.
2. Listen to the needs of your clients.
3. Make services and resources easily accessible to the clients.
4. Understand that career development programs are constantly evolving.

Human resource professionals who have a clear vision of what career development means in their organization can clearly communicate roles and responsibilities. This is especially important in the context of a workplace in which entitlements are disappearing.

Attending to the needs of the client will make a career program credible, and staff members will feel valued and respected. Ease of access is related to the issue of credibility. Key components to the program at American Express Financial Advisors are that the CEC is available after hours and that a great deal of information is available on the e-mail system. Use of e-mail also maximizes career staff time.

To be viable and relevant, career programs need to evolve with the needs of their clients. Since its inception, the CEC has made more linkages with other parts of American Express Company. In addition, the CEC is expanding its client base and developing more proactive approaches to assisting clients with their career development needs.

For example, more resources are now being provided to leaders. The materials in the section of the CEC known as the leader's corner provide leaders not only with support in their personal career goals but also with help in their current jobs and in assisting their employees in developing their potential.

One of the challenges of developing a career within a company as large as American Express Financial Advisors is to discover where the individual can best utilize his or her skills and interests. Using a proactive approach, the CEC is now developing a library of videos of in-house brown bag sessions and individual informational interviews. These videos provide employees with detailed information about the missions of various areas of the company and the types of work those areas typically perform. The video format helps employees quickly identify which areas fit best with their skills, interests, and career goals. They can then maximize their time and energy by concentrating their informational interviewing and networking efforts in the most relevant areas.

To move American Express Financial Advisors closer to its vision of becoming the Best Company for our People, the company adopted the following five-year vision statement for career development in mid-1995.

> Contribute to Employee/Advisor, Client, and Shareholder results by being a world-class Career Development organization. We will know we have achieved this when:
> - American Express Financial Advisors is renowned for "best practices" in Career Development.
> - All American Express Financial Advisors people get the career development resources, tools, and training they need, when they need it, in a way they can use it.
> - Leaders develop people and are recognized and rewarded for it.
> - Career Development happens increasingly through developmental assignments and on-the-job experience.

Questions for Discussion

1. The successful founding and operation of the CEC occurred because senior management took seriously the employees' dissatisfaction with career development resources and opportunities available to them as identified in the annual climate survey. What strategies can HR and human resource development managers take when senior management does not seek to identify, much less support, career development as a goal for the organization?

2. A company representative stationed in England reads about the effectiveness of the CEC at the corporate office in Minneapolis and expresses a desire to benefit from the center's services. What long-range, multiyear plan could be designed to offer career development services to employees nationwide, and even internationally, from a corporate operation that currently serves only the headquarters site and has only recently begun to serve satellite offices in the metropolitan area? What roles can a variety of technologies (satellite uplink, distance learning labs, Internet, and the like) play in the plan?

3. A factor that contributes to the success of the CEC is that development of direct reports counts in each leader's performance appraisal and reward system. It comes under the rubric of leadership effectiveness and has encouraged leaders to use or refer to the CEC's services. If a similar policy is not in place in your own organization, what strategies and rationale would you develop to build into the performance and reward system? Whose support would you need? What cultural and procedural obstacles would you have to identify and overcome?

4. The CEC is supported by one full-time professional staff member, supports a corporate staff of 5,000, and has begun to reach out to local satellite offices in the immediate vicinity. As publication of early successes increases the requests for more such services, what can be done to provide the same or better levels of service to satellite offices and at low cost?

5. What indicators of the interplay of the human resource development (HRD) processes of organizational development, management development, or organizational change appear to be evident in this case? How could any one of these HRD approaches and processes be a vehicle by which to address the need for organizational career development strategies and resources?

The Authors

Hilda C. Koontz is program manager for Corporate Career Development at American Express Financial Advisors in Minneapolis. She holds a certificate in career development from the graduate program of human resource development at the University of St. Thomas in St. Paul, Minnesota, and is currently completing an M.A. in counseling psychology at the same institution. Koontz has been a presenter at international, national, and state career development venues and a contributor to *Human Resource Executive* magazine and the Minnesota Career Development Association's *Communique.* She is a recipient of the American Express Human Resources Excellence Award and the Minnesota Career Development Merit Award. She has been a trainer for Womenventure, a nonprofit agency in St. Paul that provides career services for lower income women. She has also been a facilitator and group supervisor at Chrysalis Center for Women, a nonprofit agency in Minneapolis that provides a wide array of personal, crisis, referral, and legal services. Koontz is a member of the American Counseling Association, American Society for Training & Development, National Career Development Association, Minnesota Career Development Association, and the Career Planning and Adult Development Network. She can be reached at American Express Financial Advisors, IDS Tower 10, Mail Stop T1211061, Minneapolis, MN 55440; phone: 612.671.4064.

Laura. L. Theis is a senior staffing specialist at DataCard Corporation. For 10 years, Theis was employed at American Express Financial Advisors, where she served as a consultant in leadership, organization effectiveness, and staffing, delivering leadership training and consulting with leaders in the field. She also was responsible for integrating the competency-based leadership success model into field development activities, and she spent one and one-half years leading the corporate career development initiative. Theis was a member of the American Express Financial Advisors/Southwest High School Business Partnership Committee, which endeavors to inform students about realistic career opportunities, and she volunteers at Womenventure. She has been a presenter at state and national career conferences. Theis holds an M.A. in human resource development from the University of St. Thomas in St. Paul, Minnesota, and a B.A. in speech communications and psychology from the University of Minnesota in Minneapolis.

Eugene J. Audette, Ph.D., is a consulting psychologist in limited private practice, initially licensed in 1978. He specializes in organizational career development processes and issues and consults with government and private- and public-sector organizations. He is the former chair of the graduate programs in the Department of Organization, Learning and Development, and holds the title of professor in the School of Education at the University of St. Thomas in St. Paul/Minneapolis, Minnesota. He has been at St. Thomas for the past 25 years. He cofounded the university's Career and Personal Counseling Center in 1975, and managed the center and served as chief staff psychologist until 1983, when he returned to a full-time graduate faculty appointment. In 1984, he codesigned one of the first competency-based M.A. programs in HRD in the United States. He was also elected president of the university's Graduate Faculty Assembly and an associate dean. In 1991, the Minnesota Career Development Association conferred on Audette the Kerlan Outstanding Achievement Award as "career development person of the year" for his contributions to the field.

References

Feldman, D. *Managing Careers in Organizations*. Glenview, IL: Scott, Foresman, 1988.

Gutteridge, T., Leibowitz, Z., & Shore, J. *Organizational Career Development: Benchmarks for Building a World-Class Workforce*. San Francisco: Jossey-Bass, 1993.

Gutteridge, T., & Otte, F. *Organizational Career Development: State of the Practice*. Washington, DC: American Society for Training & Development, 1983.

Hall, D., & Associates. *Career Development in Organizations*. San Francisco: Jossey-Bass, 1988.

Leibowitz, Z., Farren, C., & Kaye, B. *Designing Career Development Systems*. San Francisco: Jossey-Bass, 1986.

Otte, F., & Hutcheson, P. *Helping Employees Manage Careers*. Englewood Cliff, NJ: Prentice Hall, 1992.

Rothwell, W., & Sredl, H. *The ASTD Reference Guide to Professional Human Resource Development Roles and Competencies* (2d edition, volume II). Amherst, MA: HRD Press, pp. 199–227, 1992.

Training for New Technology

Midwest Steel Company

Joseph T. Martelli

Plant modernization and technology implementation are engineering strategies corporations use for productivity and quality improvement. What happens when other functional strategies, such as human resources strategy, are not part of a corporation's grand strategy? This quasi-experimental case study in a Fortune *500 company shows the effect of failing to integrate requisite functional strategies into an overall grand strategy. The study examines the training and human resource implications in planning and installing new technology in a facility. This case study presents knowledge, performance, and financial data the researchers measured.*

Background

In March, a *Fortune* 250 steel mill and manufacturer located in the Midwest was equipped with a ladle preheater. The addition of this preheater to the melt shop was one of many changes occurring as a result of a multimillion dollar mill-modernization program, that was intended to bring the company up to state-of-the-art practices and processes in the steelmaking industry.

The company was traditionally structured and could be classified by Mintzberg's organizational structure as a machine bureaucracy (Mintzberg, 1983). The company had two primary operating divisions— one in steel production and the other in manufacturing. Each operating unit reported to a respective corporate vice president, who

This case was prepared to serve as a basis for discussion rather than to illustrate either effective or ineffective administrative and management practices. All names, dates, places, and organizations have been disguised at the request of the author or organization.

in turn reported to the president and CEO. The human resources (HR) function reported to a vice president of communications. A director of human resource management and a director of human resource development, among other administrative and staff directors, reported to the vice president of communications. The human resource development (HRD) function was responsible for management development and technical training for the organization. A manager headed each HRD function (management and technical).

Corporate headquarters and the primary operating units were located in the same city with headquarters located spatially in close proximity to the operating units. The company employed a worldwide workforce of approximately 10,000 employees, with nearly half located in the headquarters city. Other operating units were located throughout the United States and the world.

The ladle preheater represented a capital investment of approximately $150,000. Prior to the development of this preheating process and technology, ladles were not preheated. There were several expectations for this new ladle preheating method. They included producing cleaner, higher quality steel, reducing furnace delays via increased ladle turnaround, decreased overall power consumption, and the like.

For a period of several weeks prior to the preheater commissioning, various technical personnel prepared for the start-up of the preheater. Construction crews readied the foundation, maintenance people prepared utilities, and so forth. In early March, operators on all shifts began preheating ladles.

The vendor representatives at the mill during commissioning provided on-site operator training to melt-shop pouring-pit supervisors and a few hourly pouring-pit personnel (who were ultimately responsible for operating the preheater). There was no systematic approach to transferring the operating principles to personnel on the subsequent shifts.

The vendors' operator training was informal and unstructured. The training program was conducted on the job as a demonstration and lasted approximately five to 10 minutes. There was no evaluation of the training. A descriptive chronology of events over four months regarding the preheater is included in figure 1. In brief, the preheater operators' lack of knowledge and skill resulted in a significant amount of damage to the preheater.

First, the burner block was severely cracked, apparently because a crane operator bumped a ladle into the block during ladle placement. Further use of the preheater in this condition would have caused

Figure 1. Chronology of events: ladle preheater start-up.

Date	Event
3/04	Ladle preheater installation completed. Preheater was ready for operation. Vendors conducted a three- to five-minute show-and-tell training for available supervisors and operators.
3/18	Engineering department shut down two-week-old preheater because of severe damage caused by a crane operator "bumping" a ladle into the burner during ladle placement. Preheater was shut down for three weeks while a replacement block was ordered. Use of the preheater with damaged burner block would further damage electronic components on the cool side of the burner.
3/19	Because of a lack of communication, the midnight crew, not aware of the condition and status of the preheater, used it throughout the shift. Discoloration on the electronics control box indicated that heat had transferred to the cool side of the firewall through the damaged burner block.
3/20	Operations management told Training and Development (T & D) personnel that there was no need for any kind of training program and that vendor personnel trained a "few" workers on how to operate the preheater. These operators would pass along the knowledge to the other operators. Supervisors reported that vendor training took about five to 10 minutes.
4/08	Preheater repaired and operational.
4/15	Burner block redamaged. Preheater shut down again. Maintenance personnel attempted to solve the problem of damaged burner blocks and slow procurement by casting their own blocks. Preheater was altered to accept makeshift burner blocks.
4/20	Preheater (PH) repaired and operational.
5/02	While starting the PH, an operator attempted to put it in the low- and high-fire modes with the PH sealed to the ladle. This is an explosive condition, and safety relays prevent such a start-up. However, the relays were temporarily disconnected while engineering modifications were being made. Fortunately, a nearby engineer prevented the operator from starting the PH.
5/03	Preheater was in use; no operations personnel nearby. T & D observed a 12-inch gap between the ladle rim and preheater seal with the preheater in the high-fire mode. This was an incorrect, inefficient, and dangerous operating condition.

continued on page 88

Figure 1. Chronology of events: ladle preheater start-up (continued).

Date	Event
5/04	T & D observed a PH operator attempting to start the PH. Apparently, not knowing how to correctly start the PH, the operator had tripped the flame failure shutdown and safety override. Restarting the PH in this condition required a simple reset and restart procedure. The operator unsuccessfully attempted to restart the PH. After several minutes of unobtrusive observation, T & D assisted operator in resetting preheater.
5/15	Preheater was in use, preheating a ladle in the high-fire mode. No operations personnel nearby. T & D personnel observed ladle temperature at 1900° Fahrenheit. The cooling air connection to the rotary nozzle had not been made. T & D personnel corrected the faulty condition. PH could have been badly damaged by overheating.
5/15	Condition of PH refractory modules has been deteriorating as a result of inconsistent ladle sealing practices.
6/07	Preheater wouldn't start (a.m.). Operators were unable to find the problem and summoned maintenance department. The PH was shut down for the interim period. Unheated ladles were used the remainder of the shift. Toward the end of the shift, maintenance arrived. After troubleshooting, it was discovered that a tripped gas meter valve had not been reset. This was a simple operator correctable condition.
6/11	An operator thought the PH was overheating during operation. Subsequently, he opened the gap between the PH seal and ladle rim. As a result, the temperature thermocouple couldn't monitor and control ladle temperature. The PH remained on uncontrolled high fire for several hours. The thermocouple burned out, and the intense, uncontrolled heat caused slag in the ladle to melt. When the ladle was removed, molten slag poured onto the preheater, severely damaging the hydraulic hoses and other components. The PH was shut down two weeks for repair.
6/13	Condition of burner block was poor and in need of replacement. A third burner block was installed.
6/25	Structured technical training systematically provided around the clock for all operations and supervisory personnel.

additional damage to the preheater electronic components on the cool side of the firewall. The preheater was shut down for approximately three weeks while a new burner block was on order. The vendor estimated the cost of a new burner block at $1,507. The burner block had been replaced twice since the preheater was in operation. Both replacements occurred within two to three months of preheater commissioning.

Second, improper operating practices by preheater operators resulted in damage to the preheater firewall. This firewall is composed of approximately 110 ceramic fiber modules, and most of these modules had to be replaced. The cost of each module was $50.58. Total cost of replacement parts for two burner blocks ($1,507 each) and approximately 50 modules ($50.58 each) amounted to $5,543. This cost did not include shipping charges or the cost of maintenance labor to make the repairs. The exact labor figures were not made available. Assuming a cost of 50 percent for materials and 50 percent for labor, the total cost to repair the preheater within three months of start-up would have been $11,068.

Intervention by Training and Development

Shortly after initial use of the ladle preheater, Training and Development (T & D) became involved in this project. T & D's initial needs analysis revealed a need for a structured operator training program for ladle preheater operators. The needs analysis indicated that although operation of the preheater was not highly sophisticated or complex, there was a definitive body of knowledge necessary for proper and safe preheater operation.

T & D's recommendation was to curtail the use of the preheater until a training program could be implemented. This recommendation was unacceptable to melt shop operations management, which refused to curtail preheater use. As a result, preheater use continued while T & D began preparing the recommended training program. Training program development took approximately seven weeks. During this period, additional preheater damage and shutdowns occurred, as noted in figure 1.

Description of the Training Program

The initial needs analysis indicated a need for two types of training programs. The immediate goal was to train all personnel who currently were responsible for operating the preheater. This training was to occur en masse. The second goal was to provide a training medium, which would be self-instructional and enable future pre-heater operators to acquire the knowledge and skill necessary to op-erate the ladle preheater properly.

The remainder of this article describes the training program that was designed to teach all current preheater operators in the massed training program. The training program for current preheater operators was classroom based and lasted one and a half hours. Three classroom sessions were necessary to train the 30 operators. The training objectives for the preheater training program stated the following:

> After receiving the ladle preheater training, the preheater opera-tor will be able to correctly and safely
> A. place the ladle in the preheater cradle
> B. make rotary nozzle hookups
> C. start up and operate the preheater
> D. shut down the preheater
> E. remove the ladle from the cradle
> F. troubleshoot operator correctable problems as measured by opera-tor performance on the preheater knowledge test and performance test.

The knowledge test was a 14-item competency-based test that trainees took during the last 15 minutes of the training program. Trainees had to score at least 90 percent on the test before they could take the performance test.

Evaluation Design, Methodology, and Results

The researchers used a quasi-experimental, pretest, posttest, con-trol group design to evaluate the knowledge gained from the train-ing program. The evaluation design is shown in figure 2.

A true control group was not used. The pretest score from X_1 was assumed to be the same score a true control group would have obtained had it been feasible to incorporate a control group into the design. The descriptive statistics generated as a result of this design are shown in table 1.

A review of the descriptive statistics shows that the mean posttest scores (X_2 and X_3) on the knowledge test for both training groups (1 and 2) were higher than the mean scores for the pretest (X_1) and for the control group (X_4). A perfect score on the knowledge test was 14. The closeness of the X_2 mean and the X_3 mean suggests that admin-istering the pretest to X had little or no pretest sensitization effect up-

Figure 2. Research design to evaluate the structured training program.

Group 1 X_1 T X_2

Group 2   T X_3

Group 3 X_4

         Time _____

where: .

   X_1 = session 1 and session 2 pretest on the knowledge test

   T = participation in the operator training program

   X_2 = session 1 and session 2 posttest on the knowledge test

   X_3 = session 3 posttest on the knowledge test

   X_4 = control group posttest, assumed to be the same as obtained in X_1

---

on the X_2 posttest score. The inferential statistic used to determine if there was a statistically significant difference among the various pretest, posttest, and control group scores was the one-way analysis of variance (ANOVA). Table 2 shows the ANOVA summary table.

The ANOVA table shows that there is, in fact, a significant difference between the various group means. Further statistical analysis (via contrasts) is unnecessary. The significant differences exist between scores on X_1, X_4 and X_2, X_3. These results confirm that the preheater training program had a significant effect on the trainees' knowledge base.

Performance Evaluation

The next test was to determine how well the training participants actually were able to operate the preheater. A 24-step performance checklist was designed for performance evaluation. Supervisors were to fill out a performance checklist for each trainee the first time the trainee operated the preheater after completing the training program.

Table 1. Descriptive statistics calculated for the ladle preheater knowledge test.

	X_1	X_2	X_3	X_4
Mean Score	9.33	13.15	13.18	9.33
Standard Deviation	2.98	.93	.83	2.98
N	19	19	11	19

Table 2. ANOVA summary table.

Source of Variance	Degrees of Freedom	Sum of Squares	Mean Squares	F
Between Groups	3	193.64	64.55	13.25*
Within Groups	50	243.45	4.78	
Total	53	437.09		

$*p<.01$

No performance checklists were filled out for subjects prior to receiving the training program. Therefore, no comparative data are available for trained versus untrained subjects of the performance test. Fifteen performance checklists were completed and returned. Of the 360 trainee steps (15 completions times 24 steps each), a total of six steps were incorrectly performed, at which time the supervisor provided performance feedback regarding the correct action to be taken. Although a statistical analysis is not possible, examination of these results indicated that the training program had a positive effect on the trainees' posttraining performance.

Determining Cost-Effectiveness

An attempt was made to determine the actual costs of the entire ladle preheater training program. The training program was built upon the five-phase Training Technology System (TTS) (Swanson, 1987). Costs have been estimated for each of the five TTS phases, as shown in figure 3.

Note that training costs include the trainees' wages during classroom instruction. It should also be noted that the total training costs include the development of materials for the massed training session as well as for a self-instructional manual. However, this study evaluates only the effects of the massed (classroom-based) training session.

Conclusions

The purpose of this article is not to point the finger at one particular company or industry. In fact, more serious and costly tales of poor technology implementation practices exist in other industries as well (Keller, 1989). The point is that case after case of poor technology implementation practices exist and that failure to more ef-

Figure 3. Training program cost worksheet for the preheater.

	Phase		# Hours	$ Rate/Hour	Total $
1.	Analysis				
		Training Analyst	50	20	1,000
2.	Design				
		Training Analyst	30	20	600
3.	Development				
		Training Analyst	40	20	800
		Photography Staff	10	20	200
		Clerical	10	20	200
		Materials	N/A	N/A	500
4.	Implementation				
		Trainer	10	20	200
		Trainees (N=30)	20	900	
		1.5 hours each			
5.	Evaluation				
		Training Analyst	15	20	300
Total Training Cost					$4,700

fectively control this process can threaten the livelihood of a firm, an industry, and even a nation.

Technology implementation does not have to occur as it does in this case study. Poor technology management practices can undermine the intended benefits of new technology. In the case study, the poor practices caused direct and immediate financial loss and delayed the benefits of the technology (causing indirect financial return-on-investment losses). In fact, the time required to prepare and conduct training amounted to the same amount of equipment downtime due to operator damage, as shown in figure 4.

In this case, management's "default" decision that training would be handled through a vendor demonstration was actually a non-decision by management. Operations and engineering management failed to seriously consider or analyze the need for a systematic training program (at the beginning and throughout the implementation), and the results proved to be costly.

Figure 4. Cost of structured versus unstructured training.

Structured Training Cost

Total training cost (structured): $4,700
Cost per trainee: total training cost/number of trainees
Cost per trainee = $4,200/30 = $140

Unstructured Training Cost

Damage done to equipment: $11,068
Cost of unstructured (vendor) program = $0
Wages during unstructured training = undetermined, but insignificant
Damage done per operator = $368.93
Total preheater down time due to damage: about seven weeks

Total Savings: Structured Training

$11,068	Damage to equipment due to unstructured training
- $ 4,700	Cost of structured training
$ 6,368	Total savings attributable to structured training

Return-on-Investment (ROI)

$$ROI = \frac{\text{ending price - beginning price}}{\text{beginning price}} \times 100$$

$$ROI = \frac{\$11,068 - \$4,700}{\$4,700} \times 100$$

ROI = 135%

The equation for successful technology implementation has two components; one has its basis in technology, and the other in human resources. However, corporations and project managers still tend to treat technology implementation as a one-dimensional technology-based process. Organizations need to have a comprehensive concept of the technology implementation process, which includes both technical and human resource variables. These organizations also need to have corporate-level policy on the management of technology implementation.

Technology implementation project managers need to have not only a solid grounding in the engineering aspects of the technology but also in the organizational and human aspects of technology. In this case study, as in most technology implementation projects, project management is in the hands of those grounded in the engineering disciplines.

Recommendations and Findings

Companies cannot assume that unstructured, seat-of-the-pants vendor training is a viable, dependable, or cost-effective way of training operating personnel to correctly and safely operate new equipment. When they are introducing technology in their companies, they must make conscious decisions about training and other human resource issues at the front end.

The in-house development of structured training is a time-consuming process. Training personnel should become involved in the procurement of new technology at an early date. An early intervention by training personnel in the purchase of new equipment can have several positive consequences. Training personnel can examine the quality of vendor-supplied training and determine its appropriateness. Training personnel should also provide input regarding training standards for vendor training prior to the signing of a purchase order. If vendor training is not feasible, the training department can intervene early to ensure that a training program design coincides with the equipment manufacturing, installation, and start-up. Thus, training can be ready when the equipment is technically ready for operation.

Structured technical training is both cost-effective and educationally effective. Figure 4 provides the cost-benefit analysis of training for the ladle preheater implementation. The results of this case study indicate a 135 percent return-on-investment of training dollars spent.

Questions for Discussion

1. How could training have been more effectively planned for the implementation of this project as well as for the overall mill-modernization project?
2. What pitfalls of the machine bureaucracy may have influenced the outcome of the case?
3. What other organizational structures and strategies should have been incorporated?
4. What could line management have done differently?
5. What could human resource development have done differently?

The Author

Joseph Martelli is associate professor of management at the University of Findlay, in Findlay, Ohio. Martelli earned his doctorate in human resources (HR) from the University of Northern Iowa. Prior to going to the University of Findlay, he held several HR specialist and corporate HR management positions at organizations such as Kimberly-Clark and Kellogg's. He was a research scientist in the Center for Social and Economic Issues at the Industrial Technology Institute in Ann Arbor, Michigan. In addition to teaching at the University of Findlay, Martelli consults with numerous local and national businesses. He has worked in several companies including Motorola, General Motors, Ford Motor Company, Digital Equipment Company, West Center, General Electric, and Commercial Aluminum Cookware. He has published articles and monographs in various nationally recognized HR and business periodicals, and speaks at national, regional, and local professional organizations. He can be reached at the University of Findlay, Business Programs, 1000 N. Main Street, Findlay, OH 45840; phone: 419.424.4824; fax: 419.424.4822.

References

Keller, M. *Rude Awakening: The Rise, Fall, and Struggle for Recovery of General Motors.* New York: William Morrow, 1989.

Mintzberg, H. *Structure in Fives: Designing Effective Organizations.* Englewood Cliffs, NJ: Prentice-Hall, 1983.

Swanson, R. "The Training Technology System: A Method for Identifying and Solving Training Problems in Industry and Business." *Journal of Industrial Teacher Education, 12*(4), 7–17, 1987.

A Partnership for Integrating Work and Learning

Food-Processing Company

Gene L. Roth and Edward "Ted" Raspiller

There are few practical strategies for integrating work and learning in traditional manufacturing environments. This case study depicts how integration of work and learning was identified as the common ground between union leadership and the management team of a food-processing plant. It highlights aspects of a federally funded workplace literacy project. The project features learning-to-learn and team learning strategies for workers.

Background

During the next few decades, the private sector is expected to eclipse the public sector as the predominant educational institution in the United States (Davis & Botkin, 1994). Why is the private sector expected to embrace education as an important aspect of its existence? What prompts researchers to predict such an occurrence? In large part, it is because business, more so than public education, is creating changes that will help workers cope in a global economy. Leaders of the private sector are becoming increasingly aware of the connections between individual, team, and organizational learning and corporate survival. Business and citizen groups are calling on public education, in particular community colleges, to work with the private sector in workforce preparation and development.

The capacity of workers to learn is becoming a key strategic advantage for American organizations. Knowledge is doubling approxi-

This case was prepared to serve as a basis for discussion rather than to illustrate either effective or ineffective administrative and management practices. All names, dates, places, and organizations have been disguised at the request of the author or organization.

mately every seven years. In technical fields, half of what students learn in their early years of college is obsolete by the time they graduate. The need for workers to keep pace in the labor force is acute. For companies to stay competitive, and for workers to stay employable, they must continue to learn (Davis & Botkin, 1994).

The intent of this case study is neither to exalt proven practices nor lend credence to popular trends in the literature. Rather, the intent is to highlight a tripartite relationship that is premised on workplace learning. The authors depict the processes and outcomes of a partnership of a community college with the management team of a local manufacturing plant and its union leadership. Through an arduous planning process, the union and management of this plant found common ground in their respective strategic plans. That common ground was a commitment to make the development of human resources the focal point for their coexistence. Both sides identified the development of the workforce as the critical element of the plant's survival in a global market. Together they helped to create a learning center and individualized education plans for workers. This case study acknowledges the trials and tribulations of this endeavor, and focuses on lessons that have been learned.

Contextual Issues of the Project
Organizational Profile

This case study involves a food-processing facility that employs approximately 400 hourly workers. The next level of supervision in the plant represents approximately 50 workers. Over 90 percent of the workforce have completed high school. However, the employees have been out of school for over 27 years on average. The plant is located about five miles south of its closest town, with a population of 15,000 people. The plant is the largest employer in this locality and the second largest employer in the county. The county has the highest unemployment levels in the state.

Several major technological, managerial, and organizational changes were occurring with this plant. These changes indicated to plant management that all workers needed their skills enhanced if the plant was going to remain competitive. A preliminary needs assessment identified the following workplace changes and concerns that collectively merited a systematic reform in workforce development:

- As a result of a total quality management (TQM) intervention, the plant had been using statistical process control (SPC) as a method of increasing quality and reducing costs. Production workers needed skills to systematically check products and processes to ensure quality. The SPC processes required workers to be able to read charts, calculate ranges and averages, and compare results to standards.

- The plant was using team meetings as a means of identifying and solving workplace problems. Workers needed skill building in order to listen carefully and resolve conflicts within teams. Groups of workers needed to refine skills to become highly effective work teams.

- The plant had reorganized its manufacturing process from a production line system with line supervision to a number of focus factories. This move created a product manufacturing orientation as opposed to a departmental orientation. Each focus factory team was responsible for a product from its inception to its completion.

- The plant had installed computerized equipment in most areas of the workplace. These included computerized numerical control (CNC) machines; computer bar codes in production, inventory, and warehousing areas; and programmable logic controllers on equipment for tracking downtime or equipment stoppage. Workers needed to be able to read job memoranda, maintenance manuals, and computer documents.

- The plant was implementing a new method of peer evaluation for salaried employees. This process was used to annually select other employees to conduct written and verbal job reviews that would result in salary adjustments and job moves. Workers needed to refine their communication skills to participate in this process.

The Human Resource Development Function Profile

The plant's management team is composed of 10 managers, with the plant manager's title being director of operations. Six of the managers are each responsible for a focus factory and respective product line. The manager of human resources is a member of this team. The human resource component in this plant is responsible for a mix of training services for both management and hourly workers.

Involvement of a Community College

A rural community college that was founded in the 1960s serves the geographic region. The community college had a fall 1995 enrollment of 2,500 credit students and annually served over 20,000 noncredit students. The economic development officer of the community college had been working with this plant since 1988. One of the functions of the economic development officer was to write job-training plans for regional industries. Managers of this local plant were interested in creating a more comprehensive job development program. They were uncertain as to whether any of their skills training was having a worthwhile effect. Existing training programs at the plant were single emphasis training efforts that addressed employees' limited needs. Furthermore, there were minimal efforts to assess training programs. The plant manager was interested in creating a comprehensive training effort that could be coordinated at a higher level.

A Workplace Literacy Project as a Catalyst for Change

In 1994, the economic development officer of the community college became aware of a federal grant competition for workplace literacy projects. A cross section of people representing the community college and the union and management of the local plant were pulled together to initiate the grant-writing process. To gather input from a variety of constituencies for the grant application, they formed focus groups that met six to eight times.

Community college personnel presented the final version of the proposal to the plant management team with some apprehension because the proposal called for the plant to invest considerable resources in the effort. A major concern was the use of company time for employees to develop workplace literacy skills. Although there was apprehension regarding this issue, several managers viewed this expenditure as a wise investment for achieving the project's objectives.

The management team and the union leadership developed the following mission statement specifically for this project: "In order to compete successfully in a global economy, the plant must develop an integrated work and learning culture through education and educational systems, which strengthen individuals, teams and the organization."

The group then created these five goals for the "integrating work and learning" program:

- Strengthen the education and skill (basic and "soft") level of each employee to increase self-esteem for life-long learning, develop better employees which in turn strengthens the organization, and improve individual marketability through the acquisition of transferable skills.
- Tie short-term strategic business objectives to overall learning strategies as a foundation for integrating work and learning.
- Ensure that education is part of the organizational culture.
- Encompass life's educational experiences in the workplace (authentic learning).
- Re-invest the outcomes of organizational learning in people and related systems in support of continuous improvement.

Union and Management Strategic Planning: Seeking Commonalities

Key strategies employed during the project start-up had a significant impact on the success of the project. Each year the management team develops a strategic plan and tactical plan. The strategic plan spans a three-year period, and the tactical plan is for one year. For the first time, the union also developed a strategic plan. With the help of a facilitator, union and management representatives met and identified common ground in the two strategic plans. During these meetings, it became increasingly apparent that the union and the management plans had striking similarities.

The focus of the management team's vision statement was for the local plant to be the preferred supplier of its type of products. The focus of the vision statement of the union leadership was to be an irreplaceable workforce of undisputed value. The focus of the mission statement the management team developed was to continuously strive to be the preferred supplier of its products by driving down costs, providing a plant that is flexible to meet future business needs, producing products of the highest value, and providing superior customer service. This was to be accomplished through the use of empowered teams of skilled, diverse, and accountable workers. The focus of the mission statement developed by the union leadership was to inspire pride, excite people, communicate effectively, provide information, take responsibility, and share accumulated knowledge.

Areas on which the management team and union leadership agreed included safety, communication, employee involvement, security, and pride. Space constraints within this case study restrict the reporting of the components of each of the areas of agreement. For the purpose of providing an example, however, the components of the safety area included protecting people, saving money, stabilizing workforce movement in order to reduce accidents, understanding accident rates and the nature of accidents, improving ergonomics, improving safety behaviors, promoting health and wellness, and utilizing sources of expertise.

Developing a Shared Understanding

Both parties recognized education as the means for helping them achieve their respective plans. Both union and management representatives saw the workplace literacy grant as a means to achieve mutually beneficial goals. Training and development became a rallying point in the eyes of both the union and management.

One manager commented on the significance of these early planning sessions that involved representatives of the union, the management team, and the community college, by saying, "We spent several days with that activity, working through several issues and getting a lot on the table. That set the tone and jelled the working relationships that we needed."

Developing a shared understanding in the strategic planning sessions was very important. It was not only important for the union and management leaders to find common ground but also significant for community college personnel to benefit from seeing and hearing their interactions. This learning contributed to the strength of the partnership. Regarding the need for the community college representatives to gain insight into the day-to-day concerns of a manufacturing facility, one manager said, "It got the community college people familiar with our culture at the start-up of this project. It helped all of us develop a collective frame of reference."

Another timely strategy during the project start-up involved staff development. Representatives from this partnership (management, union, and the community college) traveled together to other sites to observe the operation of similar projects. It was important for representatives of these groups to listen to their peers at other sites and talk about the trials and tribulations of implementing a workplace learning project. By traveling together to observe other learning centers, a sense of unity was created and a shared understanding was forged. This was especially powerful for union representatives. They were able to hear about the benefits of such a project from other union leaders. The union hosts stressed that union and management should jointly own this type of project. They emphasized that this project would be good for union members. Union representatives came back from these trips as staunch advocates of this project. One union representative has since been assigned full-time to the grant as a promoter and recruiter. The following excerpts from a letter by the union president to the membership indicate the support for this project:

> This learning opportunity was made available through a grant from the U.S. Department of Education. The Union has been consulted at every step along the way and is in full support of this Project.
>
> Enclosed you will find a booklet titled "Labor's Key Role in Workplace Training." As you read the booklet, you will see that the AFL-CIO is involved in training programs throughout the country. This is a unique opportunity, we don't want to waste it.

Discoveries and Solutions

In most projects, discoveries are made as activities take place and time passes. During the learning center's first year of operation, the project staff made a number of discoveries and addressed several issues, such as the following:

Varied Start-Up Times

There are 54 start times per a 24-hour period for frontline workers at the plant. Workers must be scheduled into the learning center with minimal disruption of plant production. With the exception of warehouse workers, all workers who leave the line must have a replacement person to fill in for them.

The solution to the replacement worker problem was the creation of five new positions called grant relief. These workers must know and be able to operate effectively in all of the jobs in the manufacturing process. The manufacturing line is divided into two distinct areas: manufacturing and packaging. The relief workers are also divided in this manner to reduce the learning curve for each individual.

Individual Learning

The scheduling constraints associated with the manufacturing processes had an impact on the type of instruction that could be delivered in the learning center. Most of the instruction had to be designed for individuals, not classes. Several of the instructors hired for this project had minimal experience individualizing instruction or teaching in a laboratory setting.

A solution to this problem included staff development for instructors that helped them understand learning styles and the characteristics of adult learners. Numerous meetings were held to help instructors develop lesson plans for specific courses and learning experiences. Instructors participated in a satellite downlink with a comparable workplace literacy project in Massachusetts. Through this exposure to a similar program, the instructors listened to accounts of familiar obstacles that their peers had encountered during the preceding year. This reassuring interaction deflated the pressure of unrealistic expectations, and allowed the instructors to establish a comfortable pace with individual learners.

Peak Learning Times for Workers

The learning center planned and delivered workshops on learning how to learn for workers. These workshops illuminated specific attributes of the plant's workforce. Most of the learners had a kines-thetic and tactile learning style, and they preferred to learn in groups. They had specific peak learning times, and several did not have a his-tory of positive learning experiences in formal settings. A solution was to schedule workers into the learning center during their preferred learning times. The union coordinator was the person primarily responsi-ble for scheduling workers in the learning center. First, he gathered and sorted information regarding workers' preferred learning times. Next, he mastered a basic spreadsheet that allowed him to organize a schedule for the learning center. Finally, he organized the relief work-ers in a manner that would be least disruptive to plant production.

Creating Individualized Learning Plans

The project's original steering committee selected the ACT WorkKeys Assessment System as the assessment tool of choice. An initial step was to profile the 43 different jobs in the manufacturing process in the plant. These assessments indicated that the workforce was not lack-ing in basic skills of reading, writing, and mathematics to perform their jobs. However, many workers did need to enhance their soft skills, including listening, speaking, teamwork, problem solving, and crit-ical thinking.

The ACT WorkKeys assessments and job profiling provided a plan-ning base for solving workers' learning needs. Instructors developed learner objectives and assessment instruments with input from pro-ject staff, frontline supervisors, subject matter experts, and floor work-ers. They used examples and problems from the workplace in the instruc-tion. Instructors and workers jointly created individual education plans (IEPs). The IEP was initiated when the student walked into the learn-ing center, and it stressed the concept of learning how to learn. The learning path began at that point and crystallized when the worker and the instructor together discussed assessment results.

Maintaining the Motivation of Learners

Some of the workers complete their high school equivalency diplo-mas, the GED, and many complete one or more courses. However, mo-tivation does not seem to be as high as it was when the learning center first opened its doors. Some workers do not seem to have an under-standing of what this experience can do for them personally. Some work-ers are concerned that their training should be for their own personal benefit and not so much for the benefit of the company.

The project staff addressed these concerns by recognizing learners' achievements. Project staff felt that some type of formal documentation would help workers feel that they were attaining transferable skills and not solely benefiting the company. Project personnel are developing a customized program certificate that involves CEU credits, developmental education credits, and vocational education credits. The intent of this credential is to have it recognized by the local industrial base as a meaningful worker achievement.

The Significance of the Industry and Education Partnership

The central theme of this project is integrating work and learning. It has taken the individual and collective strengths of the union, management team, and the community college to pursue it. Each of the partners has contributed expertise and learned valuable lessons during the project's brief life span.

The Community College

The possibility of succeeding with a federal grant and a local industry in this rural, economically depressed area was very appealing to the community college leaders. The project allowed the college to build its capacity to better serve the region's economic development needs. Prior to receiving this grant, the college relied a great deal on brokering services that were available from external sources. The college did not have the expertise or experience to meet the varied needs of local industries. As a result of this grant, the college has been able to train its own personnel in the needs assessment process. Specifically, the college now has personnel with knowledge and experience with the ACT WorkKeys Assessment System. An administrator at the college commented on the significance of this project to related internal functions of the college:

> We are much more cohesive now in this institution. We have seen what can happen when we work together with an industry. We are redefining our roles. We are identifying our own internal and external customers and our processes.

Both the union and management representatives value the role that the community college plays in this project. The college provides an objective third-party role (on site) in a culture that has a history of intense union management negotiations. One manager stated:

What has happened is that our management and our union people do not see the college representatives as having any other agenda than education. People do not connect the college representatives with a management group. That is important, because the union might perceive management to have an agenda that is not of interest to them. The community college presence has created a neutral territory that has a great deal of power to it. It provides a completely independent source of training.

The Management Team

This project provided the management team with an opportunity to gain external support for creating a learning agenda in the workplace. This particular plant has a gain-sharing plan that is aimed at accountability at the team level. Many of the skills that are being taught in the learning center tend to enhance the skills that are needed for groups of workers to function as highly effective work teams. One manager stated:

> I am beginning to see this when I am on the floor. The workers are much more likely to talk to me about team performance and team results. In the past, I used to spend my time dealing with personnel concerns and grievances. Now, much more of the conversation that I have on the floor pertains to plant performance and team performance. We set a record yesterday for our performance from last week. Those types of things are becoming more prevalent. I attribute these performances to a variety of factors, but I am not overlooking the significance of this project.

The Union

This project has provided a means for enhancing the skill levels of its members. The union favored getting assistance in identifying major literacy problems. It embraced the notion of being able to identify people who wanted help and who were serious about improving their life skills. The union leadership saw this effort as an acknowledgment that management was moving beyond job skill training. They saw this as a means to get to the root of something that might ultimately move the production and the workforce forward. A community college administrator commented as follows about the significance of involving union representatives in the development of training:

Another key benefit has been the involvement of the production workers in the training. I have heard from a number of people that it has been a wondrous thing for them. It has been a real growth experience and it came at a good time. It has helped create better feelings about management. In addition, it has created a much greater awareness and understanding about the community college.

Toward a Common Future

At the close of the first year, this project had enrolled 30 percent of the eligible workers of the plant and had logged over 3,000 hours of training. Customized curriculum outlines were completed for six courses, and the learning center was integrated into the work culture of this food-processing facility. The collaborative efforts of the three partners paved the way for continuing success. A manager of the plant stated his optimism for the learning center this way:

> This is a true win-win proposition from my perspective. A lot of it has to do with general goodwill. So many of the things that we do pertain to improving productivity and efficiency. Many people feel that those things make people work more or harder—and there always seems to be a negative pitch to it. This project has no negative edges whatsoever. It all has to do with education and learning. It has been a very uplifting experience. People really feel good about their involvement with it.

The impetus of this effort is federal funding that served as seed money for the partners. Project personnel are hopeful that the management team and the union leadership of the plant will recognize the project's significance and find local revenues to continue its operation. Regionally, the project is gaining recognition. Local elected officials and key representatives from area businesses have toured the learning center or attended meetings that featured the project, or done both. This project is a good example of what can be accomplished if companies are given incentives to bring education, labor, and management together to explore the mutual benefits of lifelong learning and ongoing training for their employees and partners. The future of American businesses relies on the abilities of its workers to invigorate the workplace and develop competitive advantages for themselves and their organizations (Slocum, McGill, & Lei, 1994). This project has been an invigorating experience for all three of the partners.

Questions for Discussion

1. Assume that you had served in the facilitation role during the strategic planning sessions between the union and the management team. What strategies would you have used to develop the notion of workplace learning as a mutually beneficial goal for both sides?
2. What principles can community college representatives use in this case that will allow management and union to perceive them as objective and trust-gaining partners?
3. Given the gain-sharing program of this plant, what adult learning content and methods would you use with teams of workers to enhance their effectiveness?
4. Describe the key elements of an evaluation plan for this project. How would you assess the progress of integrating work and learning?
5. Describe the planning and implementing strategies that you would use to ensure internal funding for the learning center once the federal funding cycle ends for this project.

The Authors

Gene L. Roth is the director of the Office of Human Resource Development and Workforce Preparation at Northern Illinois University. He is also a professor in the Department of Leadership and Educational Policy Studies. He has published over 60 articles, book chapters, and monographs on topics such as technology and learning, learning to learn, school-to-work transition, and various elements of human resource development. He can be reached at Northern Illinois University, Department of Leadership and Educational Policy Studies, De Kalb, IL 60115-2866; phone: 815.753.1306; fax: 815.753.9309; e-mail address: groth@niu.edu.

Edward "Ted" Raspiller is director of continuing education at Texas State Technical College in Brownwood, Texas. He directed the workplace literacy project described in this case study. He is a doctoral student in the Adult Continuing Education program at Northern Illinois University. Raspiller has published several articles and presented at conferences on topics such as workplace literacy, learning to learn, and adult basic education. His research interests include distance education and contemporary issues that confront community colleges.

References

Davis, S., & Botkin, J. "The Coming of the Knowledge Based Business." *Harvard Business Review*, 165–170, 1994, September-October.

Slocum, J., McGill, M., & Lei, D. "The New Learning Strategy: Anytime, Anything, Anywhere." *Organizational Dynamics*, 33–47, 1994, Autumn.

Strategic Review of a Training and Development System

BC TELECOM

Dale Rusnell

This case study demonstrates a systematic process of reviewing the strategic function of training and development in a large organization where the review team had an open-ended mandate to recommend major changes without restriction. It also demonstrates conducting a strategic initiative through a partnership agreement by a private corporation and a public postsecondary technical training institution.

Background

The telecommunications industry in North America is involved in large-scale fundamental change resulting from advances in technology and revisions in government regulations. A new global economy is emerging that relies on communications and data transportation as a basic resource. Electronic communications and an increasing range of related applications are required for business purposes involving local and global transportation of information. Convergence of broadcast and telecommunications technologies for delivery of voice, video, sound, information, and entertainment is becoming a core resource for modern economies.

Phone companies are transforming themselves from providers of voice transportation to providers of global computer-based data transportation and value-added services and packages based on the data. Primary sources of profits are becoming less related to voice services and more related to electronic data services. There is a move

This case was prepared to serve as a basis for discussion rather than to illustrate either effective or ineffective administrative and management practices.

away from copper wire services toward fiber-optic services and increasingly toward wireless technologies where competitors can transmit data in mobile and portable services without phone company involvement.

Given these changes in technology and business competition, telecommunications jobs are becoming more complex, multiskilled, and cross-functional. Traditional career paths are disappearing, and jobs are being rolled into larger groupings with greater flexibility for rapid assignment to diverse tasks. More emphasis is being placed on interpreting customers' needs and designing high-value applications, packages, and services that provide added value for customers. Employees need new skills to perform those tasks effectively at lower costs than those of competing services.

This case study involves a telecommunications company that completed a review of its training and development activities to ensure that they were aligned with business goals and plans, and integrated with other human resources services.

The Company

BC TELECOM is a public telephone utility serving the province of British Columbia, located on Canada's west coast, immediately north of Washington State. At the time of this project, its 13,000 employees were located in many centers across the province, but the largest number worked in the greater Vancouver region. The company was restructured several times in the years preceding this project, and, during this project, it was restructured once again. The theme of the changes is the establishment of independent business units within a larger corporate structure.

BC TELECOM is engaged in making fundamental changes concerning the nature of its productivity and ways of doing business. Personnel at all levels required new understandings and skill sets to make the changes. Active learning by individuals, teams, and business units is essential for the organization to adapt to its continually changing environment. No longer a peripheral process, learning is now an essential element for corporate prosperity.

Human Resources Consulting Services (HRCS) is a headquarters unit responsible for human resources services to all BC TELECOM business units. Paul Smith, the vice-president of HRCS, reports directly to the CEO and is a key member of the BC TELECOM executive group. During this project, the human resources unit was in the early stages of adopting a consulting services approach for business units and reducing its role as a centralized corporate unit with responsibility for all corporate human resources activities.

BC TELECOM Education Centre is the unit within HRCS that is responsible for training and development activities. During this project, it employed about 140 professional and support staff and was housed in its own building, which included classrooms, instructional design and development resources, advanced equipment for telecommunications training, and centralized administrative systems for corporate training and development. In addition to serving BC TELECOM training needs with more than 500 courses in its calendar, it was engaged in marketing courses to external clients across North America and internationally. This unit has been recognized as one of Canada's leading corporate training departments for many years.

The British Columbia Institute of Technology (BCIT)

This organization is the largest public, postsecondary vocational and technical training institute in British Columbia. It employs 1,300 people and offers a wide variety of vocational and technical training programs serving 14,000 full-time and 24,000 part-time students each year. In addition, it provides consulting services and contract training for industry. The main campus is located about one mile from the BC TELECOM headquarters building and a few blocks from the BC TELECOM Education Centre. BCIT and BC TELECOM have a formal partnership agreement by which some courses employees complete at BC TELECOM may be granted credit for BCIT diplomas and certificates.

BCIT Learning Resources Unit (LRU) is responsible for design and development of curricula and instructional materials, and for professional development of BCIT instructors. This unit has an entrepreneurial style and is engaged in many contracts to develop training services and materials for external clients. It has received awards in Canada and the United States for its exemplary work in professional staff development and commitment to institutional growth.

Developing the Project Framework

In November 1994, BC TELECOM Human Resources Consulting Services (HRCS) requested that BCIT participate in a joint review of the BC TELECOM training and development system. The objective of the review, according to a BCIT/BC TELECOM memo dated November 1994, was "to provide third party validation—to Executive—that the Education Centre is adding value, and where the Education Centre needs to improve/change." For BC TELECOM the motivation was to strengthen the partnership with BCIT and to gain access to external training assessment specialists. For BCIT, the motivation to participate was to enhance its image among the business community as an organization capable of delivering high-quality services, in addition to traditional courses, to industry on a contractual basis.

To begin the process, BC TELECOM and BCIT exchanged a series of draft documents designed to list the specific objectives and scope of work. Within the corporation, there was a question of whether the review should include all aspects of learning across the organization and all its business units, or whether it should focus only on procedures and practices within the Education Centre. BCIT supported the high-level, organization-wide review. It proposed a framework for a strategic-level process and promoted it to the corporation as a study to determine if BC TELECOM was "doing the right thing, rather than doing things right." The vice president (VP) of HRCS accepted BCIT's proposal, which included a sequenced framework of activities, general procedures, a timeline, and a budget.

The major components for the strategic initiative, to which both organizations agreed, were stated as follows:

Title: Strategic Review of BC Tel Training and Development System

Purposes: Gather information to determine

1. if training and education plans are aligned with corporate strategic directions for the future
2. if training and education activities meet current and future directions for the Human Resources Department
3. if training and education activities meet important learning needs and organization requirements for delivery of services throughout the organization
4. if training and education structures, policies, and procedures reflect the best practices used by other corporations in similar contexts
5. which structures, procedures, and partnership options would ensure flexibility, cost-effectiveness, quality, and innovation within training and development activities.

Project Phases and Deliverables:

Phase I: Identify strategic needs and directions for learning.

a. Identify corporate strategic directions for the future.

b. Identify human resources development directions for the future.

c. Identify strategic needs for learning and administrative requirements for learning services across the organization.

Phase II: Identify best practices in class for training and development systems.

Phase III: Identify future options for learning services in BC Tel: structures, policies, and procedures.

The initiative was to report directly to Paul Smith, vice-president, Human Resources Consulting Services. Keith Gray, director of the Education Centre, was to be the second member of a project steering committee.

Project Team: BC TELECOM approved a three-person team of internal and external representatives who would have the following traits:

1. in-depth knowledge of BC TELECOM structure, personnel, and strategic processes
2. extensive experience and theoretical background related to corporate training practices and organizational behavior
3. broad experience conducting review/evaluation projects
4. organizational consulting skills including analytical abilities, communica-tions and interpersonal competencies
5. change-management skills including ability to facilitate change and to stimulate individuals and groups into action
6. a balance of technical and humanistic approaches to organizational growth.

Following is a brief description of the individuals selected for the team:

The BC TELECOM representative, Viki MacMillan, was a senior manager with 21 years' experience within several BC TELECOM business units, including eight years at the Education Centre and four years in other HRD areas. She was a successful project manager who had recently completed a four-year assignment to reengineer BC TELECOM construction engineering and customer service processes. As a recognized leader and team player, MacMillan maintained a network of formal and informal, long-standing contacts with personnel at all levels and units across the organization. Her important contributions for the project team included concerns for holistic integration of interunit tasks, strong change-management expertise, and keen insight into the corporate culture and individuals' views on key topics of concern to the initiative.

The BCIT representative was Bob Freeman, the director of the Learning Resources Unit at BCIT. He was responsible for improving teaching and learning processes through a team of 45 professional and production staff. Freeman was an expert in systematic instructional design, development, and materials production. As a consultant to more than 30 colleges and industries at the international level, his skills for project management and commitment to teamwork were well recognized.

The independent consultant, Dale Rusnell, was a self-employed consultant with more than 30 years' experience in education and training, including experience with evaluation of large-scale education programs and strong analytical skills. He had completed several major consulting projects with BCIT and as a former professor of adult education with special interests in corporate training, had been in contact with BC TELECOM training personnel since the mid-1970s.

Establishing the Project Team

After the organizations selected the project team, the first task was for them to meet each other and determine how they would operate as a team. This task involved several meetings to agree on the details of the contract, to develop a list and schedule for project tasks, and to establish ground rules for how the team would manage itself concerning time commitments, communications, and performance expectations. Through this process, the three team members were able to establish commitments to a common goal, levels of trust with each other, and understanding of the different work environments and cultures within their separate organizations, to which they would also have to respond while working on the joint project.

One of the first decisions was to select the team working space. Although the Education Centre had offered space, the team decided to work at the headquarters building. This emphasized the corporate-wide scope of the task and the direct relationship of the project to the VP HRCS, and the location was in the same area as other HRCS units.

Another early decision concerned the formal announcements about the project and people assigned to the new roles. To announce the appointment of Viki MacMillan to the project, the VP HRCS sent a personal message by organizational voice mail to employees. In addition, the company communications department ensured that appropriate announcements were made in corporate bulletins. These announcements were important to establish the scope and importance of the project and to provide employees with contact information if they wanted to discuss related issues.

The team's first major activity was to explain the project to all employees at a series of meetings it held at the Education Centre. It was important to reduce the unnecessary concerns or anxieties of the employees at the center by ensuring that they understood the project objectives and procedures. They conducted a series of three separate but identical meetings on different days and times so that all employees had an opportunity to attend one session. In those meetings, the VP HRCS introduced the three-team members, and then they described their own roles and responsibilities. They emphasized the following information:

- what the project is
  - —a collecting of information
  - —exploration of options for providing corporate learning objectives
  - —an identification of what is the right thing to do
  - —organization-wide
- what the project is not:
  - —an implementation of changes
  - —presentation of predetermined solutions
  - —an identification of how to do things right
  - —Education Centre focused
  - —an evaluation of the Education Centre
  - —an evaluation of personnel performance
  - —an audit of training resources
  - —a cost-benefit study of Education Centre services
  - —an excuse for downsizing training staff
  - —a first step to integration or full partnership with BCIT
  - —an excuse to implement predetermined solutions
  - —a presentation of a single-fix solution for training problems.

Phase I: Identify Strategic Learning Needs

The purpose of phase I was to identify the types of learning needed and the preferred ways to access learning opportunities to ensure that BC TELECOM achieved its strategic objectives in the future. The team gathered information concerning future directions for the corporation, trends in human resource development, type of learning, and access to learning opportunities required by employees to ensure effective performance in a highly changing business environment.

Information Gathered from People

The first activity in phase I was individual interviews with more than 40 BC TELECOM executives and senior managers. This represented a major departure from the original proposal, which was to conduct two half-day focus-group sessions with senior managers. MacMillan persuaded the project team that individual interviews would provide greater support for the project and more detailed information from all managers, even though the task required considerably longer to complete. Two team members conducted each interview, including Viki as the internal member to provide clarity for corporate issues and details, and one external member to provide opportunities to ask probing questions from the external, uninformed viewpoint. This process required more than 100 team-person hours of interviewing over a period of 10 weeks. Despite the additional time and effort required, the result provided excellent in-depth information related to future strategic directions of each business unit and resulted in strong management support for and interest in the project.

Each manager to be interviewed received in advance of the meeting a description of the project and its purposes, brief resumes of the team members, and a list of questions to be discussed. The questions were as follows:

1. What are the most important changes you expect within the company and your business over the next few years?
2. Considering those changes, what will be the impact on human resources?
3. What do you believe is the most effective way for people to obtain the training, education, and personnel development services they will need to be productive in the future?
4. If you had an opportunity to change the BC TELECOM training and development system to better align with your strategic business directions and staff learning needs for the future, what are the most important things you would do?

In addition to individual interviews, the project team conducted one focus group with Education Centre managers and another with middle-level managers from across the corporation to identify their suggestions for provision of future learning services. The focus group questions were as follows:

1. Currently, what employee competencies would significantly increase the effectiveness and efficiency of your operations?
2. In the future, what employee competencies do you project will be needed for your operation to survive and thrive?
3. What aspects/facets of the current T&D system effectively and efficiently support the learning needs of your operation?
4. What aspects/facets of the current T&D [training and development] system do not effectively and efficiently support the learning needs of your operation?
5. What do you recommend should be done to change the T&D system to ensure it cost effectively supports the learning needs of your operation?

The team completed a third procedure to gather information during the original meetings with Education Centre employees. Each employee was asked to answer a survey questionnaire that included the following two questions:

1. What changes does the entire organization have to make to meet employee learning needs of the future?
2. What major changes would you like to see implemented in the Education Centre over the next five years?

To gather information more widely from all employees, the team distributed brief questionnaires to all employees by e-mail and the weekly company bulletin asking the following question:

> Considering the significant changes in the telecommunications industry and the resulting impact on your work, describe two-three topics you need to learn about in order to be more effective on the job: (a) now (b) in the future.

Within the BC TELECOM HRCS department, several other initiatives were under way related to topics such as salary structure, management succession planning, and performance appraisal. The project team met with each of those task force groups to explore areas of common concern and preliminary findings that had implications for employee learning or needs or that would help with future integration of HRCS activities. It was sometimes difficult to identify the list of special initiatives under way within the same department or the people associated with them. One of MacMillan's major roles was to identify work of other task groups that had potential relevance for learning systems and to establish linkages to support future implementation.

As interviews, focus groups, group meetings, and the collection of documents were proceeding, the project team made as many site visits as possible to understand the work environments of all business units. This aspect of the project required more time than was available, which resulted in several parts of the organization not being contacted personally by the team. To alleviate potential problems that could arise if people felt they were not adequately consulted, MacMillan made personal phone calls to key individuals in those units.

Information Gathered from Documents

Each business unit within BC TELECOM is expected to maintain a strategic plan, which is updated each quarter. All business units gathered strategic plans and their latest updates and placed them in a central location for analysis by the project team. The team reviewed each strategic plan to identify all references to learning requirements or implications for learning that were not explicit in the plan. In addition, the team reviewed the labor relations collective agreement to identify all references to learning or related key words such as training, education, or personal development. A variety of other documents were also gathered including reports of special corporate task groups, reference materials from external organizations, and sample materials related to learning activities.

The confidential nature of strategic plans in a competitive industry raised an issue of access to the documents. A procedure was established so that all documents marked confidential were not to be removed from the headquarters building and had to be obtained by the project's secretary from locked storage and returned before the end of each day. All other documents gathered for the project were systematically stored in large 3-ring binders and kept in locked desk drawers that the team used. By the time the project had been completed, 11 binders of materials had been gathered.

Phase I Report

Phase I activities began March 1, 1995 and ended three months later. On May 31, the team submitted its first report, *BC TELECOM Strategic Learning Needs,* to the VP HRCS. The report outlined what the corporation's own managers and employees had said about future company directions and their implications for learning and what they said about the preferred ways for employees to access learning opportunities. To keep its commitment of ongoing communication about the project, the team held two meetings with Education Centre staff as well as meetings with other HRCS units to present the findings in detail. In addition, to maintain awareness and interest in the initiative, MacMillan sent personal letters of thanks to each senior manager interviewed and enclosed a copy of the report. (Detailed contents of the reports are not included in this case study as the purpose is to describe the process used rather than the specific findings.)

One of BCIT's major contributions to this project related to preparation of project reports. The BCIT Learning Resources Unit was responsible for the editing, layout, and production of all reports and produced high-quality, professionally prepared reports for all phases of the project. This commitment to quality was important in helping BC TELECOM personnel appreciate the project's importance.

Phase II: Identify Best Practices in Class for Training and Development Systems

The purpose of Phase II was to look outside BC TELECOM to identify leading-edge practices in training and development. This task was accomplished through a series of site visits to exemplary training and development systems, attendance at major conferences, review of leading-edge articles and books, and monitoring of training and development Internet discussion-group messages.

External Data Gathering

The first task in Phase II was to identify corporations with leading-edge practices in training and development. Lists of previous award winners of the Malcolm Baldrige National Quality Award and the ASTD Corporate Award provided possibilities. In addition, team members relied on their own knowledge of relevant literature and on their contacts with respected training and development professionals for much useful information.

The team used all possible occasions to contact trainers from appropriate corporations, including arranging meetings with personnel from other companies while they visited BC TELECOM on other business, attending training and development conferences, traveling on business for other unrelated projects, traveling on vacation through relevant cities, and making specific site visits to leading-edge training sites. The project team was able to make direct contact with personnel from the following organizations:

- Ameritech
- Arthur Andersen & Co. (St. Charles, Illinois)
- Bank of Montreal Institute for Learning (Toronto)
- Bell Canada Creative Communications Lab (Toronto)
- British Telecom
- Canadian Imperial Bank of Commerce Executive Development Center (Toronto)
- DDI (Toronto)
- GTE Training Center (Dallas)
- International Computers (Britain)
- Northern Telecom
- Motorola University (Schaumburg, Illinois)
- Pacific Bell
- Progressive Media Management (Vancouver)
- Rover (Britain)

- University of Southern California Center for Telecommunications Management (Los Angeles)
- US West Communications (Denver).

The site visits were designed to identify and explore the features of leading-edge systems that contributed to their reputation of excellence. In each case, the team did not make a specific list of information to gather, but let the host company explain its own system in an open-ended way. Following the hosts' presentations, the team asked probing questions about items of interest. Detailed benchmarking information was not gathered in a systematic way, but the types of metrics used and the company statistics were recorded whenever possible.

The project team attended the April 1995 Conference Board of Canada Training and Development Conference in Toronto and the June 1995 ASTD Conference in Dallas. In both cases, the team systematically identified relevant conference activities and assigned separate tasks to individuals to ensure the broadest coverage of important topics. It should also be noted that the team purchased more than $1,500 in reference books and materials at the ASTD bookstore during the Dallas conference, and subsequently reviewed them for relevant information.

The team developed the following framework to organize and describe the large volume of information gathered on leading-edge practices.

1. Trends in Human Resources Development Practices
2. Trends in Organizational Learning Frameworks
   Mission and Purpose
   Strategy
   Policy
   Resources
   Structure
3. Trends in Learning Systems Operations
   Guiding Principles for Learning Systems
   Planning Model Traits of High-Quality Learning Systems
   Analysis
   Design
   Develop
   Deliver
   Evaluate and Improve

The combination of strategic data and operating practices was an important feature of information the team gathered. From the start of the project, the team attempted to focus at the strategic level whenever possible, but it experienced continual pressure to address daily operating practices. During the collection of Phase II information, it became apparent that the operating practices of exemplary training and development systems needed to be reported. The problem of reporting operating practices without getting into minute details was solved by identifying higher level principles and traits that were noted in several of the leading-edge systems. In the final project report, the strategic data combined with exemplary operating principles provided a foundation to ensure that strategic directions recommended were supported with consistent operating practices.

Internal Focus Group

During the time the external information-gathering activities were under way, the project team was sorting and analyzing the flow of information. After several weeks of analyzing material, 65 relevant best practices for BC TELECOM were identified and sorted into the following main categories:

1. Trends in Organizational Learning Frameworks (24 trends)
2. Guiding Principles for Learning Systems (4 principles)
3. Planning Model Traits of High-Quality Learning Systems (37 Traits).

The next task was to determine the extent to which BC TELE-COM demonstrated those trends, principles, and traits. The project team needed to address carefully the sensitive issue of comparing BC TELECOM practices to those of other leading-edge companies. Many employees at the Education Centre believed they were an exemplary training organization with few needs for improvement or change. In 1992, their management training activities had been cited in *Human Resource Executive* (Drake, 1992) as one of five exemplary corporate training illustrations in North America. In addition, BC TELECOM training was at one time the second largest private training organization in Canada, and the local training community generally considered it to be at the leading edge of practice. After examining the data gathered for the project, the team recognized that BC TELECOM remained an excellent traditional system for centralized, instructor-led classes, but needed to focus more on business goals and move toward a performance consulting approach. The project team needed a strategy to develop awareness among Education Centre employees that change was needed to keep up with the leading edge of practice and that future opportunities could be expanded by moving toward a different approach to corporate learning.

The strategy chosen was to conduct a focus group with seven Education Centre specialists and two HRCS unit representatives. First, to establish a sense of pride in what they had accomplished in the past, the team asked the group to list all current best practices demonstrated by the Education Centre. Then the list of 65 best practices identified through external information sources was presented, and the group was asked to discuss and rate the extent to which each item was demonstrated in practice within BC TELECOM. Of the 65 items, the group rated two items high; 18, moderate; and the remaining 45, low. The presentation of the focus group's findings in the final report gave an important perspective in support of the team's recommendations for change.

Phase II Report

The team submitted the Phase II report, *Trends in Organizational Training and Development*, submitted to the VP HRCS on August 31, 1995. The three members discussed the report with the director of the Education Centre and the senior management team to obtain their advice before proceeding to develop a final report with recommendations for action. The team also reported the best-in-class information to middle-level Education Centre managers.

Although the project team was committed to keeping all Education Centre employees informed about progress, the team and BC TELECOM senior managers decided to delay reporting the Phase II information until the report of final recommendations was ready. That decision was made because the Phase III final report of recommendations for change was scheduled for completion only one month later, and September was a busy time for most people starting classes following summer vacation. In addition, the project team was not sure which of the trends identified in Phase II would be included in the final recommendations and did not want to raise expectations or anxieties of employees who might think that all trends listed in the Phase II report might be part of changes to be recommended. More importantly, there was a concern that some Education Centre specialists might proceed with unnecessary or misdirected work on speculation that certain best practices would be recommended in the final report.

Phase III: Identify Future Options for Learning Services in BC TELECOM: Structures, Policies, and Procedures

The project's third phase was to recommend strategic directions, guiding principles, and broad themes for action that would optimize employee learning opportunities and place BC TELECOM's training and development system at the leading edge of practice. To accomplish that task, the project team integrated all available information on future directions of the telecommunications industry, BC TELECOM, and its HRCS unit with the list of 65 best-practice trends, principles, and traits. Given future changes expected by executives and senior managers, the challenge was to identify those practices that would support and be aligned with BC TELECOM strategic plans.

First, the team developed recommendations for changes related to the corporate organizational framework for learning services. High-level guiding principles were designed to do the following:
1. outline individual and corporate responsibilities for learning
2. align a strategic plan for corporate learning with the strategic plans for the corporation and its business units
3. recommend an overall framework for training and development within the organization.

The team then developed recommendations for changes related to the learning system itself. Items in this category concerned operational-level structures, resources, and policies that linked the day-to-day practice to the macro corporate directions for learning and development, including
1. underlying themes required to sustain the learning system (e.g., ensuring the system remained at the leading edge, reskilling staff, establishing annual learning plans)
2. recommendations for each phase of the learning system planning model: analysis, design, development, delivery, and evaluation/ improvement.

Phase III Report

The team submitted its *Phase III Report, Recommendations* on September 30, 1995. It included 52 recommendations spread among the following categories:
1. strategic mission and four guiding principles for corporate learning (11 recommendations)
2. nine strategies for corporate learning (16 recommendations)
3. three learning system themes (seven recommendations)
4. five planning model phases (14 recommendations)
5. project follow-up and implementation (four recommendations).

In addition, to emphasize the integrated nature of the recommendations as a holistic approach, the project team developed a matrix that illustrated important relationships among the recommendations. The analysis and presentation highlighted that it was important to consider the recommendations as integrated sets of actions rather than individual points that could be approved or rejected without regard to their implications for the other items.

To emphasize the importance of the report and to ensure a comprehensive review without interruptions, the project team and VP HRCS dedicated one full day to discuss the recommendations in detail. Each member of the team took turns presenting the recommendations he or she was primarily responsible for developing and leading the discussion about them. By the end of the discussion, the VP HRCS had agreed to accept the full 52 recommendations and to proceed with implementation. This was a major decision because the report recommended that BC TELECOM make a dramatic change from a centralized traditional instructor-led formal class system to a decentralized, just-in-time performance support system.

After the VP HRCS had agreed to support the report and implement action, some of the options for implementation were discussed. One option was for the VP HRCS to proceed independently to make all decisions related to the human resources group and to keep other corporate executives informed, but not to ask for their permission to proceed. Another option was to present the report to the entire executive group and ask for their approval to proceed because of the widespread implications for organizational structure and need for support within all business units to succeed with the recommendations. Finally, it was agreed that the VP HRCS would present the report to four executive vice presidents who directed the four major business units of the corporation and to ask for their approval.

For the presentation to the four executive VPs, the original 52 recommendations were regrouped under 11 strategic, six resource, and two structural themes. The VPs accepted the report without change and gave approval to begin a process of implementation. Following their approval, MacMillan began a process of presenting the findings to managers of the Education Centre, discussing implications for the future, and developing enthusiasm and support for the changes.

When first proposed, this project was assumed to be a short-term assignment requiring less than three months to complete, and not much thought had been given to possible changes or implications outside the Education Centre. By the time the final report was approved, the project had taken more than seven months to complete and had become a major initiative with far-reaching implications for the entire corporation. BC TELECOM has now started a multiyear process to implement the recommended changes to ensure that its learning activities are at the leading edge of practice and are fully aligned and integrated with corporate strategic directions and business unit plans. The project team has been asked to play an important continuing role in the implementation process.

Postscript

This case study was written in January 1996, three months after submission of the project recommendations to BC TELECOM. Throughout 1996 and 1997, the BC TELECOM Education Centre was reorganized toward a performance consulting model in order to adopt the project's recommendations and become more strategically aligned with corporate operations. Although the changes were difficult and created high levels of internal stress, the Education Centre maintained its focus on quality. In the spring of 1997, it became the first corporate training department in Canada, and the second in North America, to achieve ISO 9001 certification. In November 1997, the Education Centre was awarded the Canada Award for Excellence for Small/Medium Service by the National Quality Institute and Industry Canada. This award is the Canadian equivalent of the Baldridge Award of Quality.

Questions for Discussion

1. What types of project activities are important to ensure that political support is maintained for reviews that assess the alignment of training and development units with organizational strategy?

2. This project first proposed to gather strategic-level information from senior executives using two or three focus groups, but eventually decided to gather the information through individual interviews. What issues are important in making this type of decision?

3. When a team of internal and external personnel is established for a strategic review of training and development, what qualities, competencies, and roles should the internal company team members have?

4. During a strategic review process, there is constant pressure from frontline personnel to address detailed operating problems. How can the review team maintain a high-level focus and still maintain project support from frontline personnel?

5. When making recommendations to senior managers for strategic change, what activities can a project review team include (at all stages of the project) to ensure follow-up support and action for their recommendations?

The Author

Dale Rusnell specializes in evaluation of large-scale skills-based training programs sponsored by industry, postsecondary institutions, and professional associations. Since 1981, as principal consultant and owner of Continuing Education Project People, Inc. of Burnaby, British Columbia, he has worked with a broad range of client groups engaged in assessing educational needs, developing innovative training programs, preparing program funding proposals, and evaluating educational programs. His consulting with BC TELECOM Education Centre continued beyond the strategic review project, and he is now developing a comprehensive impact evaluation system for corporate learning activities. Rusnell received his Ed.D. in adult education from the University of British Columbia in 1974. He can be reached at: Continuing Education Project People, Inc., 4608 Victory Street, Burnaby, British Columbia, Canada, V5J 1R9; phone: 604.435.4018; e-mail: drusnell@sfu.ca.

Reference

Drake, S. "Benchmarking the Best." *Human Resource Executive*, 22–27, 1992, June.

Workforce Education: A Model for Upgrading Skills of Foundry Workers

Southern Ductile Casting Company

Barbara E. Hinton

This case study describes a successful workplace education program in a foundry in Alabama. The model enabled low-skilled workers to upgrade their basic skills in response to changing technological processes. Through assistance from a federal grant, the company was able to collaborate with educators in designing and delivering a workforce education program that addressed the immediate and future basic-skills needs of their workers by developing and delivering industry-specific basic skills training.

Background

Like many other industries, U.S. foundries are faced with a dilemma. How can they utilize the increasingly complex technologies they need to remain competitive while employing workers who lack the ability to perform at the most basic educational levels? Historically, foundries, like many other low-tech industries, have been able to function with workers generally lacking a high educational level. In the past, the foundry industry has been a very labor-intensive industry, and workers were often hired more for their brawn than brain. That is no longer realistic.

Today, the foundry industry must utilize state-of-the-art technology, and frontline workers are required to read process sheets and manuals written at a high reading level. In addition, foundries, like other production industries, are asking their workers to assume more responsibility for the quality of their work and to become very knowl-

This case was prepared to serve as a basis for discussion rather than to illustrate either effective or ineffective administrative and management practices.

edgeable about their job tasks. This is especially true of plant sites seeking ISO 9000 certification.

Industry Profile

Given the changes in industry during recent years, management in the foundry industry has become very concerned with the educational skill levels of their workers. Southern Ductile Casting Company, a member of the Citation Corporation, with a 255-employee plant in Bessemer, Alabama, recognized that performance changes among its workers were essential. "If we are going to be a world-class operation, with ISO 9000 certification, we have to improve the general educational level of all employees," said David Ford, human resource manager.

HRD Function Profile

Southern Ductile had made previous attempts to address the need to upgrade its workers' basic skills. In 1992, the company administered the TABE (Test for Adult Basic Education) to all hourly employees in order to determine their basic math and reading skills. Results indicated that most workers were functioning at a low level in the basic skills necessary for competency in their jobs. The company obtained state funding for a standard education program for the high school equivalency diploma (GED), hired a teacher, and announced classes. The workers were asked to attend class outside of working hours. "Many of us expected the employees to embrace the opportunity with open arms," said general manager John Ballinger. However, only a couple of workers signed up for the classes, which were strictly voluntary and were not directly job related. Both Ballinger and Ford were convinced that investing in their workers was essential. The company decided to offer a savings bond to each attending employee. This tactic was equally unsuccessful.

In 1994, the Alabama Department of Education's Adult and Continuing Education Program received a U.S. Department of Education National Workplace Literacy Grant. The grant, called Alabama Partnership for Training, was designed to provide assistance to companies wishing to establish workplace education programs that were job specific and focused on basic skills aimed at performance improvement. Under the grant, funding was available to provide a full-time workplace education specialist (WES) who would partner with industries to assist in needs assessment and curriculum design and development. In cooperation with local adult education agencies, partner industries would be provided part-time instructors to assist with instructional delivery. Southern Ductile applied to be and was selected as one of the demonstration sites under the federal grant.

The grant required that a specific process for performance improvement be followed. The process included development of a partnership between educators and industry leaders to identify performance gaps and causes; to design, develop, and deliver appropriate interventions including job-specific curriculum; and to implement an evaluation plan. Management personnel agreed that evaluation would be essential for their purposes as well. They were very interested in linking changes in worker skills to the workforce education program. From the outset of the program, support was strong from management and union representatives. Frank Paige, union treasurer and technician in the quality assurance lab, volunteered to work as the company workplace education specialist. Paige, Ford, and Ballinger agreed that teaming with the state to develop a workplace education program that was industry specific would address their immediate needs. They also believed the partnership would provide them with the necessary skills for analyzing needs and developing their own training programs when the grant funding was no longer available.

Description of the Effort

Both management and union personnel recognized that if the plant was to remain competitive, it would be essential to upgrade the basic academic skills of the frontline workers. Technological changes in production processes made it essential that the line workers be able to read work aids, technical manuals and safety manuals; communicate effectively on the job; and perform calculations that had previously not been required. Because of prior unsuccessful efforts to put a traditional adult education program in place, the idea of focusing the efforts on work-related basic skills greatly appealed both to management and union representatives. They were convinced that targeting jobs in which newly learned basic academic skills could be immediately applied would help improve the workers' on-the-job performance and would also serve as an incentive to worker participation. They believed that designing curriculum for teaching workers basic skills that were consistent with their job responsibilities would appeal to the workers, whereas basic literacy skills programs in the past had often seemed far removed and irrelevant to the workers' everyday jobs.

Targeted Goals and Learning

The company targeted five jobs where the training needs were thought to be most acute. The company's goal of upgrading or updating the basic skills of adult workers to reflect changes in the workplace requirement, technology, products, or processes was consistent with the goals of the federal grant. A fundamental concept of the program was that there would be a partnership established between industry and educators where all events would be jointly planned and carried out. A steering committee consisting of union representatives, supervisors, management, and educators was formed early in the project, and during the following two years, that committee planned and approved all events.

The program followed a five-step process: In the first phase, the steering committee identified a present human performance gap. Committee members knew from previous testing that workers in several key jobs lacked the basic skills necessary to perform competently in the present and future work environment. In the second phase, they determined by job-task analysis and literacy audits that their workers needed specific basic skills and knowledge to perform effectively both now and in the future. Through interviews, observations, and focus groups, they were able to identify specific knowledge and skills required for five jobs within the plant. The entire team was provided formal in-service training in curriculum design and development during the intervention planning of phase three. Next, the team interviewed and hired an instructor, who was an experienced adult educator and related well to the workers. During phase four, the instructor attended training sessions on teaching techniques that emphasized the application of basic skills to the workplace. Phase five, which actually occurred throughout the program, involved planning and implementing a program and learner evaluation system. Through funding from the grant, consultants were used to provide workshops for the entire team during the first two years of the program.

Key Issues and Events

A full-time educator joined the team as the state workplace education specialist, working with Paige, the company WES, and union representatives. The two WESs, the instructor, and a steering committee made up of union, management, supervisors, and line representatives cooperatively developed a plan of operation that defined roles, responsibilities, timelines, and activities for the program. Support and involvement by all stakeholders—line workers, union representatives, and management—were key elements in the success of the program. In addition, by involving trained adult educators in the project, both industry personnel and educators learned from one another. Industry personnel learned how to design, develop, and deliver instruction from the educators. The educators learned how to make their educational efforts relevant to the needs of the workplace. During the six-month start-up period, the team further assessed workers' basic skills, identified and prioritized five jobs in which training was needed, and designed and developed curriculum to target skills required on those jobs. The 13-week curriculum for the first job, molding, covered company history and principles, safety, basic math and charting, machine-specific job procedures, ISO 9000 orientation, and reading and completing forms and process cards.

Key decisions had to be made as to when classes would be scheduled and who would attend. Scheduling was a major issue because, as in many production plants, stopping the line was not desirable. Again, the steering committee made those decisions. Job-specific curriculum was designed, and the company paid the workers overtime to attend classes. The curriculum was mandatory for all molders, and classes were scheduled one hour before each shift twice a week. By including line workers and union representatives in all phases of the planning process, there was little resistance to the program.

Because the foundry did not have a training facility, the company made a large commitment to the program by building a $200,000 two-story training facility within the foundry. It provided a quiet, centrally located classroom where training could conveniently be delivered.

At the end of the initial program, a graduation ceremony was held at which the 13 people who completed the program received a barbecue dinner and a course certificate. This was the first time many of them had ever received a certificate. This procedure of recognizing the achievements of the employees who complete the program became the pattern for subsequent courses. As the program progressed, additional jobs such as core makers, grinders, iron pourers, and ladle pushers were analyzed, and a curriculum was developed and delivered. In addition, the company purchased three computers along with computer-assisted instruction designed to improve the workers' reading and math skills. The computer-based training (CBT) was voluntary and available to any worker. However, tutoring was mandatory for very low-level readers.

For several years, the company had offered a computer purchase plan. Under the plan, workers could purchase a computer interest-free through withholdings from their checks. Prior to the CBT, participation was very limited, but after the company offered the CBT, participation tripled. After experiencing success in the job-specific training and CBT, several of the workers inquired about completing the high school equivalency (GED) program. The instructor was able to assist them through individual tutoring and referrals to the local adult education program. Several of the workers purchased study materials for their own computers to assist them in preparing for the GED test.

Evaluation Strategies

Early in the program, the steering committee worked with the grant administrators to develop an evaluation system. They collected data to measure reaction, learning, transfer of skills to the workplace, and results to the company. As part of the grant, the foundry was required to keep detailed records of learner participation and achievement, stakeholders' reactions to the program, transfer of learning to behavior on the job, and results to the company, such as safety-related incidents, scrap rates, absenteeism and turnover, machine downtime, and cost savings. At the end of year one, over half of the plants' workers had attended classes, resulting in more than 2,800 contact hours. Supervisors reported improvements in workers' reading levels, knowledge of the plant operations, and communication skills. It seemed appropriate to evaluate the program using key indicators, which the company identified, because there were no other interventions during the data-gathering period. Using the year prior to the start of the program for baseline data, the company reported the following results after the first year of the program:
- Absenteeism decreased by 10 percent.
- Turnover rate decreased by 33 percent.
- Lost-time accidents decreased by two accidents.
- Overall scrap rate decreased by 8 percent.
- Mold machine uptime increased by 8.3 percent.
- Actual cost savings was $261,957.

ASTD Models for Human Performance Improvement

The program utilized *ASTD Models for Human Performance Improvement: Roles, Competencies, and Outputs* (Rothwell, 1996) as a basis for this program. For example, the performance analysis was accomplished through literacy audits and occupational analysis of jobs in which the company had indications that the needs were most acute. Appropriate interventions included the design and delivery of job-specific curriculum. Program implementation over a two-year period allowed the team to modify and adapt the program as needed. Although management supported the program, changes were successfully facilitated through the use of a steering committee made up of representatives of all stake-holders. The partnership between industry and educational personnel was an essential component in the program in that both the "workhouse" and "schoolhouse" personnel learned from one another. By planning and collecting evaluative data throughout the program, the program team was able to adjust and adapt the interventions as needed. In addition, the company was able to show a return on its investment.

Lessons Learned

As with any collaborative effort, the industry and educational partners learned early on that communication was essential. The industry partners were sometimes frustrated by the time needed for hiring the instructor; purchasing equipment, materials, and supplies; and completing other administrative functions that typically involve more red tape in educational settings than in industrial settings. Education partners sometimes felt hurried when industry expected actions to occur rapidly. The processes involved in diagnosing needs, designing and delivering the interventions, and collecting evaluation data were time-consuming.

Some unexpected results from the interventions cannot easily be quantified. Workers became more efficient and effective in performing their jobs, and they reported that the impact on their family and community lives was positive. One worker who had functioned at a very low reading level prior to the program reported, "Miss Mary (the instructor) has been helping me learn to read Sunday school lessons. I don't know what y'all plan to do after this grant is over, but please, don't let Miss Mary leave." Another reported that he now reads to his children and that they understand that learning is a good thing because they see their dad reading at home. Publicity about the education and training efforts has earned Southern Ductile a reputation for treating its workers well. The number of job applicants has increased.

Near the end of the grant, the foundry underwent ISO 9000 certification review. Management reported that preparation for the review was greatly facilitated by the training that had been provided during the grant period. The company demonstrated a continuing commitment to education and training as the grant support decreased after the first year. Southern Ductile will continue to provide training when the grant support is over.

A final positive impact on the company is an attitude change toward learning among the workers. They are asking for more programs for the computer lab and voluntarily come to the training facility.

The efforts for developing the human resources in this foundry are paying off both in the bottom line for the company and in empowering the workers. During the second year of the program, the company received ISO 9000 certification. This company is recognized as a model for Citation Corporation plants and is rapidly becoming a learning organization.

Questions for Discussion

1. Given that this company had previously tried to start basic skills programs such as the GED, why do you think they were not successful?
2. What are the key factors that made this workforce education program successful?
3. How could the company justify making such a large financial investment in building a training facility?
4. Why is the steering committee important to the successful implementation of a workforce education program?
5. Although the initial objective of this program was to upgrade or update the workers' basic skills in order to reflect changes in technology in the workplace, what are some of the other benefits to the workers, management, and the community?

The Author

Barbara E. Hinton is a professor and head of the Department of Vocational and Adult Education at the University of Arkansas. She has extensive experience in human resource development in both business and educational settings. Areas of interest include training needs analysis, competency-based education and training, team building, criterion-referenced assessment, strategic planning, and facilitation. She has served as a consultant to governmental agencies and to many state agencies and private industries. She has served as an external evaluator for two national workplace education programs. In addition, she has delivered workshops on team building, occupational analysis, and competency-based education in Australia and Chile. At the University of Arkansas, she teaches classes in human resource development. Hinton has made numerous presentations to both national and international audiences, and her works have been published in several scholarly journals in recent years. She can be reached at the University of Arkansas, Vocational & Adult Education, 100 Graduate Education Building, Fayetteville, AR 72701; phone: 501.575.4758; fax: 501.575.3319.

Reference

Rothwell, W. *The ASTD Models for Human Performance Improvement: Roles, Competencies, and Outputs.* Alexandria, VA: American Society for Training & Development, 1996.

Evaluating Strategy Implementation in a Religious Organization: An Organizational Learning Approach

A Catholic Church

Jamie Callahan Fabian and Patrice Scanlon

This study used the Schwandt organizational learning model (1995a, 1995b) to evaluate the implementation of strategy in a Catholic parish. The leader of the organization had recently implemented a new, more participative leadership strategy and wanted recommendations for improving its effectiveness. The qualitative research design focused on the means of disseminating and diffusing knowledge within the organization. This case study discusses recommendations and outcomes of the strategy implementation.

Background

There are a wide variety of understandings about the nature of organizing (Weick, 1979). In the Western tradition, the central theory of organization has been grounded in the idea that an organization is a system that either processes information or solves problems (Nonaka, 1994). Although organizations process information and solve problems, they must also discover means to create knowledge to survive. According to Nonaka, knowledge is created by enlarging and sharing information held by individuals. Consequently, knowledge creation is only as effective as the processes of communication, or the sharing of knowledge, within an organization.

As we transform into a knowledge society, we must seek new ways to understand the strategies organizations use to create knowledge, in essence, to learn (Drucker, 1994). By using an organizational learning systems model to evaluate strategy implementation, we can see

This case was prepared to serve as a basis for discussion rather than to illustrate either effective or ineffective administrative and management practices.

the influence of strategy on an organization as it attempts to learn and survive. This evaluation began with a "pulse-taking approach" (Rothwell & Kazanas, 1994) to provide strategy improvement feedback on a new strategic leadership initiative in a nonprofit organization—a Catholic parish. The outcome was a very focused "rifle approach" (Rothwell & Kazanas, 1994) that looked specifically at the means of disseminating and diffusing knowledge within the organization in order to increase the organization's capacity to realize its strategic objectives.

Organization Profile

The organization is part of a much larger institution, the Catholic Church, which tends to take a more defensive approach to strategy (Snow & Hrebiniak, 1980). The pastor of the parish must report not only to the archdiocese but also to the Franciscan provincial under which the parish is assigned. This chain of command is the standard procedure of parishes affiliated with the Franciscan order. Under the guidance of the present pastor, the organization has grown from approximately 2,000 members in 1990 to more than 7,000 members in 1996. Unfortunately, no additional staff or pastoral resources have been allocated to the parish. As the number of members grows and the number of clergy declines in the overall Catholic Church, most parishes will continue to grow without additional pastoral resources (Bureau of Labor Statistics, 1996). Therefore, pastors must create new strategies to more efficiently lead their parishes. Because the nature of the Franciscan-trained pastors is to avoid more formal, rigid organizational structures, many have created more collaborative representations of the organization, which although innovative, still represent a means of "securing general efficiency" consistent with defensive strategies (Wilson & Butler, 1986). The organizational structure of this parish is represented in a circular fashion, consistent with the consensus-building nature of the Franciscan order, as figure 1 shows.

The core of the organization is represented as an overlap of the pastor, the Pastoral Council, and the Refounding Core Team. The Finance Committee, required by canon law to stand independent of the pastor, is adjacent to this central core. Additional functional groups supporting the parish encircle these core groups.

A Pastoral Council is required of every parish in this particular archdiocese. The council was designed to "help the pastor identify pastoral needs in the parish, help him plan pastoral programs and improve pastoral services and evaluate the effectiveness of existing

Figure 1. Organizational structure of the parish.

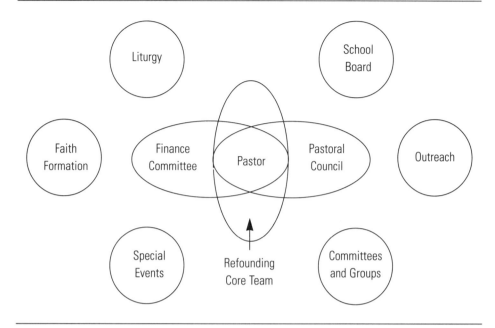

programs and services with a view to their improvement or, at times, their substitution or termination," according to a letter from the bishop of the archdiocese. (Full citation of the letter would conflict with the ability to provide confidentiality to the client.) As recommended by the archdiocese, the pastor appointed members to the Pastoral Council. He selected these members because, collectively, they represent most of the major functional groups of the organization. Further, the pastor has worked with these individuals in the past and respects their guidance even when their views differ from his own.

All parishes within this Franciscan Provincial are required to have a Refounding Core Team, whose members the pastor selects (Walsh, 1995). The refounding process consists of these seven essential elements:

1. providing leadership and vision to the parish
2. creating and expressing a mission statement, goals, and objectives
3. maintaining dialogue with all parish groups to facilitate participation and a sense of ownership among parishioners
4. establishing a collaborative ministry
5. incorporating participatory decision making
6. instilling reflection into all decision-making efforts

7. moving toward a new type of leadership involving both pastors and laity.

It is evident that the Pastoral Council and the Refounding Core Team have a substantial overlap in purpose and responsibilities. However, the organization must be responsive to both the archdiocese and the provincial. The pastor resolved this dilemma by having the Refounding Core Team provide the long-term vision for the parish and by having the Pastoral Council provide the guidance for short-term operations. This strategy of shared responsibility for providing guidance in the parish created uncertainty among leadership and parishioners about the organization's leadership roles. The pastor wanted a team of HRD consultants to evaluate the strategy and make recommendations for improvement. To accomplish this, he brought in "external and largely independent agents" to work with the organizational leadership (Glaister & Thwaites, 1993).

Methods Used

The HRD consultants selected a single-case study approach (Yin, 1994) and incorporated an action research methodology (Cummings & Worley, 1993). Action research, which is heavily influenced by Lewin's unfreezing, moving, and refreezing model of change (Weisbord, 1987), has two primary goals. The first is to help a specific organization implement a planned change effort; in this case, the HRD consultants were asked to evaluate a recent strategy implementation, identify areas for improvement, and help implement recommendations. The second is to develop general knowledge that can be applied elsewhere. The insider-outsider research team conducting the study consisted of an inside researcher who was an active member of the parish and an outside researcher who was not Catholic (Louis & Bartunek, 1992). The team met on a regular basis throughout the data-collection process and during the data-analysis stage. The report was collaboratively written for scholarly purposes. Finally, the team found practical applications resulting from the research that were not necessarily limited to the client.

The team used several qualitative methods to conduct the research, which included interviews, observations, and analyses of parish documents. The interviews were of 12 parish members, who were either functional or committee group leaders, Pastoral Council representatives, senior leader, or a combination of the aforementioned roles. The insider team member also conducted focus group interviews with seven organizational members who were not in leadership positions.

Observations of both parish council meetings and of intergroup meetings were conducted, as well as observations of events surrounding religious services. Document analysis included organizational charts, information bulletins, meeting minutes, and written guidance from institutional sources.

The Organizational Learning Model

The model used for this evaluation was Schwandt's organizational learning model (1995a, 1995b). (See figure 2.) The model uses a systems theory perspective that provides information about the connections between the individuals in the organization, the groups that make up the organization, and the organization itself in the context of a larger institution (Miller, 1978). Schwandt (1993) identifies four learning subsystems to help explain how members of organizations collectively engage in the social actions of learning in order to help the organization survive. Each of these subsystems is connected by a series of inputs and outputs called media of interchange (Schwandt, 1995a). Consistent with a systems theory approach, these subsystems do not operate in a vacuum; changes in one of the subsystems inevitably influence the functioning of the other subsystems through the media of interchange.

The environmental interface subsystem is "the informational portal for the organizational learning system" (Schwandt, 1995b). This subsystem is made up of interdependent actions that serve as filters for information brought into the organization. These actions are primarily environment-scanning efforts, including customer-survey methods, public relations, and external networks (Daft & Weick, 1984). The output from this subsystem is new information.

The action-reflection subsystem uses information as a basis for action; reflection on those actions creates valued knowledge from the information. Actions may include both day-to-day procedures and operations and also major actions that have a significant impact on the

Figure 2. Schwandt's organizational learning model.

Environmental Interface	**Action-Reflection**
Output: New Information	Output: Goal-Referenced Knowledge
Meaning and Memory	**Dissemination and Diffusion**
Output: Sensemaking	Output: Structuration

organization's ability to adapt. The reflection upon these actions creates new knowledge and may include actions such as decision-making processes, evaluations, and inter- and intragroup conflicts. Action-reflection results in the output of goal-referenced knowledge.

The dissemination and diffusion subsystem transfers information and knowledge throughout the organization (Schwandt, 1995b). Dissemination processes are the more formal elements of knowledge transfer, such as policies, communication technologies, and organizational reporting structures. Diffusion processes are more informal means of knowledge transfer and include networking, rumors, and informal communication. The output for dissemination and diffusion is structuration.

Finally, the meaning and memory subsystem is the foundation that guides and controls the other subsystems. It is composed primarily of symbols such as language and actions that stimulate a shared understanding or meaning of the culture, values, and assumptions of the organization. The memory element of the subsystem includes storage mechanisms such as the individuals, prior organizational actions, and organizational structure. The term *sensemaking* refers to the output for the meaning and memory subsystem.

Background and Key Issues

The institutional climate that prompted the necessity of involving laity in decision making, coupled with the exponential organizational growth in this parish, also prompted a need for more efficient mechanisms of information transfer. The chair of the Pastoral Council indicated that his primary purpose in advocating the evaluation was to find better ways of communicating with parishioners. He hoped to find methods that would enable the parishioners to create knowledge (Nonaka, 1994) and become more active in the leadership of the parish. Current mechanisms of information dissemination include pulpit announcements, the parish bulletin, the bulletin board, and periodic staff and group meetings. More informal diffusion of information is accomplished through such means as informal conversations among parishioners, pastoral greetings after each Mass, and coffee calls, which are occasional informal gatherings held after Mass.

Strategy evaluation efforts, therefore, focused on the learning subsystem of dissemination and diffusion. This focus enabled the HRD consultants to observe the patterns that emerged through the media of interchange. Rather than attempt to analyze every facet of this complex organizational learning model, the evaluation centered on how new information, goal-referenced knowledge, and sensemaking influenced the structuration associated with disseminating and diffusing information throughout the organization. (See figure 3.)

New Information

The organization obtained information from its environment through a variety of means. Organizational scanning efforts were consistent with Daft and Weick's (1984) undirected viewing. Because members of the parish did not operate solely within the geographic and psychological boundaries of the parish, they brought information from the external environment into the parish for consideration. These scanning efforts tended to be conducted on a personal level through casual information. For example, at the end of each Mass, the pastor would greet each exiting parishioner. The casual conversation resulting from these encounters often provided a great deal of information for the pastor. Although staff meetings and functional group meetings were used as mechanisms of information acquisition, the leadership agreed that most information was brought into the organization from its members through more informal mechanisms. The organization's informal information-gathering means differed from the institution in which it is embedded.

The archdiocese was much more "conditioned" in its interpretation mode (Daft & Weick, 1984). As a result, the organization passively accepted the information from the archdiocese. The pastor attended regular staff meetings at which regional information was disseminated. Further, guidance was regularly provided to the organization in the form of policies, guidelines, and official memoranda.

On occasion, the organization embarked on a "focused search" (Huber, 1991) in which it actively sought to gain information about potential problems or opportunities. An example of such a search was the active steps taken to resolve the issue of lack of space to ac-

Figure 3. The strategy evaluation effort.

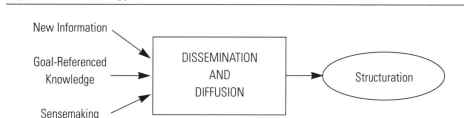

commodate the increasing membership. The parish leadership held two meetings that were open to the entire parish membership and attracted more than 200 parishioners each. Information gathered at these meetings spawned the idea of building additional meeting rooms in conjunction with the schoolhouse. This finding was followed up by a survey that the Finance Committee administered to ascertain whether or not the parish could gain the funds necessary to build the additional meeting rooms. In this organization, focused searches are the exception rather than the rule.

Goal-Referenced Knowledge

The incorporation of the Pastoral Council and the Refounding Core Team marked a conscious effort to institute at least some element of participatory decision making. Because of the size of the organization, it would be cumbersome and inefficient to involve each member in each decision. The survey to gather information on the addition to the parish school was an attempt to involve parishioners in the decision-making process. The results of the survey showed that the parishioners were in favor of building the addition and also were willing to support the endeavor financially.

The participants in this organization's decision making represented a core group of active parishioners. This core group wanted to increase the involvement of other parishioners in order to create an atmosphere of "legitimate peripheral participation" (Lave & Wenger, 1991); but better information transfer would be necessary to accomplish this goal. These members knew that involving more individuals in the activities of the organization would decrease their personal responsibilities in their volunteer roles without diminishing their power in the organization. Further, the pastor felt that increased participation would lead more individuals toward fulfillment of spiritual goals.

Sensemaking

A common set of values is the underlying force of this organization, as it is of most nonprofit organizations (Nygren, Ukeritis, McClelland, & Hickman, 1994). The leadership was consistent in referring to the organization as a family and the pastor as the father of that family. That sentiment was echoed in communications from both the archdiocese and the provincial. The family model of organizing may be a powerful alternative to the traditional bureaucratic forms of organizing. The organization as a family is grounded in the idea that members pull together out of a sense of interdependency and capitalize on individual skills as efficiently as possible for the good of the whole (Cunningham, 1983). This interdependency is created when there is a strong commitment to common values; an understanding of common values can only emerge through sharing knowledge and information. A key element in this organization that demonstrated both the dissemination of information and a reaffirmation of organizational values was the parish bulletin board.

The bulletin board, perhaps the most fundamental means of communication to anyone who walks into the parish, consisted of six partitioned areas: general information, liturgy, outreach, school, faith formation, and respect life. The leadership felt there were five basic groups representing the organization—liturgy, outreach, school, faith formation, and finance. Although all members acknowledged the importance of finance in the organization, that group was not represented in the most visible communication mechanism that the organization used. Instead, respect life—a clearly value-driven subject—replaced it. This symbolic representation reinforces the growing belief that nonprofit organizations hold core values to be the bottom line, unlike the financial bottom line of for-profit organizations.

The leadership consistently described the parish by using events that centered on welcoming others into its shared understanding of the organization. Events cited as meaningful descriptors included the initiation rites for new adult members, the outreach program serving the local community, and the come-home program that works with adult Catholics who have left the church and choose to return. By creating a sense of family in which individuals feel valued and welcomed, the organization had been moving toward its goal of spiritually fulfilling its members. This again highlights the essential nature of nonprofit organizations in which core values drive the organization toward achieving the goal of strengthening core values (Nygren et al., 1994).

Structuration

The variables and data emerging from these interchange media influenced the dissemination and diffusion of information in the organization. This subsystem can be analyzed by looking at elements of structuration, which include organizational roles, leadership, policies, and organizational structure. The leadership of the organization was consistently defined as the pastor, followed by the Pastoral Council. With some variation, most of the functional groups appearing on the organizational chart were also mentioned as elements of leadership in the organization. The Refounding Core Team, as well as the associate pastor, were conspicuously absent in discussions about the parish leadership.

As indicated earlier, the diagnosis revealed that the leadership felt that information was usually shared informally and horizontally. Perhaps peculiar to nonprofit organizations, and Catholic parishes in particular, information is not seen as credible or important unless it is received through the pastor. Given the substantial growth of this organization, one individual is not capable of personally sharing information with 7,000 members. The perception of validity of information must be changed in order to effectively communicate in the organization.

The organizational structure in figure 1 itself demonstrates some values of the organization that influence information transfer. As indicated earlier, it is structured in a circular fashion. No reporting relationships are evident in the structure. Such hierarchical structures would undoubtedly hamper the participation in an all-volunteer membership. A common metaphor for the organizational structure was a wheel with the pastor at the hub and the parishioners joined to the pastor through various functional groups represented by wheel spokes. As a result, the dissemination and diffusion of information would naturally occur through a collaborative process.

The organization was dealing with some difficulty in disseminating information. Although the Pastoral Council had to face the problem of ambiguity of information, the parishioners were often concerned with uncertainty of information (Weick, 1995). One Pastoral Council member related his experience with a parishioner who felt threatened by the Council:

> There was [sic] some hard feelings on the part of this fellow; and he's a very responsible individual. But I felt he was almost being paranoid because [he thought] there were things being done behind his back that he didn't know about but affected him. Certainly, that's not what is done nor is the Council's purpose, but it's the way he perceived it. And that's something we definitely don't need to have.

The Pastoral Council faced the difficulty of sorting through immense amounts of information to determine what was important and what had to be shared with other organizational members, whereas organizational members felt they did not know enough about what was happening in the organization. The same Pastoral Council member commented that perhaps the council should summarize the work of the various parish groups and publish the summaries in the bulletin. He hoped that such action would "prevent this business of jealousies and positions of authority."

From a more functional perspective, the additions being built in the parish represent a clear structuring mechanism for diffusing information. The leadership felt that coffee calls and group meetings were vital forums for sharing information. The new facilities would more easily enable such meetings, and even enable impromptu gatherings. As one Pastoral Council member indicated:

> These new facilities will help because they will be user-friendly facilities. People will have the opportunity to meet, to talk on a regular basis and more often. Now our facilities are booked months or a year in advance, so it's hard for committees or groups to get together. There's such limited space.

The parish was aware of the need to disseminate and diffuse information in order to maintain the health of the organization. This evaluation revealed that they have several formal and informal mechanisms to transmit information.

Recommendations

The organizational learning model was clearly useful in helping evaluate strategy implementation in this organization. Although there are a number of possible improvement areas in any organization, this model highlighted an area for improvement that can relatively easily be accomplished for maximum gain—the transfer of information. In keeping with the criteria for both action research (Cummings & Worley, 1993) and insider-outsider research (Louis & Bartunek, 1992), several key recommendations were developed for the parish leadership as they attempt to position the organization not only for the future of the Catholic Church but also for the future of their growing parish:
1. Combine the Pastoral Council and the Refounding Core Team. The essence of the Refounding Core Team is a specific process. This process could be, and should be, incorporated into the Pastoral Council (regardless of whether or not the organization chooses to merge the two groups). The substantial overlap of responsibilities that the archdiocese and the provincial outlined do not justify two separate leadership groups.

The combination of the two groups would facilitate better communication by identifying one central group responsible for establishing the organization's mission, vision, goals, and objectives. This would also serve to further legitimize the Pastoral Council by focusing attention on one central group that represents the pastor.

2. Ensure all parishioners are familiar with the members of the Pastoral Council. One of the most visible means of communication in the organization is the bulletin board system. The bulletin board segment captures the purpose of the council, with pictures of council members and their associated functional group memberships and updates of council meetings, providing parishioners with easy access to Pastoral Council information.

3. Until the culture begins to accept members of the Pastoral Council as credible sources of information, decrease the flow of functional information directly from the pastor and increase the flow of information from the council. One way this can be accomplished is through increased pulpit announcements by Pastoral Council members. Another way to accomplish this goal is to create a Pastoral Council section in the weekly bulletin dedicated to disseminating information and ensuring the pastor's section focuses on spiritual leadership remarks.

4. Increase parishioner involvement, and therefore increase diffusion of information through legitimate peripheral participation by having a systematic means of orienting new members to the activities that sustain the organization (Lave & Wenger, 1991). Because the organization contacts each new member through a registration form for information about what interests that person may have, the organization could also follow up the written contact with a personal contact from a sponsor from one of the individual's areas of interest. This would ensure that the individual was formally contacted by a member of the organization and given a support network.

5. Create a home page on the World Wide Web to increase dissemination and diffusion of knowledge. At least 500 Catholic parishes have home pages that "encourage members to participate in electronic dialogue" (Broadway, 1996). The creation of a home page could potentially involve parishioners on many levels. First, home pages enable organizations to interface with their environments by providing a virtual tour of the parish facilities and grounds. Second, home pages provide a forum for organizational members to share individual knowledge and gain access to organizational knowledge such as programs and activities. Third, home pages require creation and maintenance, which

is optimally provided by volunteers within the organization. This is yet another example of increasing "legitimate peripheral participation" in the parish (Lave & Wenger, 1991).

6. Establish a position for a volunteer development coordinator. People want to be involved in the organization; however, the parish must provide a mechanism to mobilize volunteers and help them gain easy access to the organization to facilitate structuration in the organization. The volunteer coordinator could also serve as a linking mechanism for the functional support groups not represented on the Pastoral Council.

Conclusions

Tichy (1983) points out that strategic change must address technical, political, and cultural elements. Implementation, or lack thereof, of the evaluation feedback recommendations was based on these three areas. All implemented recommendations have successfully increased the dissemination and diffusion of information in the organization and have resulted in a better understanding of the new leadership strategy in the organization.

The focus of technical change is on the mechanisms of "acquisition and application of the knowledge useful for effective performance of organizational tasks" (Argyris & Schön, 1978, as cited in Tichy, 1983). Most of the recommendations that the parish adopted dealt with aspects of technical change that were inexpensive yet highly effective. All Pastoral Council members now have name tags to identify them as part of the formal leadership in the organization. In addition, the bulletin board has been expanded to include the family model organizational structure with names and pictures of members from each of the core groups. A home page is also under construction to open communication avenues through the World Wide Web for both internal and external information sharing. Two additional organizational staff positions also have been created. An administrative assistant position was designed to enable more experienced staff members to focus on maintaining momentum on the new changes taking place in the organization. Also, a director of volunteers position was created. Although not yet filled, this position was designed to facilitate coordination between members and volunteer groups in the organization so talents are used for the good of the organization and skills are developed for the individual. A final technical change that the organization incorporated was to add a section of Pastoral Council activity updates to the weekly bulletin.

This technical change also serves a cultural purpose. The cultural norm of the pastor as sole leadership authority in the Catholic parish has a very long and very strong history. Most parishioners expect all elements of leadership, including the transfer of information, to come from the pastor. By creating a bulletin section devoted to transferring information from the new functional leadership body of the organization, organization members can begin to identify with the Pastoral Council as the source for information. The organization also implemented the recommendation of eliminating the pastor's role in providing pulpit information updates and replacing it with rotating Pastoral Council member updates.

The implementation of recommendations regarding both technical and cultural strategy change issues was successful for the organization. However, one recommendation was not implemented for political reasons. Both the Pastoral Council and the pastor felt that combining the Refounding Core Team and the Pastoral Council would create tensions with the governing bodies to which the parish is responsible. Further, combining the two groups would have eliminated some positions, which could potentially alienate some members. The result may have been a reduction in individuals' commitment to the organization. Although the two groups still maintain separate identities, the Pastoral Council has clearly been identified as the operational leadership, or management, arm of the organization. The Refounding Core Team operates behind the scenes with the pastor and the Pastoral Council to provide vision for strategic changes.

Each of these strategic change initiatives focused on improving aspects of disseminating or diffusing information. They dealt primarily with the prescribed and emergent networks of communication as change levers within the organization (Tichy, 1983). As a result, this evaluation effort became focused on a single issue of importance to organizational strategy. The initial goal of the HRD consultants was to provide general information about the original strategy implementation, whereas the key issue actually was the dissemination and diffusion of information within the organization.

This rifle approach to providing feedback enabled the organization to take manageable steps toward improving the implementation of the new leadership strategy in the parish. This organization faces the future on two fronts. Not only must it be prepared for the inevitable transformation into a knowledge society, but it must also face the uncertain future of its specific environment—the Catholic

Church. Unlike most organizations, the Catholic Church faces almost 2,000 years of ingrained organizational culture that it must overcome. The use of an organizational learning approach to identify the mechanisms enabling organization members to share knowledge offered this parish new means to effectively address its leadership strategies.

Questions for Discussion

1. This action research team chose mechanisms of information transfer as a focal point to improve strategy implementation. Using the organizational learning model as a reference, what other focal points are possible for improving strategy implementation in this organization?
2. This case study looked at a church as a nonprofit organization. Do you believe a church can be considered a nonprofit organization? Why or why not?
3. Can researchers use the same approaches to strategy evaluation in nonprofit organizations as they do in for-profit organizations? Why or why not?
4. What influence do you think the volunteer nature of the leadership in this organization will have on the implementation of the recommended strategy improvement initiatives?
5. How would you handle the implementation of the Refounding Core Team and the Pastoral Council?

The Authors

Jamie Callahan Fabian is a doctoral candidate in human resource development at The George Washington University. Her concentrations are in human development and sociology. She is also an adjunct instructor of a graduate-level course on research design. As a research assistant for the Institute for the Study of Learning, she worked on both qualitative and quantitative research projects dealing with organizational change, cohort learning, and organizational learning. Her dissertation topic is related to the role of emotion in organizational learning processes. She can be reached at The George Washington University, 2134 G Street, NW #219, Washington, DC 20052; phone: 202.994.7952; e-mail: jamiec@gwu.edu.

Patrice M. Scanlon is a human resource development doctoral student at The George Washington University. She received her master's degree in human relations from the University of Oklahoma. Scanlon has taught college-level courses as well as seminars for small businesses, government agencies, and nonprofit organizations. Her teaching experience includes courses in business communication, interpersonal communication, public speaking, and management. Scanlon's research interests include organizational change, organizational learning, organizational communication, and leadership.

References

Argyris, C., & Schön, D. *Organizational Learning: A Theory of Action Perspective*. Reading, MA: Addison-Wesley, 1978.

Broadway, B. "Flocking to the Web." *The Washington Post*, B-7, September, 1996.

Bureau of Labor Statistics. "Occupational Outlook Handbook: Roman Catholic Priests." Http://Stats.Bls.Gov/Oco/Ocos063.Thm, June, 1996.

Cummings, T., & Worley, C. (1993). *Organization Development and Change* (5th edition). New York: West Publishing, 1993.

Cunningham, M. "Planning for Humanism." *The Journal of Business Strategy*, *3*(4), 87–90, 1983.

Daft, R., & Weick, K. "Toward a Model of Organizations as Interpretation Systems." *Academy of Management Review, 2*(2), 284–295, 1984.

Drucker, P.F. "The Age of Social Transformation." *Atlantic Monthly, 274*(5), 53–80, 1994.

Glaister, K., & Thwaites, D. "Managerial Perception and Organizational Strategy." *Journal of General Management, 18*(4), 15–33, 1993.

Huber, G. "Organizational Learning: The Contributing Processes and to Literature." *Organization Science, 2*(1), 88–115, 1991.

Lave, J., & Wenger, E. *Situated Learning: Legitimate Peripheral Participation*. New York: Cambridge University Press, 1991.

Louis, M., & Bartunek, J. "Insider/Outsider Research Teams: Collaboration Across Diverse Perspectives." *Journal of Management Inquiry, 1*(2), 1992, 101–110.

Miller, J. *Living Systems*. New York: McGraw-Hill, 1978.

Nonaka, I. "A Dynamic Theory of Organizational Knowledge Creation." *Organization Science, 5*(1), 14–37, 1994.

Nygren, D., Ukeritis, M., McClelland, D., & Hickman, J. "Outstanding Leadership in Nonprofit Organizations: Leadership Competencies in Roman Catholic Religious Orders." *Nonprofit Management and Leadership*, *4*(4), 375–391, 1994.

Rothwell, W., & Kazanas, H. *Human Resource Development: A Strategic Approach* (rev. edition). Amherst, MA: HRD Press, 1994.

Schwandt, D. "Organizational Learning: A Dynamic Integrative Construct." Unpublished manuscript, The George Washington University Graduate School of Education and Human Development, Washington, DC, 1993.

Schwandt, D. "Learning as an Organization: A Journey Into Chaos." In S. Chawla & J. Renesch (editors), *Learning Organizations: Developing Cultures for Tomorrow's Workplace*. Portland, OR: Productivity Press, 1995a.

Schwandt, D. "Integrating Strategy and Organizational Learning: A Theory of Action Perspective." Unpublished manuscript, The George Washington University Graduate School of Education and Human Development, Washington, DC, 1995b.

Snow, C., & Hrebiniak, L. "Strategy, Distinctive Competence, and Organizational Performance." *Administrative Science Quarterly, 25*(2), 317–336, 1980.

Tichy, N. "The Essentials of Strategic Change Management." *The Journal of Business Strategy, 3*(4), 55–67, 1983.

Walsh, F. "Refounding...With a Franciscan Twist." *Handbook for Franciscan Parishes.* 1995.

Weick, K. *The Social Psychology of Organizing* (2d edition). New York: McGraw-Hill, 1979.

Weick, K. *Sensemaking in Organizations.* Thousand Oaks, CA: Sage Publications, 1995.

Weisbord, M. *Productive Workplaces: Organizing and Managing for Dignity, Meaning and Community.* San Francisco: Jossey-Bass, 1987.

Wilson, D., & Butler, R. "Voluntary Organizations in Action: Strategy into Voluntary Sector." *Journal of Management Studies, 23*(5), 519–542, 1986.

Yin, R. *Case Study Research: Design and Methods.* Thousand Oaks, CA: Sage Publications, 1994.

Structured On-the-Job Training: Innovations in International Health Training

JHPIEGO Corporation

Rick Sullivan, Sue Brechin, and Maryjane Lacoste

JHPIEGO Corporation, an affiliate of Johns Hopkins University, is working with medical professionals in reproductive health in Zimbabwe to implement a structured on-the-job training (OJT) program. The goal of this program is to improve the performance of family planning service providers in clinical sites throughout the country. Working with the Zimbabwe National Family Planning Council, the organization that was charged with helping to implement the system, JHPIEGO staff converted an existing group-based clinical training course to a structured OJT course and helped build support for this new training approach. The design and consensus-building activities resulted in the implementation of an effective, structured on-the-job training program. The model for implementing this innovative training approach identifies key steps from conception through pilot testing to full-scale implementation—steps relevant to a variety of training situations.

Background

JHPIEGO assisted the Zimbabwe National Family Planning Council (ZNFPC) in 1993 to develop and conduct a clinical training course for supervisors and service providers. A 1994 evaluation of this integrated program showed only limited success. Many trainees returned from the group-based course to sites where they were not able to practice their newly acquired skills because of other job responsibilities, low caseloads, or inadequate supervision. Results of this evaluation suggested that traditional classroom courses may not always be the most

This case was prepared to serve as a basis for discussion rather than to illustrate either effective or ineffective administrative and management practices.

appropriate or effective way to ensure application of new skills on the job. The assessment also emphasized the important link that needs to be made between training and service delivery. To respond to the evaluation team's recommendations and to ZNFPC's need for different training approaches that would maximize their ability to train more service providers more quickly, JHPIEGO assisted the ZNFPC, the Ministry of Health and Child Welfare (MOH/CW), and other organizations in converting the group-based clinical course to a structured OJT course in August 1995.

Organizational Profile

JHPIEGO Corporation, a nonprofit training organization affiliated with Johns Hopkins University, is funded primarily by the United States Agency for International Development (USAID) and works to develop a reproductive health clinical-training capacity in developing countries. In Zimbabwe, JHPIEGO collaborates with the ZNFPC, a parastatal organization charged by the Zimbabwean government with coordinating all family planning activities in the country, including providing technical assistance to the MOH/CW and other organizations as necessary, and coordinating training, contraceptive logistics, evaluation, communication activities, and provision of family planning services.

Industry Profile and Key Players

Currently working in approximately 30 countries, JHPIEGO assists organizations like the ZNFPC and the MOH/CW to establish pre-service education and in-service training programs to prepare clinical, advanced, and master trainers. These trainers then train clinicians to provide quality clinical services to women and men. As the focus of training is on clinical procedures, JHPIEGO trainers use a mastery-learning approach that is competency based, meaning that participants must demonstrate mastery of knowledge and skills with anatomic models before working with clients. To support this training approach, JHPIEGO produces comprehensive clinical-training packages for group-based training. These packages include a reference manual, guides and workbooks, pre- and postknowledge assessments, and performance checklists.

The ZNFPC conducts in-service family planning clinical-training courses for both public- and private-sector clinical providers. Almost all training is group based, which means that participants are brought from work sites to a central location for a specific period of time for a training course. They receive lodging in training centers or hotels, allowances for meals and incidental expenses, and reimbursement for transportation costs.

Key Issues and Events

Through in-country needs assessments, two primary issues were identified in 1994. Although the individuals who attended the group-based training course demonstrated mastery of clinical skills during training, they did not always use these skills in providing services to clients at their work sites. It appeared that the clinician was trained and ready to provide services, but that the job site was not always prepared to offer these services. In addition, the clinician's supervisor may or may not have been involved in the decision for the individual to attend training and, therefore, may not have had a strong commitment to seeing that knowledge and skills acquired during training were applied on the job.

Another issue related to the link between training and job performance. Because training was group based, participants would leave their jobs for two weeks to attend the in-service training course at a central site. Participants acquired the latest medical information, practiced skills on new anatomic models, had access to new instruments, and used their skills in the best clinics. To provide quality training, every effort was made to ensure that both classroom and clinical experiences were ideal. When the participants went back to work, however, they often were returning to facilities where they worked in less than ideal conditions. In addition, participants often were not in a position to effect change in their work environment. This resulted in skills not being applied on the job.

In light of the issues that the evaluation raised, it was apparent that either the existing group-based training course would need to be modified, or the focus of training would need to shift to the job site.

Model for Implementing an OJT Strategy

The shift from a traditional, instructor-led, group-based training approach to a self-paced OJT approach is not easy. It is often much easier for trainers to design a group-based course that allows individuals to leave their jobs for a period of time to be trained in a controlled setting and then return after being trained. Supervisors and managers may have little knowledge about what occurs during the training course, however, and may not be prepared to help the trainees apply their new knowledge and skills when they do return to work. By contrast, when training is inserted into the job site with a focus on job performance, it becomes critical to build consensus with key stakeholders and design a quality training event. Recognizing the importance of design, development, and consensus-building activities, JHPIEGO staff developed the model shown in figure 1. The focus of the left side of the model is on the steps in the design and development of the OJT training strategy. The right side of the model presents the consensus-building activities critical to the success of the design and development steps. Both sides combine to create the implementation model. JHPIEGO's position was that to implement a successful and sustainable OJT approach required a combination of design, development, and consensus-building activities. The descriptions below each of the steps shown in figure 1 summarize the approach JHPIEGO used in conjunction with the client to implement the structured OJT in Zimbabwe.

Identify the Training Need

In 1993, JHPIEGO assisted the ZNFPC in developing an in-service family planning clinical-training package and in conducting group-based courses using these materials. As discussed above, this group-based approach experienced only limited success. Many trainees returned to sites where they were not able to practice their newly acquired skills because of other job responsibilities, low client caseload for the method in which they were trained, or inappropriate and inadequate supervision. Results of this evaluation suggested that traditional instructor-led courses may not always be the most appropriate or effective way to ensure application of new skills on the job. Given these findings and the ZNFPC's need for different training approaches that would maximize its ability to train more service providers more quickly, the evaluation team recommended that JHPIEGO assist the ZNFPC in developing a structured OJT package for clinical training.

Meet With Key Stakeholders

After defining a broader clinical-training strategy to expand more quickly the numbers of service providers trained, senior managers decided to pilot test a structured OJT approach. It was imperative that all sectors involved in this type of training be consulted to garner support for the pilot test. Although ZNFPC coordinates all family planning training in the country, a number of key stakeholders have input into what kind of training is needed, where, and for whom. Meetings with these decision makers were held over a period of ap-

Figure 1. Model for implementing an OJT strategy.

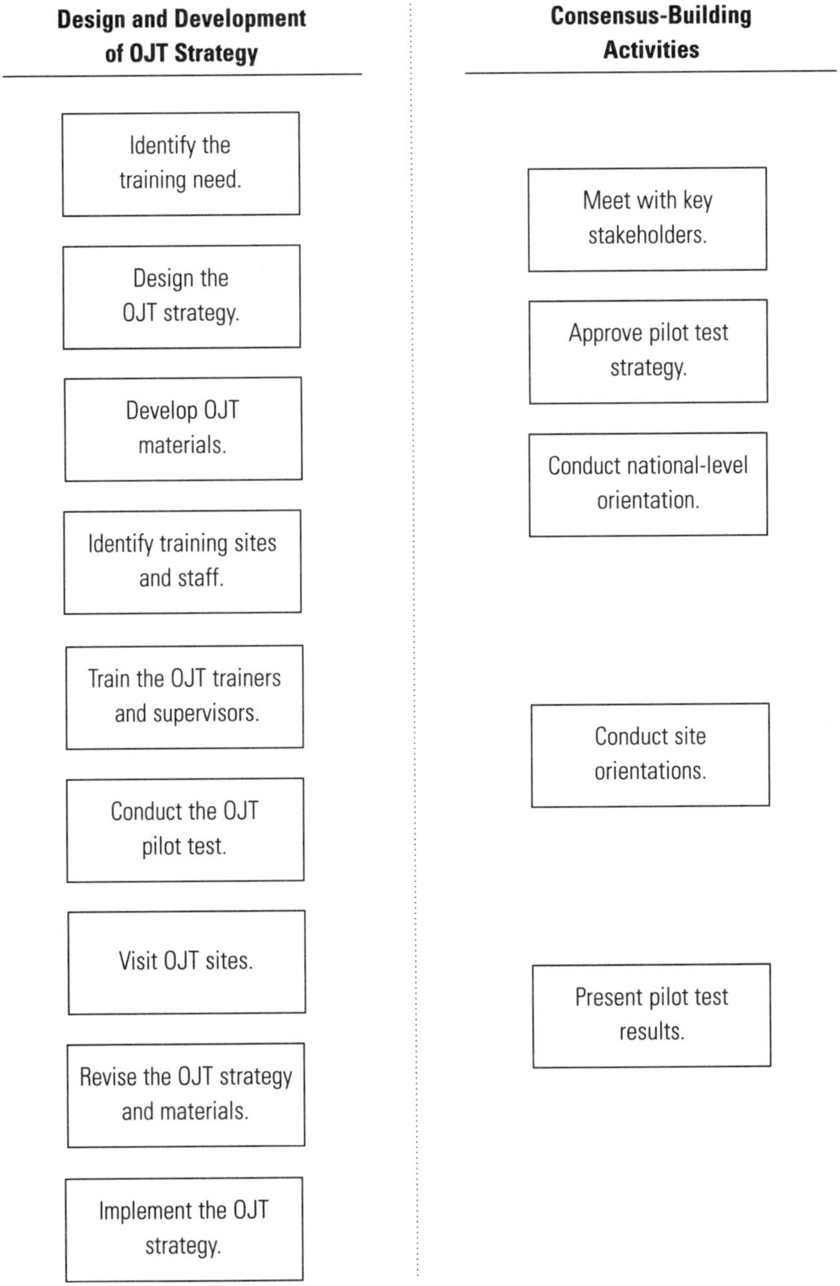

Design and Development of OJT Strategy	Consensus-Building Activities
Identify the training need.	
	Meet with key stakeholders.
Design the OJT strategy.	
	Approve pilot test strategy.
Develop OJT materials.	
	Conduct national-level orientation.
Identify training sites and staff.	
Train the OJT trainers and supervisors.	
	Conduct site orientations.
Conduct the OJT pilot test.	
Visit OJT sites.	
	Present pilot test results.
Revise the OJT strategy and materials.	
Implement the OJT strategy.	

proximately six months, until both JHPIEGO and ZNFPC felt confident that consensus on this approach had been reached and that the pilot test could move forward.

Design the OJT Strategy

Because structured on-the-job clinical training was a new training approach for JHPIEGO, a decision was made to define the approach through a strategy paper before developing needed training materials. The first step in the development of the strategy paper was to conduct a thorough review of the literature on OJT (see references at the end of this case study), which would allow staff to consider various types of OJT, advantages and limitations, training of OJT trainers, formats of materials, and evaluation strategies. A draft of the paper was circulated to staff for comments and suggestions. After several revisions, the strategy paper was ready for use in developing a specific OJT program.

The strategy paper was useful in describing JHPIEGO's general approach to structured OJT and provided readers with a clear picture of what OJT should look like. A more specific strategy, however, was needed for the OJT program being requested in Zimbabwe. With the support of key stakeholders, a workshop was held with trainers from those organizations that would be using the OJT approach. Although a centralized training office can develop a traditional, instructor-led course, development of an OJT course must involve the individuals who will be implementing this training approach. Therefore, a strategy development workshop was held in Zimbabwe to ensure that the approach was realistic and to gain the support of those who would be conducting the course at various sites.

During the workshop, participants learned about OJT and reviewed JHPIEGO's general OJT strategy. Participants then identified key personnel to be involved in the OJT approach, including the trainee, trainer, supervisor, and national OJT coordinator. Participants, working in small groups, identified the roles and responsibilities of each of these individuals. There were lengthy discussions to reach consensus on the responsibilities of each person involved in the OJT course.

The most critical discussions in the workshop centered on the process for knowledge and skill transfer and assessment. How would the trainee acquire the knowledge contained in the reference manual? How and when would the trainee be assessed? What types of activities would the trainee complete both individually and with the trainer in order to practice or apply newly acquired information? How would the trainee and trainer know when specific activities (e.g., trainee to read a specific chapter, trainer to give a demonstration) were to occur? When would the supervisor administer the final knowledge and skill assessment? The answers to these and similar questions, coupled with the results of the discussion about roles and responsibilities, helped to form the basis for the Zimbabwe OJT strategy.

The output of the strategy design phase is a clear, concise description of how OJT will work in a specific situation. If JHPIEGO were to develop an OJT approach for another country, it would have to go through the same strategy design process again. OJT will necessarily differ slightly in each setting to meet the specific requirements of the country.

Approve Pilot Test Strategy

A key step beyond meeting with key stakeholders was to gain approval both within the ZNFPC and among the various agencies in Zimbabwe to conduct a pilot test of the structured OJT for clinical training. At this point, in fact, one of the agencies that had been involved in the early stages declined the opportunity to participate in the pilot test.

Develop OJT Materials

One of the keys to the success of any training course is quality training materials. These materials are even more critical in a structured OJT course because the trainee is often working independently, and the materials must make the learning process as easy and clear as possible. In the case of Zimbabwe, an existing instructor-led course was being converted to a self-paced OJT course. This meant that there was an existing reference manual that contained all of the essential, need-to-know information. There also were pre- and posttests, skill checklists, and many other items that could be used in the OJT package.

After the OJT program was designed and the pilot test strategy was approved, a materials development workshop was conducted. The background of the participants selected to attend was an important consideration. To be able to develop quality materials, it was critical that the participants, who would be using the completed OJT package, be proficient trainers who had extensive subject matter expertise and skills. In addition, many of those attending were also involved in the development of the OJT strategy, which helped to ensure that the materials were well designed and that the participants felt a tremendous sense of ownership.

One of the first activities in the workshop was to review the existing (group-based) training package to determine which components could be used in the OJT package. The resulting package comprised six components:

- reference manual
- trainee's workbook
- trainer's guide
- supervisor's guide
- anatomic models
- supporting media.

The participants worked in small groups to develop materials for the trainee, trainer, and supervisor. Fortunately, the reference manual required no modifications, saving everyone a great deal of time and effort. The reference manual is the heart of the training package and serves as the source of information for the trainee and trainer. The anatomic models are used to allow trainees to practice skills in simulations before working with clients. Supporting media include videotapes and slide sets that show the steps in clinical procedures.

All the information the trainee needs to learn is in the reference manual. All the course design information directing the trainee, trainer, and supervisor through the OJT course is found in the workbook and guides. Table 1 presents a summary of the primary information contained in these documents. In each of these documents there is a description of the OJT course, responsibilities of those involved, course objectives, and a syllabus describing the course in detail. Both the trainee and trainer have the course pretest. The trainer has the answer key so he or she can give immediate feedback on those areas in which the trainee is strong and on areas in which additional study might be required. All three documents contain the skill checklists, which list the specific steps within the clinical procedures the trainee must master. The trainee uses these checklists first when observing the trainer demonstrate a skill. Following the demonstration, the trainee uses the checklist to practice the skill, under the coaching of the trainer, first on anatomic models and then on clients. When the trainee has completed the OJT course and is ready for the final assessment, the supervisor administers the final knowledge and skill assessments.

One of the keys to an effective OJT program is inclusion of a step-by-step guide for those involved in the course. In the Zimbabwe training package, this guide is referred to as the course outline (see table 2). The course outline serves as a guide or map for the

Table 1. Contents of training package documents.

Contents	Trainee's Workbook	Trainer's Guide	Supervisor's Guide
Overview of the OJT course	X	X	X
Responsibilities of the trainee, trainer, and supervisor	X	X	X
Learning objectives	X	X	X
Syllabus	X	X	X
Course pretest	X	X	
Course pretest answers		X	
Skill practice and assessment checklists	X	X	X
Course outline	X	X	X
Practice exercises	X	X	
Practice exercises answer key		X	
Course posttest and answers			X
Course evaluation	X	X	
OJT training-skills information		X	
OJT supervisor-skills information			X

trainee, trainer, and supervisor. The primary focus is on the steps each trainee will follow as he or she works through the course. For those steps requiring interaction with the trainer or supervisor, there are directions about what should be done. Trainees check off each step as they complete them. This helps each trainee keep track of his or her progress through the course. At key points in the course outline, the trainer will sign the outline to indicate that the trainee is making satisfactory progress.

By the conclusion of the materials development workshop, the participants had completed work on all components of the workbook and guides. Following the workshop, the materials were turned over to JHPIEGO's materials development staff for editing and formatting. In addition, to ensure that the materials were clear, training experts who were not involved in the development process reviewed the draft

Table 2. Portion of an OJT course outline.

Day	Trainee Activities	Trainer Activities	Supervisor Activities
Day 1	**Introduction** _____ Read the "Introduction" in the *Trainee's Workbook*.		
	_____ Meet with your OJT trainer.	Meet with the trainee to discuss the OJT course goals and objectives, review the training package, and then discuss the responsibilities of the trainee, trainer, and supervisor.	
		Review the OJT course outline and explain that the trainee should mark and date each step as it is completed. The trainer will sign off each section.	
		Discuss the pre- and posttraining knowledge and skill assessments.	
	_____ Complete the course pretest.	Administer and score the pretest following the guidelines found in the *Trainer's Guide*.	
	_____ Complete the pretraining skill assessment (counseling).	Administer and score the pretraining skills assessment (counseling) following the guidelines found in the *Trainer's Guide*.	
	_____ Complete the pretraining skill assessment (medical examination).	Administer and score the pretraining skill assessment (medical examination) following the guidelines found in the *Trainer's Guide*.	

Day	Trainee Activities	Trainer Activities	Supervisor Activities
	Activities completed: OJT trainer _____ Date _____	When the trainee has completed the knowledge and skill assessments, sign and date this section.	
Day 2–3	**Introduction** ____ Read "Chapter 1: Introduction to Medical Examinations" in the *Reference Manual*. ____ Complete Practice Exercise #1.		

materials. Copies were also returned to Zimbabwe for review by the individuals involved in the development workshop. Once all changes were made, copies were prepared for use during the training of the OJT trainers and supervisors.

Conduct National-Level Orientation

The newly developed OJT package was presented at a meeting of key Zimbabwean policymakers and decision makers in February 1996 to orient them to the approach and to ensure their support for implementation of the OJT pilot test. Each participant received a copy of the OJT package for reference and review. Those ZNFPC and MOH/CH personnel who developed the materials conducted the following sessions:

- overview of clinical training to date
- overview of the OJT approach and the Zimbabwe-specific OJT model
- essential training elements and the OJT program
- criteria for OJT site and staff selection
- roles and responsibilities of OJT staff
- implementation plan.

The recommendations that participants made during the course of the meeting were incorporated, as appropriate, into the OJT package and implementation plan.

Identify Training Sites and Staff

Following the national orientation, the national OJT coordinator, in collaboration with technical resource staff at the ZNFPC, worked with the MOH/CW to identify appropriate sites and personnel for the OJT pilot test. Criteria for site selection were presented in the OJT package. The OJT supervisor at each site was the nurse-manager in charge of the site, who already had supervision responsibilities. The supervisor in conjunction with provincial management selected the OJT trainer, who was generally already proficient in the clinical skills in which he or she would be conducting training. The process of selecting trainees for the pilot test varied from site to site. At some locations, the supervisor of the site selected the trainee; at other sites, service providers interested in being trained completed applications and were then interviewed by the supervisor.

Once sites and personnel were identified, ZNFPC technical resource staff visited each location to confirm the MOH's information and to ensure each site's readiness for training (for example, by assessing equipment and checking for adequate training space). ZNFPC staff also collected baseline information on the site and OJT personnel (supervisor, trainer, and trainee) that would eventually be used in evaluation of the pilot test. Key information gathered included statistics on delivery of the clinical method in which the trainee was going to be trained. ZNFPC hoped to see an increase in the number of clients accepting the family planning method following completion of training. Many of the sites selected for the pilot test were not currently offering the method. ZNFPC anticipated that this would change following training, however, and that service provision of this method would increase.

Train the OJT Trainers and Supervisors

Essential to the success of an OJT course is the preparation of the trainer and, if applicable, the OJT supervisor. In some situations the trainer may be a proficient worker with little or no previous training experience who has been designated as an OJT trainer. In other situations this individual may be an experienced group-based trainer who is now conducting training one-on-one on the job. In both situations it is critical that these trainers be prepared to conduct OJT.

Although the individuals designated as trainers at the OJT pilot sites in Zimbabwe were practicing clinicians, many had little or no previous preparation as trainers. A workshop focusing on OJT training and supervisory skills was designed and conducted for the trainers and supervisors from the pilot sites. The schedule for the OJT implementation workshop contained a number of sessions and activities to prepare these trainers and supervisors to conduct the OJT program. Participants read supporting information in their training package and then attended sessions focusing on the following:

- an approach to clinical training
- creating a positive training climate
- using interactive training techniques
- using skill-development learning guides and skill-assessment checklists
- coaching in clinical training
- combining coaching with other clinical training techniques.

Participants observed trainer demonstrations and then were given opportunities to present a clinical demonstration using anatomic models, coach another participant practicing a skill, and assess a clinician's ability to perform a skill according to the steps in the skill checklist. Each participant was then given the opportunity to deliver one or more presentations and received immediate feedback from the trainers and other participants.

In addition to the sessions described previously for the trainers, sessions specifically designed for the OJT supervisors included

• orienting site staff to the OJT program
• communicating with the national OJT coordinator
• conducting the final knowledge assessment
• conducting the final skill assessment
• conducting supervisor visits.

A significant portion of the workshop was devoted to orienting the participants to the OJT approach. Participants reviewed the responsibilities of the trainee, trainer, and supervisor. There were lengthy discussions of the OJT site-selection criteria, equipment and supply requirements, trainee learning objectives, use of the OJT course outline, and use of the pre- and posttraining knowledge assessments. Participants were also afforded many opportunities to review and use the skill-development learning guides and skill-assessment checklists. The workshop training resulted in a group of OJT trainers and supervisors prepared to conduct the OJT pilot test.

Conduct Site Orientations

During several sessions at the OJT supervisor and trainer workshop, participants discussed the status of their facility as an OJT site and set dates for site orientations. The OJT supervisor at the site conducted this orientation, which was made up of two parts: introduction of the new clinical method that would now be available at the site, and orientation to the OJT approach. Both JHPIEGO and ZNFPC felt it was crucial that to avoid misunderstandings regarding how a trainee would be spending his or her time, all staff at the site understand what would be taking place. Supervisors practiced giving these orientation sessions at the OJT supervisor and trainer workshop, and the trainers and participants gave them feedback.

After returning from this workshop, the OJT supervisors, with technical assistance from the ZNFPC, conducted the site orientations. The orientation involved all staff at an OJT site, and they had an opportunity to examine the training materials, review briefly the training schedule, and discuss how it might affect each of their roles in carrying out daily activities.

Conduct the OJT Pilot Test

The pilot test focused primarily on examining the feasibility of implementing structured OJT for clinical training. The test was conducted at 15 sites in Zimbabwe and covered a period of four months so that at least two trainees could be trained at each site. The structure of the pilot test allowed for dealing with issues that could affect training during the first trainee's learning period (such as logistics and scheduling) so that an accurate view of the feasibility of OJT could be compiled.

Visit OJT Sites

The ZNFPC monitoring activities were a key part of the pilot test. Monitoring technical assistance from the ZNFPC was multifocal. There were site visits made at the beginning of the pilot test, often concurrent with the site orientations to launch OJT. Communication (often by telephone) was maintained regularly during the pilot test, and at least two site visits were made, once during each trainee's training period. The ZNFPC, usually with a representative from JHPIEGO, visited the OJT training site, primarily to ensure that needed midcourse corrections could be made in the OJT implementation strategy if assumptions were not holding true. In fact, during these visits, we determined that trainees were closely paralleling the time estimates made for completing the OJT program (six weeks) through a variety of work-routine scheduling adaptations and that all logistics had been ensured.

Present Pilot Test Results

Synthesis of the results of the pilot test includes examining both the feasibility of implementation as well as identifying potential problem areas when scaling up to full implementation. In Zimbabwe during late 1997, these results were presented at a national forum of key decision makers in the field of reproductive health training (policymakers, program implementers, trainers, service delivery managers, donors, and implementing agencies). Key decision makers at the forum reviewed the pilot test experience, focusing on the effect of the OJT on the daily work routine (that is, service delivery), and recommended ways to expand the structured OJT approach into appropriate settings and topics for additional OJT packages.

The recommendations of the key stakeholders who attended the forum to review the results of the pilot test were then reviewed by senior managers within each agency to determine how the expansion of the existing OJT program could be effected. The process for agency approval includes determining the demand from the field sites and the appropriateness of the OJT strategy already defined for their agency.

In Zimbabwe, the national OJT coordinator has received numerous requests from other sites that have heard about this training approach and have asked to be designated as OJT sites. If the decision is made to continue this training program, these sites will be assessed for adequacy as OJT sites (by applying the same criteria used to select the pilot test sites), OJT staff will be selected, the OJT supervisor and trainer will be oriented and trained, and the site will be oriented to the approach and the clinical method, following the same implementation plan used in the pilot test.

Revise OJT Strategy and Materials

The purpose of the pilot test was to implement OJT in a small number of sites to ensure that it was a viable approach to training. Based on the results of the pilot test, revisions to both the strategy and the training materials were recommended. Fortunately, due to the time and effort invested in the design of the strategy and development of the materials, the necessary revisions were minimal.

In terms of the OJT strategy, there were two primary revisions. The first related to the way that OJT was implemented within each of the pilot sites. The approach as originally designed offered only one way for the trainee to move through the course. The course outline gave detailed steps outlining what the trainee and trainer should do at each step in the learning process. In reality, three variations on the OJT approach evolved during the pilot test. For example, the approach as designed was based on the assumption that trainees would be working within their own sites. In several sites, however, trainees traveled a short distance to a neighboring site to participate in the course. These trainees carried their materials back and forth and completed all the reading assignments and practice exercises at home. All skill aspects of the training course were completed at the pilot site. As a result, the OJT program descriptions will now include several implementation options.

The second revision to the basic strategy related to follow-up and monitoring once an OJT course has been implemented. It appears that two of the most critical elements in an OJT approach are the interaction between the trainer and trainee, and between the trainer and supervisor. To help improve these interactions, additional information will be added to the training package and to the workshops for the trainers and supervisors.

The revisions to the training materials included the following:
- **Revision of the trainee's instructions for use of the course outline.** Some trainees did not understand how to use the course outline. Although the trainer could explain it to them, it was felt that the instructions should be self-explanatory.

- **Revision of the practice exercises.** In light of the trainees' discussions with their trainers about the practice exercises, the trainers recommended several ways to improve the relevance of the exercises.
- **Correction of mistakes in the Reference Manual.** Even after several editions of the reference manual, minor errors were identified. This was viewed as a good sign that trainees really were reading the Reference Manual.

Implement the OJT Strategy

After a sound strategy has been developed, training materials have been revised, and support of the key players has been achieved, it is time to move ahead with full implementation. The implementation plan will likely include many of the steps presented in figure 1. The primary steps in the implementation plan include
- identifying training sites and staff
- training the trainers (and supervisors if applicable)
- establishing an implementation timeline
- monitoring the phased implementation of OJT
- evaluating the effectiveness of the OJT training course.

Monitoring and Evaluation

In testing a new type of training, there is a two-pronged approach to assessment of the effect. In the short term, as described briefly under the "present pilot test results" step of the model, the feasibility of implementing structured on-the-job clinical training within existing clinic settings in various organizational types (for example, MOH/CW, ZNFPC) was examined. The monitoring and evaluation strategy for this focused on a mixture of data-collection methods. Baseline data established the conditions at the work delivery site prior to the OJT pilot test. These data included documentation of existing caseloads and existing clinic stocks as well as the usual work routine at the site, and summaries of logbooks, stock records, and service statistics.

The monitoring activities (as described under "visit OJT sites") documented how the pilot-test implementation was proceeding. At each site, interviews of the OJT supervisor, trainer, and trainee (and other personnel, as available) and site visit notes from observations during the visit day documented attitudes toward the training process, perceived and actual changes in the work routine during the training period, and changes in client experience at the work site. Monitoring also included examination of the OJT Trainee Workbook and analysis of the trainee's progress to date through the dating of the completed activities (that is, comparing expected versus actual completion of a section) and review of the cases and experiences that support the structured OJT plan.

Key questions examined in the monitoring visits included the following:

- **Trainee progress:** How long does each trainee take to complete the OJT sequence?
- **Appropriateness of training topics and sequence:** How does the training sequence work? Are trainees having problems with a particular section, practice exercise, trainer-trainee practice sessions, and the like?
- **Implementation problems:** Are there problems with supplies, equipment, or other site issues that hinder effective OJT?
- **Service delivery:** What effect does OJT have on service delivery? What strategies have clinics used to minimize the disruptions?

Evaluation of the OJT pilot test experience focused on feasibility of implementation, answering the questions outlined above and using a variety of assessment tools. Information from the Trainee Workbook documented the length of the trainee's training period, the numbers of cases (by type) seen during the training period, and any problems arising that affected training. After the OJT supervisor's review, this information was submitted to the national OJT coordinator. The supervisor compiled the trainee's scores on the knowledge assessment and skills checklist and then submitted them to the national OJT coordinator.

The pilot test results were compiled through the middle of 1997. Analysis involves a synthesis of the quantitative data such as service statistics and date progression through the training outline, scores on knowledge assessments, and demonstrated competency on the skill checklist. This analysis is then supported with in-depth interview information, documenting both knowledge and skill transfer along with the success of implementing this training approach.

The longer term assessment, occurring three to six months after the pilot test, will evaluate the ability of structured OJT to produce service providers competent in the clinical skill offered in the training. This evaluation will compare and contrast clinicians trained in group-based (traditional) courses and those trained through the OJT mechanism to determine the advantages, disadvantages, and appropriate use of each training approach in Zimbabwe. The hypothesis is that there is no difference between the training approaches in producing competent clinicians.

Results

The implementation of the structured OJT approach has gone very well at 15 sites in Zimbabwe. Trainees are receiving training in a clinical skill needed for their work, and they value the training because it provided them an opportunity to receive training when they would likely never have been selected to attend a group-based training course. In addition to elaborating the ways in which the approach is being applied, we have identified the key elements that demonstrate its success and can lay to rest commonly asked questions about training that takes place at the job site.

During the pilot test we identified three different models of how OJT is being applied: true OJT, temporary OJT to train staff for other clinics, and site training for hospital rotation needs. These three models occur at different kinds of clinic sites and thus are an adaptive mechanism by the OJT trainers and trainees to use this innovative training approach.

- **True OJT:** The trainer and trainee are both at the same clinic and work together in training.
- **Temporary OJT to train staff for other clinics:** Staff travel from a nearby location to the clinic for the training period.
- **Site training for hospital rotation needs:** In some cases, trainees and trainers are working together in a location where the trainee is not assigned. The trainee has to free up time during the workday to leave the ward or clinic and go to a clinic area either to work with the trainer or work on self-study materials.

The several elements that demonstrate and support the success of implementing structured OJT in Zimbabwe can be categorized into two topics: the training approach of structured OJT and the effect of the training on the work site. As the elements are discussed under the relevant topic, the following issues and hypotheses, raised initially in the planning stages for the OJT pilot test, are discussed and dispelled:

- Trainees won't be able to find time to do the training during work hours.
- Trainees will be reluctant to do self-study (for example, reading, practice exercises).
- Trainees won't learn the theoretical knowledge first but will go straight to the practical skills work.

- Trainees won't be able to do the work at their own pace.
- OJT may have a negative effect on the work routine at the site.

The Training Approach: Structured OJT

A key element of the structured OJT program was the empowerment for many staff to be involved in training. Ownership of the training has been decentralized to the work site, and both the trainers and the trainees identify this training program as their own. Although trainee selection was more formalized at some sites (with use of an application process, for example), staff at the sites feel they are more likely to have an opportunity for receiving training with the OJT strategy than for being selected to attend a group-based training course.

The formal recognition of the training at the site by all staff meant a positive training climate and attention by all staff to ensure the success of the training. Key to this were the site orientations held just prior to the launch of the OJT pilot test.

The guided training plan for the structured OJT provided a focus for supervisors to do the training they consider part of their regular duties. Although the trainer in many instances directs the training, both trainer and trainee feel comfortable with this role and interaction.

There was a personal and professional commitment by the trainees to the training process. Trainees were able to do the work at their own pace and were motivated to progress through the training outline; they were finishing the training in about six weeks, the expected schedule. In spite of some people's skepticism that trainees would do self-study, by reading, practice exercises, and the like, the trainees were working systematically through the practice exercises, documented by the completion in the Trainee Workbook and supported in some cases by the OJT trainer's review and notes on the exercises themselves.

There was concern as well that trainees would not learn the theoretical knowledge but would go straight to the practical skills work. However, trainees did not go straight to the practical training, in part because of the value they attached to being able to receive training in the skill. The training was also a mechanism for them to interact with other staff, a situation that doesn't usually occur in their work. Interaction with the OJT trainer was, for some, "permission" for them to ask questions.

The institutional commitment to the OJT process was also demonstrated. Despite the expectation to the contrary, trainees were released during work hours to spend time reading and practicing. Most clinics configure their own work routines so training time was adjusted around the client flow and busy clinic times. This scheduling meant being able to take advantage of varying clinic hours—time available when few clients come (usually in the afternoon) so the trainee and trainer can work on practice exercises and with anatomic models, and then switching to the busy clinic times when more clients come, once the trainee is ready to work with clients.

Effect of the Training on the Work Site

The OJT taking place at each clinic has had a positive effect on clinic services and has caused a change in the service profile, disputing the expectation that OJT would have a negative effect on services because the training would take time away from the clients. At almost every site, staff felt that OJT has been a positive influence. The number of clinical procedures (the focus of the training) has increased. In some sites, word-of-mouth about the training making a new service available has meant more clients coming for this service. In addition, the trainees have added information about this new service to their initial interviews and so are able to inform new clients about an additional service. This practice within the work setting means that every client contact is an opportunity for the trainees to apply their new skills as they expand the range of services available at the clinic.

Conclusions and Recommendations

Structured OJT can be implemented in many settings. Many factors play a part in making an OJT program effective. Some of those that contributed to the success of the Zimbabwe OJT program include the following:
- development of the strategy paper
- adaptation of a group-based course
- recognition of the importance of consensus-building activities
- involvement of the end users of the program
- development of a comprehensive training package
- training of key personnel before the pilot test
- follow-up site visits.

The development of an organizational strategy paper forced JHPIEGO staff to wrestle with a number of design and philosophical issues before moving into development of materials and training of trainers. This internal consensus-building effort helped staff make key decisions before investing time and resources in other activities. Another factor was the decision to convert an existing, instructor-led course to OJT instead of developing a new course. This allowed staff to work with a proven training package and to take advantage of existing materials. Also, the trainers in Zimbabwe were already familiar with the group-based training package, thus it was easier to orient them to a converted package than to introduce a new training approach and new materials at the same time.

One of the main lessons learned related to the importance of consensus-building activities. Because OJT involves a number of job-site staff in the training process, securing the support of key stakeholders at all levels was a significant factor in the success of the program. Another important factor was the involvement of the end users in the design, development, and implementation of OJT. Once again, when inserting training into the workplace, it is important to involve both potential trainers and trainees in the development of the training approach and materials. The development of a comprehensive training package was also a significant factor that contributed to the effectiveness of the OJT program in Zimbabwe. Ensuring that those involved in OJT had complete reference materials, assessment instruments, and instructions on how to conduct training helped learning to occur as designed. Also critical to the program's success was the time and effort invested in training the trainers and supervisors before the pilot test. This helped to ensure that these key individuals understood their roles and responsibilities and were prepared to follow the guidelines in the training package. Finally, the follow-up site visits reinforced the importance of the new training approach and provided ZNFPC trainers an opportunity to observe, coach, and assist the new trainers.

The use of structured OJT is a relatively new concept in international training of health professionals. Can the lessons learned from this innovative OJT effort in Zimbabwe be applied to other training situations? Yes! It is obvious from the design and development process in figure 1 that these same steps could be applied to the implementation of structured OJT in almost any setting. Although the specific consensus-building activities would change, the importance of involving key stakeholders at various points along the way would not.

With the increasing use of electronic performance support systems, computer-based training, Internet-based training, and a myriad of other technology-assisted learning approaches, it is obvious that the shift from instructor-led training to self-paced, on-the-job training will continue. The approach used to implement structured OJT successfully in Zimbabwe can serve as a model for those interested in using structured on-the-job training in their organization.

Questions for Discussion

1. What factors led to the recognition of the need for a structured OJT course instead of a traditional instructor-led course?
2. Describe the importance of the consensus-building activities that paralleled the design and development activities.
3. What was the purpose of developing the organizational strategy paper focusing on OJT before developing the OJT materials?
4. Why was the development of the OJT-training package such a critical factor in the success of the OJT course?
5. This case took place in Zimbabwe. How could the approach used in this case be applied to organizations outside of international health?

The Authors

Rick Sullivan completed his Ph.D. in vocational-technical teacher education at the Ohio State University in 1982. Following this, he served as a professor in the Occupational and Technology Education Department at the University of Central Oklahoma, where he was responsible for the training and development degree program. Sullivan has developed training presentations and programs for numerous organizations including the Marine Spill Response Corporation, Exxon Research and Engineering Company, United States Postal Service, Exxon Company USA, and the International Ironworkers Union. He served as a training skills consultant for JHPIEGO before joining the corporation in 1994 as director of training, where he is responsible for overseeing the design and delivery of training activities for medical professionals in a number of countries. Sullivan has written several books and over 50 articles and other publications in a variety of professional journals. He has presented papers and presentations at many national conferences of organizations such as the American Society for Training & Development and the American Vocational Association. He can be reached at JHPIEGO Corporation, 1615 Thames Street, Baltimore, MD 21231-3447; phone: 410.614.3551; e-mail: rsullivan@jhpiego.org.

Sue Brechin completed her doctorate in public health (Dr.P.H.) at Tulane University in 1993, having finished her MPH there in 1983. She received her Bachelor of Science in nursing from the University of Rochester School of Nursing in 1973 and her family nurse practitioner certificate from the University of Miami School of Nursing in 1979. She has lived and worked in nine countries over the past 20 years, with experience ranging from clinical nursing and ambulatory care to rural-based health program activities, operations research, training materials development, and program management. Brechin has served as a consultant for a number of international development organizations. In 1995, she joined the JHPIEGO Corporation, where she is director of research and evaluation, responsible for monitoring and evaluation of the organization's programs in 30 countries and applied research activities to support country training program needs. She has published articles, made conference presentations, and written operations papers and evaluation reports on health aspects of international development work.

Maryjane Lacoste has worked since 1992 in the design, implementation, and management of reproductive health training programs. She currently serves in two key roles at JHPIEGO. As program development officer for the East and Southern Africa Office, she is responsible for all programming efforts in Zimbabwe, where she has played a key role in introducing on-the-job training. She also works on the development and implementation of evaluation tools for training. As a trainer, Lacoste facilitates clinical-training-skills courses both regionally for the West Africa Office and for specific countries in East and Southern Africa.

References

Jacobs, R., & Jones, M. *Structured on-the-Job Training.* San Francisco: Berrett-Koehler, 1995.

Levine, C. *Harnessing the Power of OJT Training: Getting It Right the First Time.* Paper presented at the American Society for Training and Development Technical and Skills Training Conference and Exposition, September 13–15, 1995.

Marsh, P., & Pigott, D. "Turning a New Page in OJT." *Technical and Skills Training, 3*(4): 13–16, 1992.

Martin, B. "A System for on-the-Job Training." *Technical and Skills Training, 2*(7): 2–28, 1991.

Mullaney, C., & Trask, L. "Show Them the Ropes." *Technical and Skills Training, 3*(7), 8–11, 1992.

Pacquin, D. "Skilled Trades Programs: Apprentice to Master." In L. Kelly (editor), *The ASTD Technical and Skills Training Handbook.* New York: McGraw Hill, 1995.

Reynolds A. "Individualized Instructional Approaches." In L. Kelly (editor), *The ASTD Technical and Skills Training Handbook.* New York: McGraw Hill, 1995.

Rothwell, W., & Kazanas, H. *Improving on-the-Job Training: How to Establish and Operate a Comprehensive OJT Program.* San Francisco: Jossey-Bass, 1994.

Sullivan, R., Magarick, R., Bergthold, G., Blouse, A., & McIntosh, N. *Clinical Training Skills for Reproductive Health Professionals.* Baltimore: JHPIEGO, 1995.

Swanson, R., & Torraco, R. *The History of Technical Training.* In L. Kelly (editor), *The ASTD Technical and Skills Training Handbook.* New York: McGraw Hill, 1995.

Smith, T. "On-the-Job Training Approach: Kenya Country Program." Unpublished paper, Baltimore: JHPIEGO, 1995.

Training Capacity Building
for Poor Areas

A United Nations Development Programme Project
in China

Jiping Zhang and Peter Sun

This case is unique in that it describes a training-capacity-building project for a subsector of a country. The activities were closely connected with the existing system in terms of personnel and operation. Both the design and implementation made the human resource development efforts highly relevant to the country's poverty-reduction strategy and goal. The training capacity for poor areas in China has been effective and sustainable.

Background

China has been receiving much international economic aid and technical assistance in its efforts toward economic reform and development. Poverty reduction has been one of the priority areas to receive international support, especially from the United Nations, the World Bank, and non-government organizations (NGOs). (See the list of abbreviations in figure 1.) Financial and technical assistance were mainly used for improving the infrastructure and for developing agriculture, township and village enterprises (TVEs), and human resources.

Among the various efforts toward poverty reduction, human resource development (HRD) in the poor areas was the most important. These HRD efforts included compulsory education for children, adult literacy programs, occupational and technical education and training programs, training programs for government officials and TVE managers, and various public health programs. One official of the United Nations Development Programme (UNDP) Resident Mission in Beijing,

This case was prepared to serve as a basis for discussion rather than to illustrate either effective or ineffective administrative and management practices.

Figure 1. Abbreviations.

8–7 Plan—National Seven-Year Plan for Poverty Reduction (1994–2000)

CICETE—China International Center for Economic and Technical Exchange

DTCP—UNDP Asia and Pacific Programme for Development Training and Communication Planning

EDI—Economic Development Institute of the World Bank

HRD—human resource development

IBRD—International Bank for Reconstruction and Development (the World Bank)

IDA—International Development Association

MOCO—Ministry of Central Organization

MOF—Ministry of Finance

MOFTEC—Ministry of Foreign Trade and Economic Cooperation

NGO—nongovernment organization

NTC—National Training Center

PADO—Poor Area Development Office

PTCs—Provincial Training Centers

SDR—special drawing right

TOT—training of trainers

TVEs—township and village enterprises

UNDP—United Nations Development Programme

---

who was in charge of the education and public health programs said, "Poverty reduction is one of our top priorities. We believe that the most sustainable effort in poverty reduction is to educate and train people in poor areas. So we are very supportive of education and training projects in poor areas."

The UNDP programs normally took the form of a grant and functioned as seed and model project funds to experiment and demonstrate a developmental paradigm. Local capacity building and sustainable development were the emphases of most UNDP programs. Without exception, the UNDP poverty-alleviation programs and projects in China had a strong exploratory and instructive nature. Project design and organization purposely combined international experience and practice in poverty alleviation with the local conditions in China and also combined training activities for officials, managers, and peasants with the selection, design, and implementation of the economic development projects.

In December 1990, representatives of the Chinese Government and UNDP jointly signed the project document, *Capacity Building for*

Training Managers of Economic Development in Poor Areas (known as the UNDP Training Capacity Project or simply UNDP Project). The project implementation agency was the State Council Leading Group for Poverty Reduction. The China International Center for Economic and Technical Exchange (CICETE) of the Ministry of Foreign Trade and Economic Cooperation (MOFTEC) served as the executing agency on behalf of the Chinese government. The UNDP financing totaled US$2,473,500, and the input of the Chinese government amounted to RMB 14,773,000 Yuan (in cash and kind). As cooperating agencies, the Economic Development Institute (EDI) of the World Bank and the UNDP Asia and Pacific Programme for Development Training and Communication Planning (DTCP) provided international consultants for this project.

The project objectives were to set up the National Training Center and three regional subcenters in Nanning (Guangxi Zhuang Autonomous), Chengdu (Sichuan Province), and Lanzhou (Gansu Province), and to build capacity to provide training for county and township officials in poor areas on project appraisal and management, and for enterprise managers on medium and small-enterprise management. The project anticipated that more and better training would improve the economic efficiency of current poverty-alleviation projects, absorb more funds from sources both domestic and abroad for development in poor areas, and increase the investment of new projects.

This case study describes the joint effort (from 1991 to 1996) of the Chinese government, the UNDP, and other involved international organizations for human resource development in poor areas. The HRD effort was directly serving the organization's goal—reducing poverty incidence through economic development.

Poverty and Poverty-Reduction Efforts in China

The reduction of absolute poverty was significant among China's widely recognized economic achievements since the adoption of the policy of rural economic development and the transformation from a planned economy to market economy beginning in 1978. (In 1985, the Chinese government announced the official poverty line as counties in which the rural average per capita income was lower than 150 Yuan, and later, in 1994, it announced that it put the line at counties in which the rural average per capita income was lower than 500 Yuan in 1990.) It is estimated that from 1979 to the middle of the 1980s, some 170 million Chinese escaped absolute poverty, and the percentage of people in absolute poverty in the total population declined from about one third to less than 10 percent (World Bank Group Study, 1992). The form of poverty also changed over this period, from large numbers of poor spread widely across the countryside to pockets of poverty in remote resource-deficient areas. The government's official estimation of the number of absolute poor was about 80 million during the early 1990s, which was less than 7 percent of the total population. The majority of the poor population lived in 592 poor counties designated by the State Council, the highest ranking government organization. Most of these poor counties were located in the southwest and northwest parts of the country and had the following common causes for poverty: remoteness, poor accessibility, ecological imbalances, poor natural conditions, slow economic development, backward educational and health facilities, lack of drinking water, and extreme difficulty in production and living conditions.

The Chinese government had a strong commitment to poverty reduction. Different ministries had different poverty-reduction responsibilities and projects. For example, the Ministry of Civil Affairs provided disaster relief and income maintenance support and coordinated the distribution of relief grain. The State Planning Commission administered a Food-for-Work Program. In exchange for grain from the government, poor peasants provided labor for building roads, transport, dikes, drinking water systems, irrigation works, and other capital construction in poor areas. The State Education Commission and the Ministry of Public Health were responsible for some special programs to improve the education and health status of the poor.

In the 1980s, the Chinese government enforced special policies and measures to promote economic development in the poor areas. These policies and measures included, mainly,
1. the establishment of a national leading and coordinating organization for economic development in the poverty-stricken areas.
2. the provision of 4-5 billion RMB Yuan of special funds annually to help poor areas improve the infrastructure and basic living conditions and develop agriculture, animal husbandry, and agro-based processing.
3. the adoption and implementation of an economic-development-oriented poverty-alleviation policy in place of the traditional relief-oriented policy.
4. the improvement of the management of state funding, which was provided on a project basis, by strengthening project appraisal, implementation, and management.

5. the promotion and support of mutual beneficial cooperation be-tween poor areas (most in inland northwestern and southwestern provinces) and more developed eastern regions and coastal provinces.

6. the encouragement of various government organizations—min-istries, universities, and research institutes—to establish linkages with the poor areas to help both in economic development and human resource development.

From 1985 to 1990, however, the incidence of rural absolute pover-ty did not decline significantly. Several macroeconomic reasons, such as high inflation, increased rural unemployment rate, and fiscal de-centralization, which increased the burden of poor area governments, offset the efforts of poverty relief (Agriculture Operations Division, 1995). At the microlevel, major impediments to further progress in poverty alleviation and economic development included poor pro-ject selection and management, insufficient level of education and technical skills of most officials in counties, towns, and villages in poor areas, and the lack of training of both the officials and poor peasants.

The Leading Group for Poverty Reduction in Poor Areas and Its Office

As one important institutional measure to promote economic de-velopment in poor areas, the State Council set up the Leading Group for Poverty Reduction in Poor Areas (the Leading Group) in 1986. The Leading Group was the supreme leading and coordinating agency for nationwide poverty-alleviation activities. It was a special min-istry-level government organization directly affiliated with the State Council to provide leadership and coordination across ministries.

The Poor Area Development Office (PADO) was the executive agency of the Leading Group. The Leading Group and the PADO were the principal advocates of China's rural poverty-reduction program and coordinators of annual fund allocation. Following the central mod-el, provinces and autonomous regions, prefectures, municipalities, and counties where most poor populations lived, all established Leading Groups and PADOs. The functions of those PADOs in various administra-tive levels included implementing the central government policies, receiving higher level cadres (in China *cadres* are officials or managers who work for the government), allocating poverty-alleviation funds, and doing various work relating to local economic development and poverty reduction, including training.

Each year, the State Council allocated a large amount of funds for production development in order to increase peasants' income and employment opportunities in poor and remote areas and in regions with dense minority populations. Both the domestic and international resources for poverty alleviation were allocated through various projects. It was essential to train the county and township levels of officials in the knowledge and skills of identifying, preparing, evaluating, and implementing economic development projects as well as in managing township enterprises. Five percent of the development fund for poor areas, which amounted to about 50 million RMB Yuan (about US$6 million) per year, was mandated to be used in various kinds of cadre training. Therefore, the building up of the capacity for training managers of economic development in poor areas became critical to the overall government poverty-alleviation strategy.

The National Training Center and the Provincial Training Centers

The National Training Center for Cadre of Poor Areas (NTC) was one of the three organizations under the leadership of the Leading Group and the National PADO. The NTC was established in 1990 to be responsible for providing guidance and coordination of training activities to cadres in the poor areas. In the beginning, it had fewer than 10 officials and supporting staff to implement several mandated training events per year at the national level, or across provinces. Two major forms of cadre training were a conference and study tour. The former could hardly be called training because it provided no knowledge or skills training.

Before the UNDP Training Capacity Project, only a few provinces had established training centers for cadres in poor areas. In late 1990, the cadre training centers of the Guangxi Zhuang Autonomous and the Sichuan Province were established in Nanning and Chengdu, respectively. The cadre training center of Gansu Province was established in Lanzhou in 1991. Similar to the NTC, at the early stage, all these provincial training centers (PTCs) had only an office and a few staff members with an adjunct director, who held another full-time position in the provincial Leading Group or PADO. The PTCs organized training activities by getting participants and providing logistic support. The training content was left to the instructor who normally came from a university.

At both the national and provincial levels, real training capacity building was badly needed to bring the NTC and the PTCs into full functionality.

Goals of the UNDP Training Capacity Project

The UNDP Training Capacity Project brought the necessary financial resources and technical assistance to China's poverty-reduction efforts in a very timely manner. The immediate objectives and expected outcomes of the UNDP Project were as follows:

1. to establish and enhance the capacity of the National Training Center and the three regional subcenters in Nanning, Chengdu, and Lanzhou

2. to develop, organize, and manage training programs for county and township officials and enterprise managers in poor areas

3. to develop a model training program for county and township officials and for enterprise managers in poor areas, respectively

4. to disseminate to other training institutions for use in training activities on the project cycle the training materials that the National Training Center and the subcenters produced.

The deputy director of the National PADO served as the project director, and the director of the NTC served as the project deputy director. The NTC functioned as the project office to handle the daily work of the UNDP Training Capacity Project.

Exploratory and Preparation Stage of the UNDP Project

The UNDP Project was the first UNDP-financed, large-scale training-capacity-building project for a specific sector in China. The Economic Development Institute (EDI) of the World Bank had conducted a lot of training seminars in China since that country reassumed its membership in the bank in 1980. Although EDI emphasized institutional building of its partner institutions (normally colleges and universities), a comprehensive training-capacity-building program across provinces and organizations was still a new experience. The poverty-reduction sector itself was lacking experience in training, not to mention experience in training-capacity building. So, the first one and a half years of the implementation of the project was an exploratory and preparation stage, which was longer than the expected schedule.

The preparatory activities to establishing external working relationships and conditions included drafting the following:

1. the report to the Ministry of Finance to apply for the government matching fund, which was agreed to in principle when the project document was signed

2. the report to CICETE to establish a working relationship and a general implementation plan and management procedures

3. the report to the Leading Group of the State Council for the government's formal approval and a budget to expand the establishment of the NTC and the three subcenters of the UNDP Project
4. the bid document for subcontractors.

There was a lot of internal preparation in organization setup, personnel recruitment, and understanding of the mission and goals of the project. The UNDP project start-up conference took place in Guangxi Zhuang Autonomous from April 4 to 7, 1991. Directors and staff from the participatory organizations studied the project document to reach a common understanding.

Along with the progress that each training center made in recruiting new staff and teachers as well as local advisers and adjunct teachers, the NTC organized four working seminars and two field-investigation activities in poor areas to make the project participants understand the poverty situation and specific training needs of cadres in poor areas. Seminar participants also discussed the training material development plans. As an output of the field-investigation activities, more than 50 cases about poverty reduction were developed and published later in three casebooks titled *Enlightenment Gained from Development Cases.*

In November 1991, the EDI and the DTCP were finalized as cooperating agencies to provide consulting services. Consultants from EDI visited the four training centers and started to organize the first comprehensive course for training of trainers (TOT).

From April 27 to July 27, 1992 in Shenzhen, 36 participants attended the three-month TOT. These participants were full-time teachers who worked at the NTC and three subcenters, and adjunct teachers who worked full-time in other organizations relevant to agriculture, rural development, or management. Professors from the Chinese University of Hong Kong and consultants from the World Bank and DTCP taught economics, project management, enterprise management courses, case method, and basics of adult education. The Shenzhen course was the first one of a series of TOT activities of the UNDP Project. Training of trainers was the core human resource development effort of this human resource development project. Most of the participants of the Shenzhen TOT course received further training later and became key managerial and teaching staff of each training center.

Participants at the fifth working seminar, which was held at the Beijing Sanyuan Hotel on October 8-15, 1992, decided to develop three sets of training materials on project appraisal and management, TVE management, and rural economic development. They also selected the task force, including chief editors and working staff. The project could now move to its key activities and work on its major output.

Targeted Goals and Key Issues

To achieve the objectives, implement the activities, and obtain the output described in the project document, it would be necessary to develop an operational work plan that could be modified according to the changing environment. During the exploratory and preparatory stages, the general goal of establishing the training capacity for the poor areas became clearer and more concrete to the management of the project. Finally, it was summarized visually and briefly as six *Yi*s ("a" or "one" in Chinese):

- a training base
- a teaching task force
- a set of training materials
- a curriculum for the project and enterprise management training programs
- a model for managing training activities
- one thousand officials to be trained.

The first five *Yi*s constituted the training capacity. The last *Yi* was to test, take shape, and drill the training capacity through real training tasks. The NTC developed a detailed work plan and schedule to specify a series of activities with expected output under each subgoal. The EDI consultants used the illustration in figure 2 to get consensus on project goals and to coordinate major activities of the UNDP project.

Build the Training Base

The physical infrastructure of the training centers included housing (office space, training rooms, participants' dormitory, and living quarters for full-time staff and teachers) and training equipment. The housing construction was the responsibility of the provincial government as part of the local input of the matching fund of the UNDP project. At the beginning, each training center operated in rental space. Later the three subcenters all received government funding to build their own facilities. The purchase of imported training equipment, such as copy machines, projectors, fax machines, computers, audiovisual equipment, and two vehicles for each training center, was made possible from UNDP's budget and was tax free.

The infrastructure of human resource development of the training base also expanded because of the UNDP Project. PADOs applied to provincial governments for permission to hire more staff and teach-

Figure 2. Major activities of the UNDP Training Capacity Project.

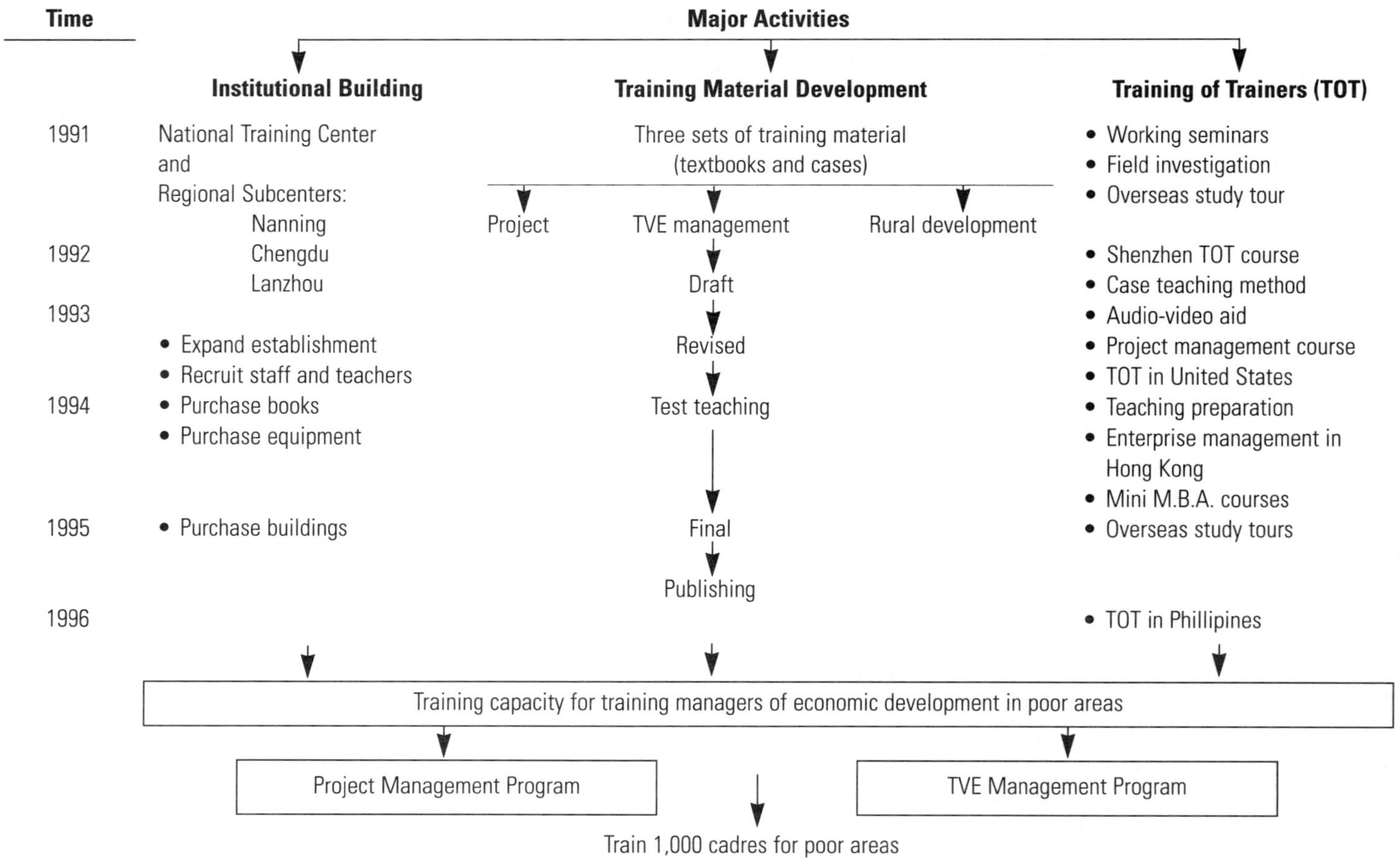

ers, and their salaries and positions counted as matching funds of the project. The provincial government approved the expansion, and included it in its budget.

The UNDP Project was the catalyst for the institutional building of the training centers. It gave the training centers priority in applying for government resources mentioned above. It also provided scarce foreign currency to purchase training equipment, obtain foreign consultants, and pay for overseas training.

Even though the training centers had many things in common, each had its own model to fit into its institutional environment, especially the relationship with the provincial poverty-reduction system. The Nanning Subcenter was set up as a division within the PADO of the Guangxi Zhuang Autonomous, and the vice chairman of the autonomous region who was in charge of agriculture was the honorary director of the training center. This arrangement showed that the top administration in this province paid some special attention to the UNDP Training Capacity Project. The new staff and teachers were recruited under the name and the establishment of the Nanning Subcenter. The subcenter was under the management of the director of the PADO and was operated the same way as other government units. All staff and teachers did the routing work of the PADO office. The advantage of the Guangxi model was that the staff and teachers could get the same treatment and benefits as other officials who worked for the government because the PADO was responsible for their work assignment, promotions, and employee benefits. In China, the most important employee benefit was to get low-rent living quarters from the working unit.

The Chengdu Subcenter was set up relatively independently of the PADO of Sichuan Province. It was located in a different building, its staff and teachers did not do routing work for the PADO, and it operated more like a school than a government unit. However, employee benefits and career development were uncertain. After several years in operation, the Chengdu Subcenter finally changed to the Guangxi model and became a part of the provincial PADO.

Recruit, Train, and Drill the Teaching Task Force

The normal practice of an organization's training unit was to use university professors as adjunct teachers or temporary outside instructors as the major teaching force. A few full-time teachers in the training center organized and managed training activities as training officers.

In China, there were no trainers who worked as independent consultants. Off-campus teaching provided a second income for many professors. With the limited training budget of the poverty-reduction system, however, it would not be possible to hire professors on a regular basis to prepare and deliver the training needed in the poor areas. To satisfy the capacity requirements of the UNDP Project, the four centers could not rely on outside instructors but had to have an adequate number of qualified teachers with professional knowledge of project management or enterprise management. The strategy for establishing a teaching task force was to rely mainly on full-time teachers at the centers who would be capable of teaching and management, and to complement them with adjunct teachers who could provide teaching according to the needs of cadres in poor areas.

The strategy for choosing full-time teachers was to target young graduate students who had the potential to teach and manage training. For adjunct instructors, the focus was on individuals who wanted a long-term working relationship. The typical adjunct teachers were government officials, research fellows, and university professors who had a close working relationship with the poverty-reduction system. The UNDP Project gave both the full-time and adjunct teachers training opportunities locally and overseas.

The training of trainers was organized to match work assignments closely to training material development and teaching. On the basis of the organization's need, personal background, and preference, the full-time and adjunct teachers in the four training centers were assigned to either a project management or enterprise management team. Each team took training courses at a domestic university on subject matter knowledge, received training on general knowledge and skills of instruction and training management, had workshop and individual supervision on training material development and teaching notes preparation, and got supervision and feedback on their test teaching.

Develop Training Material Suitable for Training in Poor Areas

Training typically used materials from domestic and overseas publications, but these publications could not reflect the characteristics of project management in China's poor areas in terms of sources of funds, ownership, project contents, and management procedures. University textbooks on enterprise management and economic development were not easily applicable to practice and were not suitable to the education and professional background of officials in poor areas. The project had tried to invite university professors to develop textbooks for use in poor areas, but their outlines and sample chapters were not very different from those they wrote for university students.

Finally, the NTC made a tough decision that the teachers of the four training centers would compile the training materials with the help and supervision of local and international advisers. Such an adjustment increased the project activities significantly and added to the staff's heavy workload. Internal teachers compiled two textbooks and one work manual for project management and seven textbooks for the TVE management. In addition, outside economists and technical specialists edited and wrote a series of books on rural economic development, covering such subjects as poverty and development, community institutional building in rural China, rural community development plans, management and development of small drainage areas, rural cooperative economy and management, rural energy, and establishment of land systems in rural China.

Special features of these training materials were an integration of theory with practice, an accurate depiction of the situation in poor areas, and an emphasis on scientific work procedure and operationalization. They introduced the World Bank concept, methodology and experience of project cycle management, and the new concepts and practices of enterprise management in easy-to-understand writing. It was the first time the poverty-reduction system had such a quantity of training material of such high quality.

Design a Curriculum for the Two Model Training Programs

After the training materials were compiled, a two-week model training program, which was expandable to a longer duration for training cadres in poor areas, was designed, first on project management and later on TVE management. In 1994, the World Bank's first poverty-reduction loan project in southwest China (Guangxi, Guizhou, and Yunnan Provinces) was under preparation. The provincial- and county-level cadres who were working in the poverty-reduction system badly needed an understanding of the World Bank project cycle, basic knowledge about the feasibility study, and a financial and economic analysis of the project. To satisfy these real and urgent training needs, the project management course focused on the identification, preparation, and feasibility study of the investment project. The enterprise management course gave emphasis to marketing, production, finance, and organizational development.

The curriculum of the two model training programs included a description of target trainees, an analysis of training needs, a statement of training objectives, major content on subject matter knowledge, introduction of relevant teaching methods, a list of textbooks and other reading materials, and course schedule with instructors' names. The curriculum was revised and improved according to participants' feedback during test teaching. Together with the Teacher's Manual containing much more detailed teaching notes and visual aids completed during the test teaching courses, the curriculum offered a complete model design and instructional file for the project management and the TVE management training programs.

Teachers of the four training centers participated in the whole process under the close supervision of international and domestic consultants. Through preparing and delivering real training sessions, they learned how to design a quality training course and prepare the teaching. They could adapt the two basic models to the changing needs in their own province.

Establish a Model for Training Management

Before the UNDP Training Project, the training for cadres in poor areas consisted mainly of conferences and study tours. Some short courses were organized to have the outside instructors lecture on a given title or theme on the basis of their knowledge and skills. There were no formal management procedures and requirements.

The EDI consultants brought to the project training management experience in such areas as needs assessment, promotion, recruitment, budgeting, logistics, and evaluation. They also introduced various teaching methods suitable to adult learners, especially the case teaching method. The DTCP consultants brought into this project various participatory teaching methods and preparation and use of visual aids for teaching.

The following practices were implemented in each training course conducted in the UNDP Project:

1. *Course director and course manager.* Each course director was responsible for the instruction of the course, and the course manager was in charge of the logistic service and management of participants. The course director normally came from the NTC if the course participants came from different provinces, and the course manager normally came from the local host unit (provincial training center or PADO).

2. *Course document.* Each written course design stated the training needs and course objectives as well as the detailed design of content and activities.

3. *Participants' organization.* Each course had participants' groups and group heads as well as a class monitor who represented the participants in giving suggestions and feedback to the course director.

4. *Course evaluation.* Each course used EDI evaluation forms to get participants' comments and feedback on the training. The evaluation results were announced to the class at the end of the training course.

All managerial procedures were written down, and together with various forms, were compiled as the *Training Manual for Training Officers in Poor Areas.* This training management model was demonstrated in various provinces during the test teaching and training period. These formal and practical management procedures told the inexperienced training officers how to do their jobs, and enhanced their effectiveness and efficiency. As a result, the total quality of the training activity was improved and ensured.

Train 1,000 Officials and Managers in Test Teaching and Training

To fulfill the task of training 1,000 cadres in poor areas, six test teaching and 11 training courses were held in more than 10 provinces. Three test-teaching courses were organized for the project management and the TVE management, respectively, right after the relevant training textbooks were ready.

In test-teaching courses, every member of the team (project management or TVE management) was required to participate in the whole two-week course, even if each teacher only taught one module (one or two days). Because the teachers lived and worked in different provinces, the international consultant or the local adviser, or both, who were subject matter experts and experienced instructors, jointly conducted a one day preworkshop. At the workshop, teachers reported to the team on their preparation and teaching plan, and their peers and the experts gave them suggestions. The coordination and integration gained from the preworkshop helped teachers understand better their teaching objectives and the relationship with the whole course. They also got to see the course design and how others were going to teach.

During the course, the team sat in the back of the classroom to observe their colleagues' teaching. Each team member used an evaluation form adapted from DTCP to evaluate the instruction from various aspects—objective statement, content selection, teaching method, participation, visual aid, and delivery skills. Both the written evaluation form and the discussion from peers and experts helped in improving the teaching quality.

Each teacher prepared teaching notes of his or her module in a standard format and incorporated necessary revisions into them. After three test-teaching sessions, a teacher's manual for the training course was compiled. With the Teacher's Manual, each teacher in the team could share the material and teaching experience and adopt the teaching content of other modules. The manual was also a measure to control the teaching quality.

Only about one-third of the teachers in the team taught in each training course following the test teaching. No fee was paid for their instruction because all the teachers were considered to be internal (adjunct teachers received free training from the UNDP Training Project). The travel costs and working time were much less than in the test teaching.

The training material, training content and design, participatory teaching method, and training management model were also disseminated in provinces that were not part of the project, such as Shanxi, Hunan, Inner-Mongolia, Yunnan, Xinjiang, and Hebei. In Shanxi Province, the director of the training center was so impressed with the quality of the training that she sent her three young teachers to participate in the UNDP Project activities, thereby enhancing the training ability at her center.

Accomplishments

After about six years of continuous effort (1991–1996), the project achieved several major accomplishments and started to make important contributions to the goal of the poverty-reduction sector—poverty reduction through economic development.

Established Training Capacity for Economic Development in Poor Areas

With the following elements of the project in place, the training capacity was in shape and started to function effectively:
- institutional setup and building of the National Training Center and three subcenters
- the qualified teachers who were specialized in poverty-alleviation training
- the two most needed training courses and relevant training material
- a model to manage training activities.

Putting the hardware and software together, the NTC had gradually built up its capacity for coordinating and guiding the subcenters to provide training for county and township officials and enterprise managers. In the meantime, the NTC had attained the ability to implement and manage foreign assistant training projects. Through project implementation, the three subcenters in Nanning, Chengdu, and Lanzhou gained the capacity to organize, manage, and adapt model training programs of project management and TVE management.

Developed Human Resources for the Poverty-Reduction Sector and Poor Areas

The most important contribution of the UNDP Project was the human resources it developed for the poverty-reduction sector and poor areas. The immediate beneficiaries were staff and teachers at the NTC and three subcenters and relevant senior officials who worked closely with this project.

In late 1996, there were 22 qualified teachers (two-thirds of them were key instructors in training courses) and 50 adjunct teachers (about a quarter of them were very active in training). The trained teachers had a good understanding of conditions in poor areas and were familiar with poverty-alleviation theories and policies. Equipped with professional knowledge and skill in relevant subject matter, they were able to teach in project management and enterprise management by using the model training programs and teaching materials that the UNDP project developed. The intensive teaching tasks made them experienced instructors in a short period of time.

Because these teachers were also government officials of the PADO, they participated in various poverty-reduction activities, especially the World Bank poverty-reduction loan project in their province. Twelve teachers trained in the UNDP project got promoted to a deputy division chief position or even higher in PADO during 1995–96. The teachers of Nanning and Chengdu Training Centers became key professionals of the World Bank projects in Guangxi and Sichuan Provinces. Two were promoted to vice director of the World Bank Loan Project Office and became local consultants. The practical working experience made them better training instructors.

The overseas training held in the United States and Philippines enhanced the teachers' English-language ability and computer proficiency. Many of them became versatile cadre of the poverty-reduction sector. More than 20 senior officials and about half of the teachers participated in six overseas study tours to gain experience in rural development and poverty reduction in other developing countries.

The teaching task force trained by the UNDP project had itself trained about 1,200 PADO officials and TVE managers who were in charge of economic development and TVEs in poor areas. The participants in Guangxi and Sichuan applied what they learned in the training course directly to their World Bank loan project preparation. When the first test teaching was held in Nanning in March 1994, the county magistrate of one of the World Bank loan project-covered counties brought the 18 cadres from his office to the training. He said, "You delivered the training to us just in time!" Guangxi Autonomous, which took advantage of the training, was always ahead of the other two provinces in the World Bank's Southwest Poverty Reduction loan project.

Although positive results from the training capacity building and the actual training from the UNDP Project were obvious, it was difficult to calculate the direct and indirect benefits on economic development in poor areas due to the officials' and managers' enhanced knowledge and skills. As time went on, the benefits would become clearer.

One benefit became evident when the government introduced a program in 1994. In recognizing the difficulties and problems confronting economic development in the poor areas and the new challenges that emerged as a result of the establishment of the socialist market economy, the Chinese government prepared a national poverty-reduction plan. It was decided that during the seven years from 1994 to 2000, human, material, and financial resources would be concentrated and used in a planned way to address the basic needs of the remaining 80 million poor population. This plan was known as the 8-7 Plan.

Two emphases of the 8-7 Plan were to make the benefit reach to the poor households and to develop the human resources in the poor areas. The formulation and implementation of the 8-7 plan reinforced the importance and justification of the UNDP Training Capacity Project.

Gained Experience of Implementing Comprehensive Training Capacity Building Program

The experience of training capacity building is valuable not only to the poverty-reduction sector but also to other sectors and organizations. The experience, including lessons and learning, of setting up the hardware and software of a training base, the selection and training of teachers, the development of training materials, the design, delivery, and management of training activities, were all real and concrete. People could see the physical and visible output, talk to officials and teachers, and read all the documents that recorded the practice and procedures.

More provinces had been established or were preparing to set up the provincial or county training centers, or both, for cadres in poor areas. With the experiences of Nanning, Chengdu, and Lanzhou before them, other provinces' jobs would be easier. Other ministries with similar projects came to the NTC to ask what was done and how the UNDP Project was implemented.

Improved the Investment Environment of Poor Areas in China

The poor areas were not only poor in money and natural resources but also in human resources. To improve the investment environment and draw more funds, it was critical that they enhance their institutions and people. The UNDP Project built valuable assets for the Chinese poverty-reduction sector. The human resources developed had become an important component of the investment environment of poor areas. As mentioned above, the UNDP Training Capacity Project prepared quality economic development officials for the World Bank poverty-reduction loan projects. The following projects ensued:

- The World Bank approved special drawing right (SDR) 128.6 million ($200 million equivalent) International Development Association credit, and a US$47.5 million equivalent International Bank for Reconstruction and Development loan to the Southwest Poverty Reduction Project in 1995. (Note that SDR, which means special drawing right and was first issued by the International Monetary Fund in 1970, is a special measure of a nation's reserve assets in the international monetary system.) The beneficiaries were 35 poor counties consisting of 290 townships and 1,798 administrative villages in Guangxi, Guizhou, and Yunnan Provinces.
- The Qinba Mountains Poverty Reduction Project was approved in 1997 with IDA credit of US$150 million (equivalent), and an IBRD loan of US$30 million. The beneficiaries were 26 of the poorest counties in Western China, consisting of about 2.6 million upland smallholders. The World Bank credit and loan would finance about 50 percent of the estimated project cost. Counterpart funding from the central, provincial, municipal, prefectural, and county governments and from beneficiaries would provide the other half of project costs.
- After a senior UN consultant visited Chengdu Subcenter in 1996, another UNDP poverty reduction project—Sichuan Yilong County Small Credit Project—designated it as a local consulting firm. The UN consultant was very impressed by the vision and knowledge of the Sichuan PADO director and the quality of the teachers he met.
- Since 1995, the National Training Center has become the managing institution of the International Environment and Develop-

ment Training Program financed by the Rockefeller Foundation. In 1996, the NTC undertook the task to design, organize, and implement the government's training plan called *1996–2000 Training Plan for Cadre in Poor Areas,* which was formulated and approved by the Ministry of Central Organization (MOCO), Ministry of Finance (MOF), and the Leading Group of the State Council. This was an aggressive plan of training 3,000 county-level officials and 3,000 young cadres from the 592 state-designated poor counties in a five-year period.

Evaluation Strategy of the UNDP Project

With completion of major activities of the UNDP Project, the evaluation and summary report began in the middle of 1996. The internal evaluation was divided into two steps. The first step was to examine the output of the project against the project document requirement. The quality evaluation focused on the two training curricula developed and taught on project management and TVE management, as well as the training materials developed and used in training. The second step was to evaluate the project's relevancy, effectiveness, and sustainability.

Evaluation of Project Output

The project output exceeded the tasks stipulated in the project document in terms of quantity and quality. It built the capacity of training managers of economic development in poor areas and fulfilled the objectives of the project. The evaluation of the two model training programs included evaluation forms that participants completed after their training, follow-up surveys, interviews with the participants' supervisors, and assessments by domestic consultants who compared the UNDP training sessions with executive training sessions they had seen involved in other settings. EDI used a six-point-scale rating system (Oxenham, 1995) in which six means "exceeded expectation"; five, "fulfilled expectation"; four, "worthwhile"; three, "inadequate"; two, "much below expectations"; and one, "not at all." The average overall ranking of the 17 training courses delivered by the UNDP Project to cadres in poor areas was 4.9, with the highest rating 5.53 and the lowest rating 4.5. The project management and the TVE management courses were popular, and many nonproject provinces requested them. In December 1995, a TOT on project management for new teachers from more than 20 provinces was held in Shijiazhuang, Hebei Province. This was an extra activity of the UNDP Project, and the second wave of teachers for cadre training in poor areas received training from their "big brothers and sisters" under close supervision of EDI consultants.

The evaluation of the training materials included evaluation from participants, domestic experts such as university professors, and a publisher. Participants gave the training material an average rating of 4.90, which was a high score compared to those of other EDI/China training courses, which normally use a collection of translated papers as training material. The project management and TVE management textbooks were popular in the training courses, and participants bought extra copies for their colleagues. The reputable People's Publisher expressed strong interest in reprinting the TVE management textbooks. The series of 12 books on rural economic development had not been used in training yet. However, the important and popular topics it covered, and the "combining theory with practice" style made these books valuable in the forthcoming training for county-level senior cadres.

Evaluation of Relevancy, Effectiveness, and Sustainability

The evaluation of the project's relevancy focused on the following:

- location of the NTC and subcenters and their relationships with the poverty-reduction sector, especially the PADOs of various levels
- the direct and indirect impact of the HRD efforts of the UNDP Project to the cadre training and poverty-reduction investment projects
- the training models' and materials' relevance to the training needs of the poor areas
- the training content and methodology's relevance to the participants from poor areas.

The evaluation of effectiveness of the project looked at the following:

- the effectiveness of the training capacity established (Does it work? How well does it work?)
- the completely different quality level of the training for economic development in poor areas, which the UNDP Project brought
- the project's major contributions to the national and provincial poverty-alleviation efforts.

The conclusion was that the UNDP Project was a relevant and effective contribution to the poverty-reduction sector of China. The institutions built and the human resources developed have played a more and more important role in poverty-alleviation activities and will continue to do so. They helped improve not only the identification, preparation, and management of the ongoing investment projects and enterprises, but also the investment environment, and they drew more funds for the economic development of the poor areas.

The evaluation of sustainability of the project examined the training centers' internal motivation and ability to exist and develop as well as the external environment and demand for their existence and development. Many organizations that are established for and supported by a special project lose support and demand at the end of the project and die. They do not have sustainability. The National Training Center and the three subcenters continued after completion of the UNDP Project for the following reasons:

1. The four training centers had powerful backing from the central government and other levels of government, all of which were committed to training and to poverty reduction. The 8-7 Plan emphasized human resource development, especially the economic management training of officials and practical skill training to peasants. The *1996–2000 Training Plan for Cadres in Poor Areas* issued jointly by the MOCO, MOF, and the Leading Group made the training activity systematic and regular as a part of the government plan and budget. The NTC had been designated to lead the implementation of this plan.

2. The driving force behind the four training centers' continuous development was the sustained and huge training needs of the poor areas. The gap was huge between the 1,200 cadres whom the UNDP Project trained and the other training needs of the poor areas. To make effective use of the central government's training budget of 50 million Yuan per year, as well as the local government input, there was a lot of work that the training centers could do.

3. Continuous participation of international agencies in China's poverty alleviation was another important backing force to the newly established training capacity.

4. The four training centers were competitive in the training market because of the quality teaching and management they could offer.

5. Key teachers were getting promoted, the employee benefits were ensured by the PADOs, so the personnel was stable, and the morale was high.

The sustainability indicated that the training capacity established had gotten into a positive cycle. Any additional investment would achieve higher effectiveness and efficiency. The UNDP Resident Mission in Beijing and CICETE had responded positively to the proposal from the NTC for another project focusing on training capacity building that would reach households in poor areas.

Three major weaknesses and limitations of this project were as follows:

1. The three subcenters were supposed to serve as regional training centers and disseminate training to neighboring provinces. However, they could only function as provincial centers, limited by the personnel and budgeting systems in China. Therefore, the NTC bore the responsibility to organize, coordinate, and guide training activities across provinces.

2. The amount of teachers trained was not adequate. If more teachers had recruited and received training in the early stages of the project, resources would have been utilized to train more qualified young teachers.

3. The training materials and model training programs so developed were aimed at the demands of county officials and TVE managers. No consideration was given to meeting the demands below the township level, such as village cadres who were directly involved in poverty reduction in rural areas.

4. Because of the limited project objectives and funds, this project did not address the huge training demand of poor rural households in using poverty-reduction funds and applying agricultural technology.

Experiences and Lessons

Several important lessons were learned, and several important experiences were gained from this project.

Good Project Design and Document Preparation Lay Foundation for Successful Implementation

Good project design and document preparation were critical to implementation of this multiyear, multi-institution, and multimillion dollar project. Although revision of activities could be made later according to the changing environment and conditions, the general goals and basic strategy would not be changed. When the UNDP and Chinese government signed the project document, it became the basis by which the multi-institutional group understood, coordinated, and implemented the project for several years. *Capacity Building for Training Managers of Economic Development in Poor Areas* was a successful design for a project of this kind. It remained vital for almost a decade in China's very dynamic and rapidly changing environment because of the following strengths:

1. It captured the priority of priorities, the essence of key issues— build training capacity to develop human resources for economic development in poor areas in order to help achieve the government poverty reduction goals.

2. It diagnosed and prioritized accurately the training needs for training managers of economic development in poor areas—project management training for government officials in the poverty-reduction sector, and TVE management training for TVE managers.
3. It combined the training-capacity building activities with the actual training task—using the newly built training capacity to train 1,000 officials and managers.

Although many revisions were made later in how to implement the project, the general goals and basic strategy and framework remained unchanged. This project document also left enough room for a creative implementation. The six *Yi*s of training capacity building were a collective innovation of the people in this project.

Link Human Resource Development to Organizational Strategy

The ultimate measure of a human resource development (HRD) investment should be the contribution or impact it makes to the organization's output—economic development and poverty reduction in this case. It takes time to see and measure the contribution and impact. The people involved must work hard to increase the relevancy of the HRD efforts to the organizational strategy and goals. In the UNDP Training Capacity Project building case, what if a College of Cadre Training for Poor Areas was built in Beijing, following the model that every other ministry had already used? What if two or three young teachers from each training center had been sent abroad to study for a master's degree during the project implementation period? What if the provincial subcenters had been built as a part of a local agriculture university, but not part of the PADO? It should be quite obvious that the relevancy of the HRD effort to the organizational strategy and goals would be different under each alternative of building the training capacity. So the link of the HRD function to the organizational strategy and goals would not occur automatically. In this project, special efforts including creative thinking, optimal design, and careful implementation were necessary to create the link.

The institutional arrangement of the four training centers with the PADOs was one of the key success factors of the UNDP Project because it ensured a high relevancy and set up a rational institutional environment for the HRD efforts.

Integrate Training and Personal Development with Organizational Development and Career Development

HRD means "the integrated use of training and development, organization development, and career development to improve individual, group, and organizational effectiveness" (McLagan, 1989). Training and personal development could be useful and optimized in terms of the organizational goals only if the person was located in a proper position in a rational organization. Part of the training offered during the early stage of the UNDP Project did not contribute to the building of training capacity because of the changes of job assignments and even work units of the trainees. Without a rational organizational environment gained through organizational development, it would have been hard for the training and personal development to make real contributions to the organization's strategy and goals.

Career development was the bridge and managerial tool to link organizational goals with personal development. Full-time teachers and adjunct teachers were motivated and willing to stay in the poverty-reduction sector when they could achieve career development by working hard for the organizational goals.

Demand Sustainability from the Foreign Aid Project

Without the ability of sustainable development, the institutional building and human resource development efforts of a foreign aid project would have very limited effect. The question of what happens after the support of the UNDP project has ended should be asked during the whole process, from project formulation to implementation. Sustainability would amplify the efficiency of the seed fund, and the rate of return of the investment significantly.

Tips and Traps

Following are some tips to help people involved in similar projects avoid traps.
1. Get to know in-depth how the local system (specific sector and subsector) works, such as personnel management, resource allocation, and management. The institution building and HRD effort of the project has to fit well with the existing system.
2. Combine project activities with the routine work of the organization so the project can get routine budget provision and manpower from the organization.
3. Clear and effective communication among different parties of the project is critical. Various instruments, such as slogans and newsletters, could be used to interpret the project document and to coordinate activities. The six *Yi*s and figure 2 were important in the UNDP Project.
4. Close supervision of the project activities was as important as the formulation and design of the project.

5. Important characteristics of international training consultants include bilingual ability, knowledge of the relevant subject matter, strong communication skills, coordination of tasks and organizations, and management ability.

6. Use both short-term and long-term consultants in a multiyear project to ensure continuity of work and ideas.

Questions for Discussions

1. In the efforts of poverty reduction, what is the role of human resource development in general and the training in particular?

2. What is training capacity for an organization?

3. How can you build the training capacity in an effective and sustainable way?

4. How can you evaluate the impact of this project?

5. If you were an international consultant of the UNDP training capacity project, what would you do in project design and implementation to make the maximum contribution to the poverty-reduction sector of China?

The Authors

Jiping Zhang is currently an Ed.D. candidate at the School of Educational Studies, Oklahoma State University. She has been an independent consultant for various executive and government official training programs jointly sponsored by Chinese Government and international organizations since 1990. In the UNDP/China Training Capacity Building Project, she was EDI consultant from 1992–1996. Jiping Zhang had her undergraduate education and master's degree from Tsinghua University (China) in civil engineering. She was a faculty member of the Economic Management School at Tsinghua University from 1981 to 1988 and was a visiting scholar of Richard Ivey School of Business at the University of Western Ontario (Canada) in 1986–1987. She can be reached at 1701 N. Washington Street, Stillwater, OK, 74075; phone and fax: 405.377.0931; e-mail: zjiping@rocketmail.com.

Peter Sun is currently consultant, senior agricultural economist of the World Bank. He received his M.S. and Ph.D. degrees at the University of California at Davis, had hands-on work experience for agricultural and rural development for more than 30 years, including 10 years with the Asian Development Bank, and 17 years with the World Bank. From 1986 to 1996, he had worked for the Economic Development Institute of the World Bank as a senior training officer responsible for designing and conducting training activities in many developing countries in the fields of integrated rural development, poverty alleviation, and participatory irrigation management. For years he has done intensive work in China and received from the Chinese Government a National Friendship Award in 1997.

References

Agriculture Operations Division, China and Mongolia Department, East Asia and Pacific Regional Office. *China: Southwest Poverty Reduction Project.* Washington, DC: The World Bank, 1995.

McLagan, P. *Models for HRD Practice.* Alexandria, VA: ASTD, 1989.

Oxenham, J. "Evaluation at EDI." *EDI Review,* Washington, DC: The World Bank, 1995, January–March.

World Bank Group Study. *China: Strategies for Reducing Poverty in the 1990s.* Washington, DC: Author, 1992.

Moving to Manufacturing Professionals

Michelin North America, Inc.

Barbara E. Hinton

To achieve its purpose of providing high-quality tires for its customers at the lowest possible price, management at Michelin North America adopted the Manufacturing Professional Concept, a method for staffing and operating a manufacturing professional (self-directed work team) environment. Goals included increasing production, lowering cost, and increasing the quality of the product. This study describes how the human resource development (HRD) and workforce education partnership was linked with strategic planning to move the Michelin tire plant in Dothan, Alabama, to the Manufacturing Professional Concept. The plant utilized HRD efforts through a workforce education model to support retraining workers and to facilitate major strategic changes in a manufacturing workplace.

Background

Michelin North America's stated purpose is to provide high-quality tires for its customers at the lowest possible price. To achieve this, the company strives to increase production, lower cost, and increase the quality of its products. The company had long been aware of the need for training and has provided various training programs to its employees since opening the plant. In 1989, the company tested the academic skill level of the entire staff using a standardized test, the Test of Adult Basic Education. Results from that assessment indicated a need for worker training. A sister plant had developed a basic skills curriculum, which the Dothan site adopted. The Dothan plant

This case was prepared to serve as a basis for discussion rather than to illustrate either effective or ineffective administrative and management practices.

maintained a training center and strongly encouraged workers to use it. Although workers were compensated for up to 10 hours of work in the center per week, they did not voluntarily comply with the company's desire for self-directed instruction. Those who did comply were not able to complete the assignments satisfactorily without the aid of an instructor, who was available only nine hours per week. The classes and curriculum were loosely structured, and the content was not necessarily job specific. Although the plant offered training, it did not have a highly structured training program in place.

Organizational Profile

Michelin, a French-owned tire production company, has operated its plant in Dothan for over 15 years. This nonunion plant employs approximately 650 persons and operates three shifts with four crews rotating through the shifts in a rather complex rotation. The plant manager stated that the company's values of quality, safety, and cost were the driving forces for the planning cycle of the plant. Although the plant described itself as a "plant at risk" in 1987, through the successful process of linking human resource efforts to the strategic plan, that has changed. Today it defines itself as an expanding plant.

Industry Profile

The nature of the tire industry is that of keen competition in a world market. Michelin has long been known as a manufacturer of the highest quality tires. The challenge Michelin faced was an increasingly competitive market. The tire and rubber industry is rapidly changing, and plant management recognized the need to be flexible and responsive to changing forces in the environment. The plant needed to maintain quality and productivity while reducing production costs in order to maintain its edge in the market. As one manager stated, "We know how to make a perfect tire. But making one perfect tire will not keep this plant open. We must find ways to do more with less. We believe the answer is in a better trained workforce."

HRD Function Profile

HRD efforts had been ongoing since the early years of the plant. The training function had been seen as important, but there was no systematic training program in place. "In the past, our HRD strategy was to aim, adjust, and fire," said A.J. Blankenship, human resource manager. This was a time-consuming process, and many times the "targets" moved before the adjustment process was completed. Michelin management recognized that the human resource development (HRD) efforts must become more timely. Blankenship said, "That strategy had to change to aim, fire, adjust." For example, there had been traditional adult education classes available to workers. But the basic skills training curriculum, which had been developed at a sister plant, was outdated because of the rapid changes in the workplace. There was little acceptance of the classes among the workers, and redeveloping the curriculum did not appear feasible. In other isolated training efforts such as a statistical process control (SPC) training curriculum, people were falling through the cracks, according to Fred Blackwell, personnel director. There was no systematic coordination of training efforts, and the workers did not understand why they should attend training classes. They saw no connection between training efforts and their jobs.

As management determined that organizational changes would occur, they decided that HRD efforts would be key to successfully implementing these changes. Because management had determined to move many of the tasks traditionally assigned to supervisors down to line workers, they knew that there would be an increased need for training at the line level. At about the same time, funding became available from a National Workplace Literacy Project grant, administered by the Alabama Department of Education, Adult and Continuing Education Program. Management saw this as an excellent opportunity to develop a partnership of industry and educators, and to provide a comprehensive HRD system for its workers.

Approaches to Strategic Planning and HRD Design

Strategic planning at the plant was conducted through a team approach. The plant's chief executive officer strongly supported the notion that the plant must be reorganized and that it should become a high-performance workplace. This meant that a better trained workforce was essential. Management teams met often to determine the strategies necessary to reach the organizational goals.

Initial decisions included the move from mechanics being responsible for machine maintenance to line workers becoming certified as "operator/maintainers." The operators would handle their own minor maintenance tasks and repairs on their equipment, with "troubleshooters" (skilled mechanics) concentrating on major repairs. Through management team meetings, additional plans for change had developed, including moving from traditional manufacturing to the Manufacturing Professional (MP) Concept.

Restructuring would mean a flatter organization with fewer hierarchical layers between wage and salaried employees, and fewer functional boundaries between the various skill areas. The MP concept would reduce the number of middle managers and would result in placing business unit responsibilities with the line workers, when practical and cost-effective. As strategic planning progressed, it became evident that the many changes in the plant would affect all the workers. Questions arose about how to get the workers' buy-in and how to prepare them for the major changes that were to occur. Issues included the departmental approach versus the plant approach to production, what knowledge and skills the new assignments would require of the workers, and how effective interteam and intrateam communication should be developed and maintained. There was concern about how the MP levels should be designed, how workers at each level should be trained, and what the effect of these changes would be on salaried employees and on hourly workers. In essence, the number of middle-management personnel would decrease as those workers were reassigned to production jobs.

Management was very aware that workers might view major changes in the way the plant was operating either as a threat or an opportunity. Early on, they made it clear that as responsibilities were redistributed there would not be mass layoffs. Workers were given an opportunity to be a part of the change process by taking on new roles and responsibilities. Most took that offer. Although the size of the workforce was reduced by attrition, turnover rate at this plant continues to be very low and wages are high for the area.

As the possibility of entering into a partnership with educational entities presented itself, the company saw an opportunity to put into place a workplace education and training model that could support the strategic plan. In addition, management saw a chance to learn from educators and establish a strong, ongoing training program.

Description of the Effort

The Alabama Partnership for Training (APT), funded through a National Workplace Literacy Project grant and administered by the Alabama Department of Education, Adult and Continuing Education Program, was the vehicle through which Michelin chose to support its strategic plan. APT provided a workforce education and training model through a three-year partnership of industry and educational leaders. Although not unique, the model focused on a train-the-trainer concept in which industry and educational partners worked together to develop and implement job-specific workplace education and training. The partnerships required agreed-upon common goals, benefits, and expectations; provisions for shared governance and ongoing partner involvement; support from upper management and line supervisors; and worker incentives. A state-supported workplace education specialist (WES) and a company-supported WES would partner with an adult education instructor, contracted through the local education agency to design and deliver an industry-specific program. The grant provided in-service training for the WESs, instructor, and administrators. It required, through use of a steering committee, a jointly developed and approved operational plan to provide the conceptual framework guiding the project activities to produce expected outcomes. In addition, the operational plan would guide the process whereby targeted workers were identified and a recruitment plan was developed. Finally, the grant required that partners formulate and carry out an evaluation plan.

Targeted Goals and Learning

Goals of the grant were to
- provide training in adult literacy and other basic skills, services, activities
- provide adult secondary education services and activities leading to workers' completion of GEDs
- meet the literacy needs of adults with limited English proficiency
- upgrade or update basic skills of adult workers to reflect changes in workplace requirements, technology, products, or processes
- improve the competency of adult workers in speaking, listening, reasoning, and problem solving
- provide educational counseling, transportation, and child-care services for adult workers during nonworking hours while workers participated in the program
- develop a cadre of qualified WESs to serve as core instructors to expand workplace literacy.

Key Issues and Events

The APT model required several steps: needs assessment, job-task analysis, literacy audits, curriculum design and development, and evaluation. As part of the partnership agreement, industry partners were asked to identify areas where they perceived the greatest need for worker training and to determine if indeed there was a training need. Those identified areas were given priority for training development. Prior to any of the curriculum development, a steering committee was formed, consisting of the WESs, the adult education instructor, the local adult education director, the plant personnel manager, and representatives of the line workers and supervisors. Development of the operational plan was the first order of business. Problems that arose included adaptation of the industry partners to the bureaucratic requirements of educational institutions. For example, materials and equipment purchased through the grant had to be ordered through state agencies, greatly increasing the time required for purchases. Both the "schoolhouse" and the "workhouse" sides of the partnership had to learn new vocabularies and adapt to the different ways of teaching and working. During the needs assessment and job-task analysis phases, the educators became familiar with the production processes at the plant through observations, questioning of workers, and focus groups in which workers assisted educators in conducting job-task analysis. Through workshops funded by the grant, the plant partners learned how to design, develop, deliver, and evaluate workforce education and training to address the company's specific needs. In summary, the grant allowed the educators and industry partners jointly to plan and implement a systematic approach to HRD that was aligned to the plant's strategic plan.

An initial concern in the partnership was how to best increase workers' participation in the program and ensure their acceptance of the classes. Several tactics were used, including paying the workers for training, making sure the training was specific to their needs, and utilizing plant communications systems to inform the workers of the training. The company made a large investment in renovating the training center and held a widely publicized open house when the renovation was complete. Door prizes were awarded and refreshments were served. The plant newsletter and in-house video system carried information about the classes and emphasized their job-related content. Workers who completed training received certificates.

Consequences

As the plant approached the end of its third year of the program, there were many key indicators of success. Of the original 62 workers needing basic workplace skills, only two had not completed the program. The plant hosted a luncheon to celebrate the success of those who finished. GED instruction continued to be available on site, with expanded opportunities available through the local community college. The current curricula focuses on upgrading skills to reflect changes in the workplace. Because of the move to high-performance work teams, 30 modular curricula were developed. Training was designed to cover writing skills, stress management, time management, facilitation, communication, team building, operator maintainer, manufacturing professional design (three levels), peer input, and interviewing skills. Some modules have been adapted to computer-based training (CBT) delivery. This has made the training program much more flexible as workers can work on the CBT modules individually. As the restructuring process continued, other needs were identified and curriculum designed and delivered to address those needs. It is significant to note that the workers requested several training topics, including writing skills and time management.

Evaluation Strategies

The company maintained careful records to evaluate its investment in its workers. HRD staff gathered data to determine workers' reactions, learning, and behavioral changes on the job. Michelin determined that since the beginning of the program, production increased 9.5 percent, quality improved 15 percent, personnel was reduced by 13 percent, and costs were reduced by 5 percent. The program provided decision makers with instruction and tools needed to expand the training program, allowed them to build a well-equipped training center, and provided valuable Michelin-specific workplace curricula. In addition, the program allowed Michelin to implement a restructuring process that directly affected the plant's production capabilities and supported the workers who needed training. Although Michelin managers are quick to point out that training is not the only thing that had an impact on their success, they note that without training they could not have implemented the strategic changes the restructuring process necessitated. The plant has recently received ISO 9000 certification. Michelin managers are convinced that the successful achievement of this certification was directly related to the successful training program.

Lessons Learned

As Michelin completed the restructuring process, management noted that although change is never easy, it was smoothly accomplished by tying the HRD efforts for supporting the workforce to the strategic plan. The personnel manager, Blackwell, has summarized the many benefits of the workforce-training program. He noted that partnering with educators as they planned and implemented the strategic plan produced positive results both in the plant and in the community. The partnership allowed six of its management team members to become competent in job-task analysis, job-specific curricula design and development, and computer-based training design and development. The company now has the ability to apply the transferable model to all of its training efforts.

Some unexpected outcomes also resulted from the partnership. Through working with local adult educators, there is now closer communication between business and local educational agencies, resulting in a better understanding of industry needs and an increased presence of educators at the plant campus. The methods and materials developed at the Dothan Michelin plant are being exported to sister sites, reducing the need for other plants to develop their own curricula. Both educators and industry personnel have increased their skills through better understanding and collaboration. The two groups now have a stronger political base when lobbying for funds for adult and workforce education. Most important, the once at-risk plant is now an expanding plant, contributing needed stability and important economic support to the local community.

Questions for Discussion

1. What are the ethical issues involved in restructuring the workforce in this case?
2. How did Michelin utilize HRD efforts to address "threats" to the workers in this case?
3. How can a company justify investing so heavily in a workforce education program?
4. What are the advantages and disadvantages to partnering with educators in developing and delivering workforce education?
5. What are the indicators that this plant will or will not continue its training program after support from the grant is no longer available?

The Author

Barbara E. Hinton is a professor and head of the Department of Vocational and Adult Education, at the University of Arkansas. She has extensive experience in human resource development in both business and educational settings. Areas of interest include training needs analysis, competency-based education and training, team building, criterion-referenced assessment, strategic planning, and facilitation. She has served as a consultant to national, state, and local governmental agencies as well as to private industry. She has served as an external evaluator for two national workplace education programs. In addition, she has delivered workshops on team building, occupational analysis, and competency-based education in Australia and Chile. At the University of Arkansas, she teaches classes in human resource development. Hinton has made numerous presentations to both national and international audiences and has published articles in several scholarly journals in recent years. She can be reached at the University of Arkansas, Vocational & Adult Education, 100 Graduate Education Building, Fayetteville, AR 72701; phone: 501.575.4758; fax: 501.575.3319.

About the Editor

William J. Rothwell, Ph.D., is professor of human resource development (HRD) in the Department of Adult Education, Instructional Systems and Workforce Education and Development, in the College of Education on the University Park Campus of The Pennsylvania State University. In that capacity he directs a graduate program in HRD. He is also director of Penn State's Institute for Research in Training and Development.

Before arriving at Penn State in 1993, Rothwell was an assistant vice president and management development director for the 28th largest life insurance company in the United States (of 1,200 companies) and a training director in a state government audit agency. He has worked full-time in human resource management and employee training and development since 1979. He thus combines real-world experience with academic and consulting experience. Rothwell was chairperson of the ASTD Publishing Review Committee when the *In Action* series was authorized and remains a strong supporter of the concept of providing real-world cases to practitioners and academics.

Rothwell's latest publications include *Mastering the Instructional Design Process* (2d ed., 1998, with H.C. Kazanas), *Beyond Instruction: Comprehensive Program Planning for Business and Education* (1997, with Peter S. Cookson), *Beyond Training and Development: State-of-the-Art Strategies for Enhancing Human Performance* (1996), *The ASTD Models for Human Performance Improvement* (1996), *The Self-Directed on-the-Job Learning Workshop* (1996), *The Just-in-Time Training Assessment Instrument* (1996), *The Just-in-Time Training Administrator's Handbook* (1996), *Developing the High Performance Workplace: Administrator's Handbook* (1996, with David Dubois), and *Developing the High Performance Workplace: Organizational Assessment Instrument* (1996, with David Dubois).

Rothwell has been author, coauthor, editor, or coeditor of numerous other publications, including: *Strategic Human Resource Planning* (1988, with H.C. Kazanas), *Strategic Human Resource Development* (1989, with H.C. Kazanas), *The ASTD Reference Guide to Professional Training and Development Roles and Competencies* (1989, 2 volumes, with Henry J. Sredl),

The Strategic Planning Workshop (1989), *The Structured on-the-Job Training Workshop* (1990, 2 volumes), *The Workplace Literacy Primer* (1990, with Dale Brandenburg), *Mastering the Instructional Design Process: A Systematic Approach* (1992, with H.C. Kazanas), *The ASTD Reference Guide to Professional Human Resource Development Roles and Competencies* (1992, 2 volumes, with Henry J. Sredl), *The Employee Selection Workshop* (1992, 2 volumes), *The Employee Discipline Workshop* (1992, 2 volumes), *The Complete AMA Guide to Management Development* (1993, with H. C. Kazanas), *Improving on-the-Job Training* (1994, with H.C. Kazanas), *Human Resource Development: A Strategic Approach* (1994, rev. ed.), *Planning and Managing Human Resources: Strategic Planning for Personnel Management* (1994, rev. ed.), *Effective Succession Planning: Ensuring Leadership Continuity and Building Talent from Within* (1994), *Practicing Organization Development: A Handbook for Consultants* (1995), and *The Emerging Issues in HRD Sourcebook* (1995).

Rothwell earned his undergraduate degree at Illinois State University, completed a master's degree and all course work for a doctorate in English at the University of Illinois at Urbana-Champaign, earned an M.B.A. with specialized courses in human resource management from Sangamon State University (now the University of Illinois at Springfield), and (in a second doctoral program) completed a Ph.D. in human resource development at the University of Illinois at Urbana-Champaign.

In 1996, Rothwell completed "A 21st Century Vision of Strategic Human Resource Management," an unpublished research report from a project sponsored by the Society for Human Resource Management, the Research Committee of the Society for Human Resource Management, and CCH Inc.

Accredited for life as a senior professional in human resources (SPHR), Rothwell has been a consultant for over 30 *Fortune* 500 companies. He can be reached at 647 Berkshire Drive, State College, PA 16803; phone: 814.234.6888; fax 814.235.0528.

About the Series Editor

J ack Phillips has more than 27 years of professional experience in human resource development and management and has served as training and development manager at two *Fortune* 500 firms, senior human resources executive at two firms, president of a regional bank, and management professor at a major state university. In 1992, Phillips founded Performance Resources Organization (PRO), an international consulting firm specializing in human resources accountability programs. Phillips consults with clients in the United States, Canada, England, Belgium, Sweden, Italy, South Africa, Mexico, Venezuela, Malaysia, Indonesia, Australia, and Singapore. PRO provides a full range of services and publications to support assessment, measurement, and evaluation.

A frequent contributor to management literature, Phillips has been author or editor of 15 books, including the following: *Return on Investment in Training and Performance Improvement Programs* (1997); *Accountability in Human Resource Management* (1996); *Measuring Return on Investment* (vol. 1, 1994; vol. 2, 1997); *Handbook of Training Evaluation and Measurement* (3d edition, 1997); *Conducting Needs Assessment* (1995); *The Development of a Human Resource Effectiveness Index* (1988); *Recruiting, Training and Retaining New Employees* (1987); and *Improving Supervisors' Effectiveness* (1985), which won an award from the Society for Human Resource Management. Phillips has written more than 100 articles for professional, business, and trade publications.

Phillips has earned undergraduate degrees in electrical engineering, physics, and mathematics from Southern Polytechnic State University and Oglethorpe University; a master's degree in decision sciences from Georgia State University; and a Ph.D. in human resource management from the University of Alabama. In 1987, he won the Yoder-Heneman Personnel Creative Application Award from the Society for Human Resource Management for an ROI study of a gain-sharing plan. He is an active member of several professional organizations.

Jack Phillips can be reached at Performance Resources Organization, P.O. Box 380637, Birmingham, AL 35238-0637; phone: 205.678.9700; fax: 205.678.8070.

Other Books Available in the Series

The ASTD *In Action* series examines real-life case studies that show how human resource development (HRD) professionals analyze what worked and what didn't as they crafted on-the-job solutions to address specific aspects of their work. Each book contains 15–25 case studies taken from many types of organizations, large and small, in the United States and abroad. Choose from case study collections on the following topics:

Measuring Return on Investment, Volume 1

Jack J. Phillips, *Editor*

Who's going to support a training program that can't prove itself? This volume shows you case after case of trainers proving that their programs work—in dollar-for-dollar terms. Each of the 18 case studies shows you the best (and sometimes not-so-best) practices from which every trainer can learn. Corporations demand bottom-line results from all branches of their operations, including HRD. This volume hands you the tools—the hows, whys, and how-wells of measuring return-on-investment—to mark that bottom line.

Order Code: PHRO. 1994. 271 pages.

Measuring Return on Investment, Volume 2

Jack J. Phillips, *Editor*

This second volume contains even more case studies focusing on the issue of return-on-investment. Authors reflecting several viewpoints from varied backgrounds examine their diligent pursuit of accountability of training, HRD, and performance improvement programs. The 17 case studies cover a variety of programs from a diverse group of organizations, many of them global in scope. As a group, these case studies add to the growing database of return-on-investment studies and make a unique and significant contribution to the existing literature on the subject.

Order Code: PHRE. 1997. 272 pages.

Designing Training Programs

Donald J. Ford, *Editor*

These days, training techniques must consist of more than setting up flipcharts, handing out manuals, or plugging in audiovisual aids. Organizations are asking instructional designers to create innovative learning systems that use a wide range of methods and media to spark participants' interest and increase retention and use on the job. This volume showcases 18 real-life examples of customized and artful programs that improve learning and staff performance. Computer-based training, distance learning, and on-the-job training are just a few of the many methods used by the contributors to this book.

Order Code: PHTD. 1996. 340 pages.

Transferring Learning to the Workplace

Mary L. Broad, *Editor*

The 17 case studies in this volume cover a wide range of organizational settings. Specifically, the real-life training examples feature dramatic, large-scale knowledge and skill transfer applications that affect overall organizational performance, as well as smaller programs that affect individual employee effectiveness. As more training and HRD professionals struggle to implement learning transfer support activities, this collection of field experiences will be an invaluable source of ideas and advice.

Order Code: PHTL. 1997. 332 pages.

Leading Organizational Change

Elwood F. Holton III, *Editor*

HRD is concerned fundamentally with change, which is traditionally in individual knowledge, skills, and abilities. Today, however, organizations face an ever-increasing rate of change and struggle to manage change processes. HRD professionals have the opportunity to become key players in leading organizational change efforts. Covering a wide range of organizational types, change strategies, interventions, and outcomes, these 14 case studies show that HRD professionals can and should lead change.

Order Code: PHLO. 1997. 260 pages.

Creating the Learning Organization

Karen E. Watkins and Victoria J. Marsick, *Editors*

It's time to take learning organizations out of the think tank and into the real world. This volume of 22 case studies from a cross section of organizations—international and national, industry and service, government and private sector—shows you how to create the learning organization as HRD professionals move beyond theory and into practice, transforming organizations into businesses that perform, think, and learn.

Order Code: PHCL. 1996. 288 pages.

Conducting Needs Assessment

Jack J. Phillips and Elwood F. Holton III, *Editors*

How can you fix performance problems if you don't know what they are? This volume gives you the investigative tools to pinpoint the causes of performance problems—before investing time and money in training. Each of these 17 case studies provides real-world examples of training professionals digging deep to find the causes of performance problems and offers real-world results.

Order Code: PHNA. 1995. 312 pages.

Managing the Small Training Staff

Carol P. McCoy, *Editor*

These 12 case studies explain the challenges and opportunities small training departments face and describe specific success strategies and tactics that proved useful. The book contains practical ideas for action and in-depth examples of what training departments of varying sizes can accomplish. By following the strategies outlined in this book, lone trainers can survive and thrive in today's challenging business environment.

Order Code: PHMS. 1998. 227 pages.

Developing High-Performance Work Teams

Steven D. Jones and Michael M. Beyerlein, *Editors*

Increasingly, companies are experimenting with teams in some area of their organizations. The push for teams comes from market forces that reward efficient companies that are highly responsive to and innovative with changes in their organizations. These 14 case studies present a variety of approaches to implementing high-performance teams in the workplace.

Order Code: PHDH. 1998. 265 pages.

ASTD

1640 King Street
Box 1443
Alexandria, VA 22313-2043
PH 703.683.8100, FX 703.683.81
www.astd.org